Governing New York State

D0925905

Governing New York State:
The Rockefeller Years

Proceedings of
The Academy of
Political Science

Volume 31
Number 3

May 1974

Edited by Robert H. Connery and
Gerald Benjamin

The Academy of Political Science
New York, New York

Contents

POLICY ISSUES

Contributors

DONALD AXELROD is chairman of the Public Administration Department, Graduate School of Public Affairs, State University of New York at Albany. He is co-author of *Dollars and Sense: Budgeting for Today's Campus*.

GERALD BENJAMIN, associate professor of political science at the State University College at New Paltz, is author of the forthcoming *Race Relations and the New York City Commission on Human Rights*.

BLANCHE BERNSTEIN is director of research on urban social problems at the Center for New York City Affairs, New School for Social Research. She is the author of *Social Benefits in New York: Adequacy, Incentives, and Equity*.

ALAN CHARTOCK, a consultant to the New York City Police Department, teaches political science at the State University College at New Paltz.

WILLIAM G. COLMAN, former director of the Advisory Commission on Intergovernmental Relations, is a consultant to state and local governments. He is also a visiting lecturer in government at the University of Virginia.

ROBERT H. CONNERY is professor of government in Columbia University and president of the Academy of Political Science.

DONALD H. HAIDER, who teaches at the Graduate School of Management, Northwestern University, is the author of *When Governments Come to Washington: Governors, Mayors, and Intergovernmental Lobbying*.

RAYMOND D. HORTON teaches at the Graduate School of Business, Columbia University. He is the author of *Municipal Labor Relations in New York City: Lessons of the Lindsay-Wagner years*.

RICHARD J. KALISH is associate professor of political economy at the State University of New York at Albany. He has written extensively on environmental economics.

FRANK S. KRISTOF is director of the Division of Economics and Housing Finance of the New York State Urban Development Corporation and adjunct professor of planning at the School of Architecture, Columbia University.

ARTHUR L. LEVIN is a physician who has served as a consultant to the surgeon general of the United States and to the commissioner of health in New York City.

FRANK J. MACCHIAROLA, assistant vice president for academic affairs, Columbia University, is on leave from Bernard M. Baruch College, the City University of New York, where he is associate professor of business.

BARRY MAHONEY is a lawyer currently directing a research project on bail reform under the auspices of the National Science Foundation and the National Center for State Courts.

STEPHEN P. RAPPAPORT is a graduate student in the Department of Political Science in Columbia University.

DONALD M. ROPER, recently a liberal arts fellow at Harvard Law School, teaches history at the State University College at New Paltz.

SEYMOUR SACKS is professor of economics at the Maxwell School, Syracuse University. He is coauthor of *Metropolitan America: Fiscal Patterns and Governmental Systems*.

DONNA E. SHALALA, associate professor of politics and education at Teachers College, Columbia University, is the author of *The City and the Constitution: The 1967 New York Convention's Response to Urban Problems*.

MICHAEL D. USDAN is professor of education at Bernard M. Baruch College, the City University of New York. He has written extensively on education and has served as a consultant to numerous educational organizations.

STUART K. WITT is professor of political science at Skidmore College. His special interest is state legislatures.

JOSEPH F. ZIMMERMAN is chairman of the Department of Political Science at the Graduate School of Public Affairs, State University of New York at Albany. He is the editor of *The Crisis of Mass Transportation*.

Preface

This volume explores the ways in which the major institutions and processes of the New York State government have operated in the past decade and a half, examines how these have changed, and considers the implications of suggestions for future changes. It also examines New York's role in the intergovernmental system, its relationships with the federal government, with local governments, and with other states. Finally, it assesses the state's recent record in some of the fiscal and substantive policy areas that have been most pressing throughout the 1960s and early 1970s.

Although New York is one of the nation's largest states and experts have acknowledged its leading role as an innovator in the federal system, the state's political processes and public policy performance have not been subject to comprehensive analysis in recent years. Indeed, the politics of the state have received much less scholarly and popular attention than those of its largest city, though, as one contributor to this volume argues, much of what happens in the public sector in New York City is determined, or at least delimited, by decisions made in Albany. Thus, in one sense, this collection is an attempt to redress the imbalance of scholarly attention given to New York. By doing this, it is hoped, the functioning of all levels of government in New York State will become clearer to both students and practitioners.

Although the essays in this volume are about the governance of one state, the collection takes on national significance for several reasons. New York has been and remains a vanguard state. Traditionally, it has been among the first to confront emerging problems, and its solutions have often been emulated by other states. In recent years, the political leadership in New York has taken a major role in attempting to redefine the place of the state in the federal system. Moreover, this volume is the first analysis of the fifteen year gubernatorial record of Nelson A.

Rockefeller. The ways in which Rockefeller approached the central problems of New York during the period of his governorship and the techniques that he used to help make the state's political system responsive to the demands of its multifarious population have made him a national figure. Consequently, New York's experience takes on major importance for those interested in state govrnment throughout the nation.

The scholars who contributed to this volume were selected because they are experts in their fields. Some of their papers were delivered at a conference on "Governing the State: Programs, Policies, and Politics" sponsored by the Academy of Political Science on November 16, 1973, at Columbia University. The Academy serves as a forum for the dissemination of informed opinion on public questions, but it makes no recommendations on political issues. The views expressed in this publication do not necessarily reflect those of the Academy, the editors, or the governmental or academic institutions with which the authors are affiliated.

ROBERT H. CONNERY
GERALD BENJAMIN

Nelson A. Rockefeller as Governor

ROBERT H. CONNERY

As governor of New York, Nelson A. Rockefeller was a major figure in shaping not only the course of government in his own state, but also the role of states generally in the federal system. Moreover, he was a perennial presidential candidate and consequently an important national figure. There is no doubt that he dominated New York State government during his fifteen years as governor, an office that is almost unique among state executives because of the wide formal powers it confers. But the reasons for Rockefeller's enormous impact upon government, both within and outside New York, go beyond the formal powers of the office and must be sought, in large measure, in the qualities of the man himself, his style, and the manner in which he used the resources available to him.

Rockefeller had certain advantages not usually possessed by a governor. He added long tenure, abundant energy, great wealth, and an exceptionally wide acquaintance in industry and the arts to the prerogatives and strong party leadership role that go with the governorship in New York. Rockefeller also brought to the governorship a conviction that major social and economic problems could be solved by state government and that aggressive executive leadership from the governor's mansion could help find these solutions. He was, to use James David Barber's phrase, an "active-positive" executive.[1] To

---

This paper is based on the New York State Administrative Policies Studies, now in progress, sponsored by the Academy of Political Science.

[1] James David Barber, *The Presidential Character: Predicting Performance in the White House* (Englewood Cliffs, N.J.: Prentice-Hall, 1972).

be sure, in later years, as state resources were strained to the limit, Rockefeller came to believe in the necessity for massive federal action and funding in many major policy areas, but he remained convinced of the central role of state and local government in the actual administration of programs and delivery of services.

Rockefeller's appearance on the New York political scene provided few clues to his future success. He had served in the federal government during World War II as assistant secretary of state for Latin American affairs and under Eisenhower as a special assistant to the president. This administrative experience in appointed posts, with the inevitable conflicts with other officials regarding policy—particularly over Latin American relations and the extent of the resources that should be allocated to the national defense—had not been an entirely happy one. When Rockefeller left Washington in 1956, he decided that he would seek elective office with its much greater scope for independent leadership.

On his return to New York City he consulted with a number of Republican leaders about the possibility of running for office. Their initial reaction was cool. Former Governor Thomas E. Dewey, elder statesman of the party, thought Rockefeller was not known well enough to seek statewide office and therefore advised him to run for Congress from his home district in Westchester County. When Rockefeller showed no enthusiasm for that undertaking, Dewey suggested that perhaps he could induce President Eisenhower to name Rockefeller postmaster of New York City. This alternative seemed even less inviting to Rockefeller.

Soon afterwards, an opportunity developed that would give him statewide exposure. Governor Harriman and the Republican legislature were at odds concerning the composition of the bipartisan Committee on the Preparation of the State Constitutional Convention, which was scheduled to meet in 1958. The Democratic governor and Republican leaders of the legislature could not agree on a chairman. L. Judson Morhouse, the Republican state chairman, suggested Rockefeller for the post, and Harriman, who had known Rockefeller for years, agreed. This appointment provided Rockefeller with the unusual opportunity over the next two years to make an intensive study of the state government. He visited every county in the state in company with Malcolm Wilson, one of the first Republican leaders to view him as a potential candidate for high state office. This assignment gave him two important assets: familiarity with the operations of the state government and exposure to grass roots Republican leaders. In addition, it gave him the opportunity to assemble the nucleus of a staff that served him well in both the campaign and as governor. Two central figures in this group were George Hinman and William Ronan.

Even this experience did not make Rockefeller a front runner for the Republican gubernatorial nomination in 1958. The call for a constitutional convention in New York failed to be ratified in a statewide referendum and did not take place. Harriman later inadvertently focused the spotlight on Rockefeller. At the annual Albany correspondents' dinner, when various party leaders were cited as potential gubernatorial timber, Harriman said jokingly, "There is one who sits among you whom you have not named, who has the greatest potential: Nelson Rockefeller."

In the election of November 1958, Harriman, as the incumbent governor with seemingly widespread political support, appeared to be a difficult candidate to defeat. While several senior Republicans yearned to be governor, they were not sure that Harriman could be beaten. Republican leaders were therefore willing to accept as their candidate an attractive young man new in state politics but with the financial resources to wage an effective campaign. Thus the Republican convention nominated Rockefeller, and he won the election by a vote of 3,126,929 to 2,553,895.

Powers of the Governor

Comparative studies of state executives place New York's governor first among his peers in the extent of his formal powers.[2] Administrative activities are combined in twenty departments, each headed by a commissioner who holds office at the governor's pleasure. Only the State Education Department, where state activities are directed by a board of regents elected by the legislature, is outside of the chief executive's control. Even there the governor has a powerful input through the executive budget, which includes funds for education. Moreover, while the legislature may reduce items in the budget proposed by the governor, it may only increase the budget through separate items which are subject to the governor's line item veto. The governor appoints persons to fill some 8,000 positions which are exempt from the Civil Service merit system. Finally, New York, unlike some states,

[2] See, e.g., Joseph A. Schlesinger, "The Politics of the Executive" in Politics in the American States, eds. Herbert Jacob and Kenneth N. Vines (Boston: Little, Brown and Co., 1971), and Thad Beyle and J. Oliver Williams, eds., The American Governor in Behavioral Perspective (New York: Harper & Row, 1972).

has no limit on the number of times a governor may succeed himself. Rockefeller was elected in 1958 for a four year term and was reelected in 1962, 1966, and 1970. When he resigned in December 1973, he had served as governor for fifteen years. In New York only George Clinton in the late eighteenth century had served a longer time.

The veto is a final major formal power of New York's governor. To be sure, his vetoes can be overriden by a two-thirds vote of both houses of the legislature. But, in fact, most important legislation is passed in the closing days of the legislative session, and then the governor has thirty days either to sign the bills into law or to veto them. Since the legislature has adjourned by that time, the effect is to give him an absolute veto of end-of-the-session legislation.

Wide as the formal powers of the New York governor are, Rockefeller's informal powers and his personal background made him an even more influential chief executive. He was fortunate, compared to other governors, in having available the services of an unusually large and able staff. Traditionally in New York the governor's principal staff assistants were the secretary to the governor, the counsel, and the director of the budget. In the course of his administration, Rockefeller added an appointments secretary, a director of communications, and a director of planning services. For temporary assignments he used special assistants. The Division of the Budget was staffed by civil servants under the merit system except for the director and his immediate assistants.

In the last year of the Harriman administration there were fourteen professional posts in these staff offices. At the end of the Rockefeller administration the number had increased fourfold, and the total staff of professional and clerical personnel numbered about 200, excluding the staff of the budget division. To be sure, the increase of activities in all of the states had led to an increase in governors' staffs. New York was unique only in absolute numbers.

Like the staffs of most governors, the New York group were selected for professional competence, not because of party position. Few had been active in party politics before their appointment to Rockefeller's staff. In the main, they were younger men than the heads of the administrative departments, as was true in most of the states. The New York staff was considerably better paid than most. Indeed, a newspaper tabulation reported that each of the four top staff positions had salaries larger than those of governors of forty states.

The counsel to the governor was responsible for legal matters, particularly those concerned with new legislation. The appointments secretary made nominations for the offices (except judgeships) that the governor was empowered to fill. The director of communications maintained contacts with the news media and advised on public relations in general. The secretary was the principal channel between the governor and administrative agencies, but he had a unique role in defining state problems and proposing innovations.

The unusual aspect of staff operations came about in the systematic way that they explored state problems and developed possible solutions. During the year, reports flowed from the administrative departments to the secretary's office and were channeled to his five or six principal assistants, who were called program associates. They also monitored the national press in an attempt to discern problems as they were developing in other states. In September the program associates put together a list of state problems, broken down by functional areas, with suggestions for solutions. Some ideas might be omitted as contrary to established policy—if, for example, a proposal was made that the state cease making grants for school aid. In the second step the laundry list was sent to the governor's top advisers for discussion, and then the list was returned to the program associates with instructions that certain items be further developed. With the help of the line agencies and of special study groups, the original list was expanded with arguments pro and con, an exploration of fiscal implications, and the positions of various interest groups. These were again reviewed by the senior staff. Finally, a "position book" was put together and sent to the governor with the recommendations of the staff.

The governor was not limited to what the staff might recommend. He had additional resources, personal friends, and political advisers, and consequently he would add his own preferences. Moreover, as the length of his tenure increased, Rockefeller came to be the most informed man in the administration on state issues and was thus less dependent than most elected officials on expert staff. From extensive staff work and gubernatorial review, the annual State of the State Message would be developed. In preparation for more important conferences in Albany, Washington, or with fellow governors, Rockefeller's staff would put together a massive volume of position papers covering every item likely to be discussed. Few governors have had this kind of research support.

It is worth noting that Rockefeller was careful to keep his own staff separate from that which he used for his political campaigns. During the campaigns the state staff continued to operate out of Albany, and an entirely new group with separate headquarters was organized to handle both the gubernatorial and national campaigns. Gubernatorial staff people essential to the campaign were temporarily removed from the state payrolls and paid from campaign funds during preelection periods.

To support the permanent staff and stage agencies, Rockefeller used study groups to a greater extent than any former governor of New York and much more frequently than did governors in other states. These study groups fell into three categories: task forces; temporary study commissions; and governor's conferences. The task forces might be recruited wholly from state personnel or wholly from outside the state agencies or from both sources. Temporary commissions dealt with long range problems. The governor's conferences were larger meetings used to get a broad cross section of views. During his administration Rockefeller named some seventy task forces, appointed five temporary commissions, and convened sixteen governor's conferences. There were also a number of temporary commissions whose members were named partly by the governor and partly by legislative leaders.

One can postulate many reasons why Rockefeller made study groups such an important part of his staff operation. In-house task forces such as the one that developed the Pure Waters Program enabled the governor to cross established bureaucratic lines and join members of his personal staff with agency officials to provide a fresh look at a state problem. By bringing in outside authorities, the governor could tackle issues that his own staff might not possess the expertise to handle. In defining problems and providing the governor with new knowledge, a study group could act as a "credibility addition." Thus a broad-based panel of experts who would define a problem and propose a program would help Rockefeller build public support for it. At the same time, study groups did not bind the governor to a decision that he might not approve.

Another resource that Rockefeller used for helping in formulating and implementing policy was his large reservoir of friends, business acquaintances, and confidants outside the government. New York State, and particularly New York City, is a national headquarters for finance, labor, and the arts. The governor moved freely in these circles and thus had access to unique ideas and advice. Moreover, New York City, headquarters for the news media, provided a platform from which he could test public opinion.

Finally, the governor made extensive use of public opinion polls for input in public policy making. Polls were used by Rockefeller during election campaigns in order to identify potential supporters, to pinpoint voter concerns, to measure his own strengths and weaknesses and those of probable opponents in the eyes of the voters, and thus to develop campaign strategy. Frequent polling during campaign years also permitted measuring trends in the electorate as they occurred; five polls were commissioned by the governor during the 1970 race.

Beyond this, Rockefeller and his aides used polls as a management tool to discern the overriding concerns of the people of New York in nonelection years and to act to meet them. Though some critics argued that Rockefeller was too responsive to the vagaries of his private polls, he ignored them as often as he heeded them, for he saw it as his responsibility to lead, as well as to respond to, public opinion. Polls, however, were one way that the governor could have information input beyond that which would come to him from pressure group leaders and others that sought to overtly influence executive decisions.

Besides an unusually able staff and many outside sources of information, Rockefeller had extensive patronage to increase his informal powers as governor. It is sometimes said that Governor Rockefeller controlled appointemnts to 40,000 state positions. This figure is far too high, since appointments to many of the positions were made by departmental commissioners.

During his first days in office, Rockefeller, who had campaigned on a good government platform, was not comfortable with his patronage-dispensing role, but he soon came to recognize patronage as an essential tool for governing and controlling the party. By the late 1960s he was wielding it skillfully. Although he came to understand and value the use of patronage, Rockefeller insisted that his appointments secretary and the Republican state chairman realize that high professional competence was the underlying consideration in making appointments. Patronage, the governor said, must meet party needs within the constraints of this criterion. The operation of this principle sometimes meant that a Democrat be chosen to fill a major post. In the closing days of his administration, the commissioner of transportation and the chairman of the Power Commission were both Democrats. Exceptions to the partisan rules were most often made at the top level of appointments. For middle level posts, qualifications were more broadly defined and party loyalists were more easily found. Another factor that limited the patronage power was that certain commissionerships, such as health, mental hygiene, and welfare, were held by men nominated by professional societies. Rockefeller's appointments record was exceptional in that he appointed few men who were later found guilty of graft or corruption.

The popular view of the state patronage system as a well oiled machine was simply not accurate. Although instructed to do so, departments frequently did not report vacancies which could be filled outside the Civil Service. Some departments, like the State University, had a tradition of political independence. Others, like Mental Hygiene, had no centralized control of appointment, which was vested in superintendents of various state hospitals. These were among the largest employers outside the merit system.

Often, too, available positions were not filled because the jobs themselves were not desirable, either because of their location in the state or because of their low status. Most of the positions in the Office of Parks and Recreation and in the Thruway Authority were upstate and not attractive to New York City residents. Indeed, in the Harriman administration, the Democratic governor found it necessary to fill many of these appointments with Republicans because few Democrats were interested in them.

The patronage system failed to be the overwhelming tool of gubernatorial power that it would seem to have been not so much because of the small number of positions, but because the governor had neither the desire nor the means to manage the system. There were about 8,000 posts, many of which were honorific and did not carry salaries, that were controlled from the office of the appointments secretary. About 2,000 of these became vacant each year. Although the governor had the potential for influencing appointments to some 40,000 other posts, most of the decisions regarding these were left to lower levels in the administrative and political process.

One evidence of Rockefeller's increasing sophistication was the way in which he used administrative reorganization to advance his goals. When he took office in 1959 his secretary, William Ronan, a former professor of public administration, proposed extensive reorganization of the state's administrative agencies based on "sound principles of management." Although the governor supported these plans to provide for a more symmetrical structure, few of them were accepted by the legislature. In Rockefeller's later years as governor, he was more inclined to use reorganization as a means of infusing fresh leadership into programs in which he was interested, and he was not as concerned about theoretical considerations. After launching the Pure Waters Program he created the Department of Environmental Conservation in 1970 from the existing Conservation Department and parts of the Health Department. Thus not only were all areas of environmental concerns brought under one agency, but fresh impetus was given to the program.

Relation to the Party

Two important aspects of Rockefeller's political relations were vital to the success or failure of his programs. One was his relation to his own party, the other to the state legislature. There can be no doubt that, from the moment of his election as governor, he was the accepted leader of the Republican party in the state. To be sure, the opinions and wishes of Republican United States senators from the state had to be considered, particularly in the area of state-federal relations. Republican congressmen were important in matters affecting their districts, but rarely in statewide politics. Republican leaders in the legislature, especially in the early years of the Rockefeller administration, sometimes took an independent stance. But on party matters within the state Rockefeller had few challenges to his leadership, and none were successful.

Rockefeller courted Republican county leaders and was keenly conscious of the pressures to which party leaders were subjected because of criticism of various state programs. He recognized that support was a two-way street and that he had a role to play when local leaders were under attack. He said, "Public good will is like a bank account, which can be built up at certain periods and then drawn upon to get important things done. However, like a bank account, it can be rebuilt."

For example, when local Republican leaders came to Rockefeller and reported mounting criticism about the operations of the Long Island Rail Road, Rockefeller took the pressure off of them by going to meetings and taking full responsibility for the railroad's operations, predicting that it would shortly be the best commuter railroad in the country. Later he admitted, "I got carried away and I really had not intended to say that, but I did buy time until the operations could be turned around." While he was roundly criticized for his remark, over the next two or three years more money was available for the railroad, labor problems were worked out, productivity increased, and the governor's credibility on Long Island was rebuilt.

The Governor and the Legislature

The legislature convened each year in early January. The governor presented his annual State of the State Message, which in the Rockefeller years was a brief document made up of little more than a list of problems and programs that he would detail later in special messages. Then came the budget, which the legislature had to act on by April 1. During the early months of the session the two houses marked time awaiting the governor's programs, but the tempo of business increased in late April and May, ending with the massive legislation in early June.

In all but four of Rockefeller's years in office the Republicans had control of both houses of the legislature. Moreover, unlike many state legislatures that normally had a one-third turnover at each session, the New York legislature had little change in membership from year to year except for the Johnson landslide in 1964 and the redistricting that followed the one man, one vote decision of the Supreme Court. Largely because of the permanent character of the membership, the party leaders had good disciplinary control over the members at least until the last years of the Rockefeller governorship, when increased turnover in the legislature began to erode party loyalty. Many of the more prominent members had interim committee assignments which gave them a certain amount of patronage and staff.

Rockefeller, working closely with the two majority leaders, usually had little difficulty in getting his programs through the legislature. What the legislature lacked, however, was the ability to develop new programs, and this was the principal input of the governor.

Since most programs originated in the governor's office, one might say the governor proposed and the legislature disposed. Many of the major undertakings of the Rockefeller years—expansion of the State University, the Pure Waters Program, the Metropolitan Transportation Authority, the Council on the Arts, and the Urban Development Corporation—were initiated by the governor and accepted with few changes by the legislature.

Generally the governor left relations with individual members to the leaders in each house unless they requested his aid. It was virtually impossible for an individual legislator to obtain passage of bills in which his district was interested unless he went along with the leaders on most matters. Rockefeller's main problem, however, was that on his more liberal legislation, the Republican majority, coming largely from upstate districts, were not enthusiastic about his proposals. Social measures meant increased state spending and increased taxes, which had little attraction for upstate Republicans. Although most votes were on party lines, on social measures the governor could usually count on some Democratic as well as Republican votes. On the other hand, occasionally the Democratic state chairman, by insisting on making issues partisan, caused the Republicans to rally to Rockefeller's support.

Frequently, Rockefeller was criticized in New York City for being too favorable to upstate interests; upstate he was criticized for being too responsive to New York City problems. It was part of his philosophy, however, to broaden the base of support for his legislation by including aspects that would have some appeal upstate and other items that would have some appeal to New York City. For example, in regard to various transportation bond issues, he provided some money for mass transit not only in New York City, but in upstate cities, as well as funds for highway construction and aviation aid.

Rockefeller said that he was more interested in the substance of the issues than in strict partisanship. During the short period in which the Democrats controlled the legislature, he was almost as successful in getting his programs passed as he was when the Republicans were in control. Although his main tactic in dealing with the legislature was persuasion, an art in which he was particularly effective, he recognized the political realities. He was not above using patronage to influence a member's vote, and he could occasionally act with aggressive effectiveness to compel legislative compliance with his wishes.

His action in 1968 in regard to the housing problem is a good example of this type of coercion. The Mitchell-Lama program, which gave tax advantages to private housing developers, had lost its effectiveness in providing an incentive for major new housing. Racial problems, local zoning, building codes, difficulties in acquiring sites for large developments, all made it increasingly difficult for private sponsors. David Rockefeller, the governor's brother and chairman of the board of the Chase Manhattan Bank, made a speech in Washington saying that low- and middle-income housing should be built on the basis of four dollar's worth of private capital to one dollar's worth of government aid. The governor read the speech in a newspaper and called his brother the next morning and said, "David, I've got the 20 cents if you've got the 80 cents." David Rockefeller had not worked out his proposal in any detail, so he and the governor set up a small committee to study the problem. Meantime, the governor invited Edward Logue, who had been successful in managing public housing in Boston, to confer with him. Logue said that no program would work until somebody got power to override local zoning and local building codes. The governor offered him the top position in a state program, and Logue agreed *if* the governor could overcome these two weaknesses.

The governor proposed legislation to establish the Urban Development Corporation, but met considerable opposition from suburban legislators. Nevertheless, he thought that he had reached an agreement with the legislative leaders to support his program. When Martin Luther King was assassinated, Rockefeller chartered a plane and invited eighteen black legislators to go with him to the funeral. The legislators agreed to pass the legislation while he was away, along with two other acts in which black members had an interest. On the way back from the funeral, Rockefeller called Albany hoping to be able to announce to his companions that the legislation had been passed. He discovered, however, that the measure had been defeated in the assembly on a vote of 86-54 and that the Republican legislators from the suburbs had reneged on their agreement. The governor was furious. He telephoned the Republican minority leader, and told him that he would refuse patronage and veto legislation in which the rebels were interested. The leaders then rounded up the members of the legislature, held a session, and at midnight the assembly reversed its vote and passed the urban development bill giving the corporation power to override local zoning and local building codes and also to set up subsidiaries which would have the same power. No authority like this had ever been given to a state agency.

Relation to the Public

Rockefeller was a confirmed believer in consensus building and in the value of public opinion as a political resource. He was convinced that if reasonable men were presented with all the facts involved in a problem, they could be moved to support his program. In press conferences and television appearances he avoided emotional appeals. He used his staff to ascertain the facts. Once briefed, he had excellent recall. Although he read his annual messages and more formal addresses, he was much more effective in informal presentations, though even then he relied on charts, graphs, and other visual material to support his arguments.

The press sometimes attacked Rockefeller for not being accessible, especially during legislative sessions. Indeed, he did not hold as many press conferences as some governors had, but he felt that open controversy with the legislature in the press was not the way to succeed in getting his programs approved. He once said, "If I am to do a good job, I've got to get the legislature to pass the bills that I think are important for the state. The press may criticize me for not being available sufficiently, but I would rather be successful in my dealings with the legislature."

Rockefeller's firm belief in the reasonableness of the average citizen led him on occasion to tackle problems that his staff had advised him would ruin him politically. When the Urban Development Corporation's plan to build low-cost housing in Westchester County developed bitter local opposition, he held a "town meeting" there and argued strongly in support of the corporation. Although he was unsuccessful in getting his program accepted, his courage in facing the issue did not lead to political disaster.

In addition to more formal media, Rockefeller used direct appeal to the citizens. On occasion, some groups of approximately twenty-five people in various parts of the state were invited to meet with him in what he called leaders' meetings. When he had a particular message that he wished to communicate to the voters, he would spend a week or ten days holding five or six successive leaders' meetings a day in various parts of the state. More infrequently, he convened "town meetings" at which an invited group of 200 might be present, but which would also be open to the general public. There the attendance might vary from 500 to 800 people. Sometimes at a town meeting Rockefeller would receive rough criticism from the floor. Such criticism provided him an opportunity for a remark such as, "What a wonderful, democratic system we have here in America, where people of courage can stand up and openly criticize their governor! I wish to compliment the gentleman for his frankness." His grasp of facts and quick wit usually enabled him to offset criticism thus openly made.

Conclusion

The Rockefeller style was to determine what the problem was; sort out alternative solutions; seek the best possible professional advice; decide on a program capable of being carried out; seek consensus among interested groups, compromising, if necessary, on details; and carry the issue to the people. He believed that if one did not succeed the first time, one should be persistent and keep trying until success was achieved. No-fault automobile insurance was a good example of his persistence. His proposal was defeated in two sessions of the legislature but passed in the third.

All of Rockefeller's initiatives were taken in the context of a firm commitment to the viability of the federal system and reflected the governor's conviction that the state government could function to meet the needs of a heterogeneous, largely urban, society. In some policy areas, notably education, the state sought to help with increased aid to local governments. In others, transportation for example, it assumed new operating responsibilities as emergencies arose. As the demands upon state government increased and as New York reached the limit of its resources, Rockefeller made a major contribution to the effort to have the federal government contribute increasing resources to the states through revenue sharing and categorical grants programs. All of these efforts reflected Governor Rockefeller's view that, given the resources, New York and other states could do the job.

How Rockefeller's political style and methods of operations worked can best be evaluated by the achievements and failures of his administration. Certainly on the achievement side of the ledger he would place the expansion of the State University, the Pure Waters Program, and the land use plan for the Adirondacks. To these he would probably add the reform of the welfare system. Both the federal government and almost half of the other states followed the example of New York in similar reform in welfare. The governor held high hopes for the Urban Development Corporation as a means of providing low cost housing outside of New York City. The legislature clipped the wings of the corporation in 1973, although its accomplishments have still been substantial.

The failure to control the traffic in illicit drugs was certainly the most conspicuous shortcoming of Rockefeller's regime, although it must be acknowledged that no other government, state or federal, has yet found a solution to this problem.

Perhaps Rockefeller's greatest legacy to New York will prove to be his redefinition of the scope of the office of the governor. During his tenure, the responsibilities of state government were greatly increased, and the capacity of the governor to get things done increased with them. Future governors of New York will be acting in an institution defined by Rockefeller, and his expansive interpretation of the guber-natorial role provides a model of "what might be" for chief executives of other states as well. The devices Rockefeller used to expand the powers of his office and the record he made in using these powers in various policy areas are explored in greater detail in the essays that follow.

The Governorship in History

DONALD M. ROPER

A great variety of men have served as governor of New York over the past two centuries, and personal charisma has often been offered as a reason for their political success. Theodore and Franklin D. Roosevelt, for example, are recalled as most charismatic men. Yet charisma can be overrated, as the jokes about Thomas E. Dewey's campaigns indicate. ("Smile for the cameras, Governor." "I thought I was smiling.") Herbert Lehman even lacked Dewey's skill at organizing a formal address to compensate for his lack of personal magnetism. The lack of public appeal, however, did not prevent Dewey and Lehman from succeeding at the polls. It was their image of positive liberalism rather than their personalities that, in the final analysis, was the critical factor.

As used here, "positive liberalism" is defined as the belief that the state should promote the welfare and protect the rights of as many of its people as possible. The use of a broad definition is advisable since it allows for adjustment to changing conditions of the past, such as shifts in the electorate. Moreover, what may not seem like positive liberalism to one age may to a previous one. The ultimate test of positive liberalism is the degree of social justice meted out to the politically powerless and unpopular elements of the population. This test marks the ability of a governor's political security to withstand attacks from groups with political clout when they disagree with him.

It is to be noted that this paper is but a hypothesis. Only educated guesses will be possible until the completion of the long-called-for study of Al Smith's governorship, an examination of the Lehman years, and an updated study of Dewey's administration.

A positive liberal posture has often put a governor at odds with a legislative majority that represented a more provincial constituency, but the need to win the governorship led party and legislative leaders to seek out positive liberal candidates and to endorse some of their programs. There have, in fact, often been discrepancies between the rhetoric of conservative leaders who oppose positive liberalism and their willingness to accept state support for their constituencies—witness contemporary highway building and public education programs.

While there will be no evaluation of positive liberalism here, it is worthwhile, if somewhat risky, to try to understand the sources of that position by casting an imprecise social profile of the governors before Rockefeller. Not surprisingly, most of these governors came from comfortable circumstances. The best line along which to make a division is between self-made men and those of independent wealth. The problem with this grouping is that the former category is so comprehensive as to include those who pulled themselves up by their bootstraps from close to the poverty level (Al Smith), as well as those who had a good deal to start with and added to it (DeWitt Clinton). Independent wealth presupposes high social status and perhaps *noblesse oblige*. There have indeed been aristocratic governors with demonstrated concern for less fortunate people, but they did not have a monopoly on social consciousness. *Noblesse oblige*, moreover, can be only a limited explanation, for it overlooks self-interest. Compromise does not adversely affect the one making it, and the one needing help finds himself being compromised. Rather than stressing social status and *noblesse oblige*, then, it is more helpful to consider that New York governors have generally had considerably higher exposure to reformers and reform movements than their counterparts in other states, and since reformers have often been among the governors' influential supporters, the result has been concern for social justice by osmosis.

Historically there is a notable exception to the generalization as to the prevalence of positive liberalism. What should be borne in mind is the strong countertrend of negativism. In its classic and extreme form, negativism means that government which governs least governs best. As with positive liberalism there have been variations of this theme corresponding to changing historical circumstances. One basic premise was that government's function was largely to promote and protect free and fair competition. It was thought that the positive state bred corruption, because a selected few profited rather than the many. So went the rationale of negativism in New York during the Jacksonian Era. Yet this line of reasoning had the seeds of positive liberalism within it, as seen in the Working Men's party demand for equal educational opportunity. In the post-Civil War period the example of urban services à la "Boss" Tweed caused negativism to emphasize civil service reform, the premise being that good government by good men was a panacea for society's problems. These good men were to do as little as possible. With the entrenchment in this century of positive liberalism, what remained of negativism was largely rhetoric, with the possible exception of its stress upon personal integrity. When a party in power lost its credibility with the electorate, the power brokers on all sides claimed that their "Mr. Clean" could eliminate the mess in Albany. This ritual of political cleanliness, to belabor the obvious, is done at the demand of the voters. The question is, For how long and to what extent are they willing to see retractions in services until credibility returns?

For purposes of convenience, the history of the governorship can be roughly divided into five parts. Part one, the Era of Establishment, covered the first forty-five years of the state's government, from 1777 to 1822. Part two spans the period from 1823 through the Civil War and is labeled the Flourishing of the Two-Party System. An apt term for the third phase extending until Theodore Roosevelt became governor in 1899 is the Age of Industrial Giants. Part four, the Progressive Transition, lasted from Roosevelt's ascendancy to 1919 when Al Smith became governor. Smith's assumption marked the beginning of part five, the Triumph of Positive Liberalism, which has continued to the present. Proceeding chronologically, with focus on eight of the "great" governors and their interaction with the electorate, it is possible to demonstrate the positive liberal tradition. The selection of "great" governors is purely arbitrary and does not constitute judgment as to their accomplishments. The basic criterion used in compiling this list was adherence to positive liberalism. The three-part format used to ascertain commitment is the extent to which they were heeded by their party, the degree of their positive liberalism, and the degree of their independence. In each case, the extent and degree are general. The list in chronological order is DeWitt Clinton, William H. Seward, Theodore Roosevelt, Charles Evans Hughes, Alfred E. Smith, Franklin D. Roosevelt, Herbert H. Lehman, and Thomas E. Dewey. In addition, because of the precedent-setting significance of his administration, it is necessary to look at the first governor, George Clinton, even though his commitment to positive liberalism was ambivalent. Finally, it is assumed that the stance of positive liberalism has been accompanied by a considerable amount of political sagacity. The paradigm example of what awaited a failure to exercise political discretion was the premature declaration of independence from Tammany by progressive-minded William Sulzer after his election in 1912. (Sulzer was the only governor in the state's history to be impeached.)

The Era of Establishment

The tone of the governor's office was established at approximately the same time that its authority and weight came into being. New York's first constitution, drafted in 1777, was a bundle of compromises, as most constitutions are. The moderate-conservative consensus which first shaped the executive office rejected designs that would have made it what policy makers would have liked the colonial governor to have been—a creature of the legislature, with little or no patronage at his disposal, and executive discretion tightly constrained. Given the maladministration that stamped colonial governors in the minds of New Yorkers, the desire for a eunuch-type executive is understandable, but the exigencies of the moment, with the state a battleground and its heart occupied by the enemy, caused second thought. The result was creation of the first strong state governor in the country, though with limitations.

The constitutional provisions creating a strong governor seem unremarkable today. He was to be selected by the electorate for the state senate, which was confined to those males owning property worth £100. While this meant a limited electorate (19,369 men were eligible to vote for governor in 1790), the fact that the legislature did not select the governor was unique. His term was for three years, which is not notable in itself, except that rotation in office was then the rule. Moreover, while there was no provision for reelection, neither was there any prohibition against self-succession. Thus, when George Clinton completed his first tenure as governor he had served eighteen years. By this time (1795) the larger states, Virginia, Pennsylvania, and Massachusetts (which had established the strong governor by its 1780 constitution), had all gone through a myriad of chief executives. Neither did the constitution restrain the governor with an executive council as those of other states did.

There were restraints, however, in the form of a plural executive, consisting of two councils—the Council of Revision and the Council of Appointment. The former, consisting of the chancellor of the state and members of the supreme court, as well as the governor, exercised the veto function. Since the judicial officers were appointed for life (up to age sixty), as political parties developed the governor was sometimes in a minority on the council. In such instances, however, the Council of Revision majority was often at odds with a majority of the legislature, and there was thus a better chance to override vetoes. Moreover, since the judiciary rather than the governor was responsible for unpopular vetoes, the judges unwittingly served as a lightning rod for the executive. If anything, then, the Council of Revision served to strengthen the governorship by strengthening party discipline, necessary to overcome infrequent judicial vetoes. A glaring exception to the above assertion was DeWitt Clinton's decision not to seek reelection in 1822, partly because of hostility created by his joining Federalists on the Council of Revision to delay calling a constitutional convention in 1820 to bring about badly needed reform, including the abolition of the Council of Revision.[1]

The Council of Appointment operated much differently. Unintentionally, this council turned out to be tailored for promoting the party system. The senate was divided into four large geographical districts, and the assembly selected one senator for the council from each of the four districts. These four senators, along with the governor, composed the Council of Appointment. Control of both legislative houses, but particularly the assembly, then, meant control of the state's patronage, and it became important that a gubernatorial candidate provide a coattail effect for legislative candidates of his own party. To be sure, the governor came into conflict with senators of the opposition party on the council. The lesson was clear to the politicians—the governor and the legislative majority must be of the same party. Finally, it is to be noted that the governor had an advantage over his fellow councillors, since they were limited to one-year nonsuccessive terms.

The unfolding of the two councils' roles was still very much in the future when George Clinton became governor. Given the historian's retrospect, one can see that Clinton had an opportunity to shape as he would and as he could. Again, the framers of the first constitution seem prescient, although they definitely did not have the first governor in mind when they deliberated in 1777. Yet a phrase from the fourteenth article of the constitution, "a wise and discreet freeholder

---

[1] It should be noted that Clinton was elected in 1824 and reelected in 1826. Under the constitution of 1822 the governor's term was lowered to two years.

of this state shall be, by ballot, elected governor," seems a most apt description of George Clinton. Compared to the great landholders like Philip Schuyler, Robert R. Livingston, and John Jay, his station was modest. Compared to the bright, young officers coming out of the war like Burr, Hamilton, and Brockholst Livingston, his intellectual capacity was limited. Clinton was, of course, well-to-do when he became governor, and he increased his fortune remarkably while in office. If not an intellectual giant, he possessed an uncommon political shrewdness befitting a man of wide experience, and he wielded patronage and land grants with skill.[2]

George Clinton emerged from the popular Whig element of the revolutionary generation, and throughout his lengthy stay in office represented the "politics of opportunity" against the "politics of privilege" of the great landholders. The "politics of opportunity" was flexible enough to adjust to the significant changes in the electorate that were taking place even at that early date. This malleability makes it difficult to place George Clinton in either the positive liberal or negative category, and it is enough for now to note that constantly updating the "politics of opportunity" can lead to positive liberalism without much difficulty, and George Clinton seemed headed in that direction in response to a changing electorate during the last years of his first long stay in office.

George Clinton owed his first narrow election in 1777 to the state's yeomen farmers, and they continued as the bulwark of his support in subsequent campaigns, although in some elections he ran unopposed. Naturally Clinton was concerned with the welfare of the constituency that served him and had made it futile at times to run an opposing candidate. Accordingly, he recommended aid to education and a transportation system to enable his farmer supporters to get their commodities to market. He also carried out a land policy designed to get the vast acreage recently euchred from the Iroquois into the hands of actual settlers, which he felt could best be done through speculators rather than "land jobbers"—admittedly a fine distinction. Clinton was particularly reluctant to place any tax burden on his agrarian supporters. Programs undertaken thus had to pay their way, and his opposition to the federal constitution of 1787 can be traced to an unwillingness to surrender impost duty revenues protecting yeo-

[2] This account of George Clinton's governorship is based primarily on Alfred F. Young's superb study, *The Democratic Republicans of New York: The Origins, 1763-1797* (Chapel Hill: University of North Carolina Press, 1967).

man landowners from taxation.

George Clinton, then, appears as the personification of negativism. In 1794 and 1795, however, there was a significant transformation in his attitude toward reform. Where once he had been content to recommend action in the area of public education, Clinton later pushed through the common school act of 1795. It was something of a landmark, though Clinton himself considered it a failure. Similarly, the reform of the criminal code enacted in 1796 represented fruit from seed that Clinton had sown in the preceding two years, even though John Jay was by that time governor.

Clinton's shift to reformism was, as noted, owing to a changing electorate. Since its founding as New Netherland the population had been ethnically and economically diverse, a condition that continued throughout the colonial period. The Revolution, of course, halted population development, but by the 1790s, with renewed immigration, diversity was renewed. The influx of artisan immigrants from England, Ireland, Scotland, France, and the German states touched off a wave of democratic humanitarianism that swept New York City, a leading factor in Clinton's transformation. The essence of this change was the addition of reformism to the largely negative Clintonian anti-Federalist party to make it into the Clintonian Republican party. No longer concerned with simply keeping the "great and opulent families" at bay, which it had successfully done for eighteen years, the party of George Clinton possessed the potential for positive liberalism that came to be successfully exploited by his nephew DeWitt. In short, operating in a political world much different from the one of today, George Clinton was largely responsible for laying the foundations for a strong party system and strong executive through political acumen and skilled utilization of his powers; well might he refer to "our excellent constitution."[3]

If the concept of reformism essential to positive liberalism emerged during George Clinton's time, the concept of positivism came to fruition with DeWitt Clinton. By 1817 the rapid geographic growth of the state subsided, and the element of geographic diversity was added to population diversity. The commercial needs of burgeoning agricultural regions demanded an effective system of transportation to supplant the extensive but inadequate turnpike networks. So strong was this demand that DeWitt Clinton, because of his outspoken commitment to the building of the Erie Canal, was drafted by his party. The

[3] Ibid., p. 22.

strength of this need is demonstrated by the fact that the Republican party (Jeffersonian or Clintonian, to distinguish it from the GOP) leadership had emphatically placed DeWitt Clinton in political exile. But when popular Daniel D. Tompkins, happily known as the "farmer's boy" and a four-time winner, became vice president, the acts of political apostasy by Clinton, which had caused his banishment, were momentarily put aside, if not forgiven, and he became governor virtually by acclamation.

DeWitt Clinton had imbibed of the democratic humanitarian swirling of the 1790s, and as a consistent friend of Irish immigrants had, while in the United States Senate, helped change the citizenship residence requirements back to five years from fourteen. Consequently, Irish-Americans remained his supporters throughout his lengthy political career. The main source of his support, however, was the following he attracted by advocating positive government. Besides his well-known advocacy of internal improvements, there was Clinton's championing of state support for agriculture via a supervising board empowered to provide funds. In a real sense, then, DeWitt Clinton provided the model for positive liberalism to be followed by subsequent governors and, as a consequence, was able to maintain maximum independence, even to the extent that he became the "divider of parties."[4] This ability was partly owing to the appeal of the positive state to some Federalists, while some Republicans (Martin Van Buren, for example), opposed the concept of positivism. To be sure, there were purely personal factors—Clinton had a knack for alienating politicians —but, at any rate, Clinton had a party of his own.

The Flourishing of the Two-Party System

Chronologically, DeWitt Clinton straddled the era of the establishment and the flourishing of the two-party system. Aside from the campaign of 1822, which he chose to sit out, he was elected and re-elected until he died in 1828. Even before Clinton's death the American party system had begun to emerge in New York, with the elements that subsequently became the Whig and Democratic parties acting in at least amorphous cohesion against each other. Furthermore, the realignment of the American party system into the Republican and Democratic parties during the 1850s was accomplished in New York al-

[4] Dixon Ryan Fox, *The Decline of Aristocracy in the Politics of New York, 1801-1840* (New York: Columbia University Press, 1919), p. 194.

most unnoticed, if one looks only at the gubernatorial election returns. This period was marked by extremely close elections, with a
turnover so frequent as to resemble a children's game of "king-of-the-
hill." That this surface picture is deceptive is too obvious to mention.
There was at least one other factor of great importance, one that is
central to this paper's hypothesis. The two major parties did indeed
flourish during this era, but so did minority parties. Among such
parties were the Anti-Mason, Antirent, Free Soil, Know-Nothing, Lib-
erty, and Working Men's. That these forces might be labeled pressure
groups rather than parties does nothing to blunt the point that a pluralistic society existed, and, more important, that many of its diverse
elements sought to make their interests cared for via the political process. Furthermore, these groups succeeded to the extent that the two
major parties made significant efforts to encompass minority positions, which provides at least a partial explanation for the divisions in
the Whig and Democratic parties and partly explains why the Republican party came into existence and why it had an apparent reform
quality in the antebellum period. Finally, the difficulty of appealing
to this dynamic pluralistic electorate explains in part the constant rotation of the governorship.

William Henry Seward provides the paradigm for examining the
flourishing of the two-party system. Seward was not in such demand
as DeWitt Clinton had been, yet the infant Whig party needed him
to get itself off the ground in the gubernatorial election of 1834, and
although unsuccessful against incumbent William Marcy, Seward kept
the race close. Seward sat out the campaign of 1836, but, in a return
match with Marcy in 1838, was successful. In his quest for office, Seward had a major advantage, since the Whig party's major strategist,
Thurlow Weed, was also Seward's firmest supporter.

Seward, like DeWitt Clinton, sought to bring George Clinton's
politics of opportunity into effect for all men, and, like DeWitt Clinton, advocated extensive positive action by the state. Seward seems to
have been genuinely caught up in the nation-sweeping reform movements of the pre-Civil War generation, but the needs and demands of
three downtrodden groups—blacks, tenant farmers, and Irish immigrants—were more than the existing divisions in the Whig party structure could then withstand, and his desire to be "both humane and
politically realistic" (to borrow his biographer's phrase)[5] ended with

[5] Glyndon G. Van Deusen, *William Henry Seward* (New York: Oxford University
Press, 1967), p. 63.

reality prevailing. For his support of the unpopular, particularly Irish educational aspirations, Seward found his victory margin of 1838 sliced in half when reelected in 1840, and this diminished popularity was a factor in his decision not to run in 1842. Seward's failure was more than personal; rather, it reflected the inability of a pluralistic society to make its weight felt, with notable exceptions like the anti-renters. For example, New York blacks were constitutionally disfranchised until after the Fifteenth Amendment, newly created labor unions were snuffed out during the depression of the late 1830s (which is not to say that workers would have voted for Seward), and, contrary to optimistic expectations, the New York Irish remained in the Democratic party.

The Age of Industrial Giants

The next period marked a time of preparation, a time spent by various groups building up their political strength to an effective level. Tammany Hall not only symbolized the age, but machines like Tammany, by providing services—jobs, sometimes living necessities for poor immigrants, and urban facilities needed by business—served to delay a renewed call for positive liberalism. Obviously, there were indeed such clamors by social reformers, but they tended to be muted and isolated by the hustle and bustle of industrialism and by the failure to mobilize. In an age when the likes of the bipartisan Black Horse Cavalry wheeled and dealed in the state legislature, it is small wonder that integrity in administering negative government would seem a viable alternative to what was going on. Appropriately, the best remembered political leader of the era is Grover Cleveland, who as mayor of Buffalo, governor of New York, and president of the United States, was the personification of integrity in administering negative government. It is not surprising, then, to think of this period primarily as the age of industrial giants.

The Progressive Transition

While social reformers never take a holiday, the relatively widespread awakening to the problems brought by industrialism during the progressive era (roughly 1900-17) makes it seem as though reform had been dormant during the previous generation. Such was not the case, however, in New York. Rather, newcomers from abroad by the millions formulated the ideology and means by which there would be an opportunity for all to succeed. East European Jews were particularly effective in hammering the plans and means for success. Generally rejecting the quasi-private relief provided by Tammany and the private relief of organized charity as inadequate, these newcomers moved vigorously for positive action by the state to ameliorate society's ills through organizations such as the clothing workers' unions. The result was the firmest positive liberal consensus to develop in the state's history. Almost simultaneously came the awakening by significant numbers of the middle and upper classes to the inadequacy of government as it existed to deal with society's problems. And while still placing greater emphasis on reforming the institutions of government, because of either altruism, guilt, political pressure, or fear of revolution (or various combinations thereof), these progressives, too, supported positive liberalism. This political cobelligerency, rather than alliance, of the progressive era provided the climate for the governors' reasserting positive liberalism. More important, other politicians were to learn from the experience of this era, including future Governors Smith, Roosevelt, and Lehman.

Theodore Roosevelt was still associated with the negativism of his goo-goo ("good government") supporters when elected governor in 1898, but when his single term was finished and he was on the way to Washington as vice president, he had made important steps up from the negativism he had flaunted while a freshman assemblyman in the 1880s. Although Republicans had been almost habitually successful in late nineteenth century gubernatorial elections, the party's "easy boss," Thomas Collier Platt, became impressed with the need to replace the lackluster and corrupt Frank S. Black administration with Roosevelt. It was not only that the rough rider colonel was the hero of San Juan Hill, but also that he would attract the New York City Republican and independent votes. Roosevelt was ambitious and a constant party regular with the exception of the aberration of 1912. Moreover, he realized that he would need party support to reach his ultimate goal—the White House. Because of Platt's rigorous opposition to social reform, Roosevelt's roles as "honest broker" for labor, champion of conservation, and vigorous fighter for effective corporation taxation and pioneering urban housing legislation are meaningful. Moreover, Roosevelt, once in the White House, was able to obtain a degree of control over the state party that had not been possible when he was in Albany, and from this position he was able to provide Hughes with a modicum of independence.

It was President Theodore Roosevelt's insistence that New York Republicans rectify their reversion to the habit of nominating hacks that led to Charles Evans Hughes's nomination in 1906. Hughes had roused New Yorkers through his hard hitting and even-handed exposure of wrongdoing in public utilities and insurance industries in 1905. The image of the unsullied prosecutor of the public interest has a negative connotation coinciding with his goo-goo supporters. Prior to the campaign of 1906, Hughes's views on social reform were unknown, but in that campaign against William Randolph Hearst, Hughes found it incumbent to appeal to working people. By the time he left office in 1910, he had justifiably earned the applause of social reformers like Homer Folks for his efforts to bring about improved working conditions. While it might be argued that Roosevelt and Hughes should be labeled dynamic conservatives rather than positive liberals, the point is that their pragmatic response to social problems— testing the ideas of reformers—indicated a fair degree of educability.

The Triumph of Positive Liberalism

If Theodore Roosevelt and Hughes had been educated up from "googooism," so Al Smith was educated up from Tammany. But where the two Republicans had made it a point to be *aware* of what social reformers thought, Smith *relied* on the advice of social reformers like Belle Moskowitz, though this reform influence came to be countered in his later years at Albany by his "golfing cabinet" including the General Motors magnate John J. Raskob. While Smith was undoubtedly educated as to the problems of society by such traumatic events as the Triangle Shirtwaist Company fire of 1911, a more forceful educator was that the assemblyman from New York City came to realize (as his mentor, Boss Charles F. Murphy, of Tammany would) that social reform legislation meant votes.

In 1918 Al Smith was the best known Democrat in the state, and, as demonstrated by his work at the constitutional convention of 1915, he was the best informed person in the state on the operation of government. He was, moreover, well known for championing social justice in the assembly, notably as the first New York City Tammany Democrat to serve as speaker. In short, he was his party's logical gubernatorial candidate, particularly since the Democrats had been successful only twice (1910 and 1912) in over twenty years. Aided by an upstate influenza epidemic that reduced the Republican vote and the failure of incumbent Charles Whitman to fulfill his positive liberal promises, Smith narrowly won his first gubernatorial election. Unable to withstand the overwhelming Harding victory of 1920, he was the only candidate the Democrats could put up in 1922—that is, if they hoped to win—and he was easily reelected in 1924 and 1926. Smith established a pattern of longevity followed until today. In the fifty-five years since 1918, only seven governors have been elected, and only two did not succeed in getting reelected.

Smith was the personification of positive liberalism, with its limitations and strong points, and his first state message in 1919 is a model of that persuasion. Still remembered as an outstanding administrator, Smith accomplished much in providing services for many of the people, and in those areas (such as public power) where legislative accomplishment was not forthcoming, he provided an education for the public upon which Franklin D. Roosevelt was able to build. While bringing positive liberalism into full bloom, Smith also succeeded in solidifying the governor's independence. Enlightened Boss Murphy well understood that he needed his one-time protégé and indeed Tammany had no other choice but to accept Smith on his terms. Even before Murphy died in 1924, Smith was de facto head of the New York State Democratic party, evidence of which is his unequivocal refusal to allow the powerful newspaper publisher William Randolph Hearst on the ticket in 1922, despite entreaties from party leaders, including Murphy.

Smith laid the foundation for Franklin D. Roosevelt and Lehman, yet in 1928 he needed Roosevelt. While it was indispensable that the Democrats replace Smith with a candidate who promised to continue the course that he had charted, it was important to the presidential candidate that he have a gubernatorial running mate who would help carry the nation's most populous state. Enter FDR, who exceeded expectations (and Smith's vote total) by winning the election. Because of his physical condition, Franklin D. Roosevelt was a reluctant candidate, but his disinclination to run was overcome partly by the promise of Lehman as his running mate. The latter indeed became "the other governor," in FDR's phrase, and in turn became the natural successor to Roosevelt. In building upon Smith's foundation, FDR and Lehman found that the depression demanded more of the state than had previously been needed, and they responded in what was essentially first a preview and then a microcosm of the New Deal.

Because of Tammany's antipathy for them, FDR and Lehman further projected the image of independence. Despite their own success at the polls, however, they usually had to operate with Republican legislative majorities, indicating the unrepresentative quality of the districting. True, Lehman might have been able to project his own "prodigious sense of public stewardship" to defeat a particularly recalcitrant upstate Republican legislator like Horace White, but this was rare. There was, however, an effort by Republicans to assume the mantle of progressive liberalism, with moderate liberals like Irving Ives moving into legislative leadership roles. This change in image would serve to make Thomas E. Dewey's task of obtaining party control easier. How much help he required is questionable, however, because he was so badly needed by the party that Dewey's domination was secured even before he was elected governor.

If ever a party needed a candidate, the Republicans needed Dewey in the late 1930s to challenge Lehman. Dewey was possibly the best known person in the state. As special prosecutor of New York City rackets, he projected the image of "Mr. District Attorney . . . Defender of the People" (as a favorite radio program of the period called itself). But Dewey's promise of "me-tooism" in the realm of social justice was also a factor, indeed an essential one, in his success. Narrowly defeated in 1938 by Lehman, who had to be truly drafted, he was victorious in 1942, when the Democratic leadership, unable to coax Lehman into just one more term, cast aside the model of positive liberalism that had served the party so well. The election of Dewey, then, could not mean a turning off of the positive, if the Republicans hoped to retain control of the executive mansion. Though World War II provided the final cure for the Depression, the Dewey administration followed through with measures supported by Lehman. Thus, for example, New York became the first state in the union to have a Fair Employment Practices Act, an indication that black voters were finally in possession of sufficient political clout to get positive action.

There is irony in the solidification of the positive liberal state during the Smith-Roosevelt-Lehman years, being perpetuated down through the Dewey era to today. So firmly has the concept become entrenched that it is a necessary part of any gubernatorial pledge to the electorate, if the candidate wants to win. Thus the issue now is which party the electorate will choose to run an executive branch that is expected to be positive liberal, and the difficult onus is on the Democrats to prove that they can do it a good deal better (not just better), because of widespread antipathies rooted in that party's urban base.

Scholars have recently been told that they spend too much time on the past. In this instance, however, the past explains why a party must still project a positive liberal image in a gubernatorial campaign. Because a positive liberal governor has been needed, and in turn because the office has been traditionally strong in New York, this strength, both formal and informal, has been continually increased. The end result has been a fair degree of government for, if not by, the people. As the great lawyer Charles Evans Hughes observed while governor, "I am here under a retainer. I am here retained by the people of the State of New York."[6] Whether a traditionally strong governor projecting a positive liberal image is a valid substitute for at least a reasonably representative legislature is another matter.

[6] Robert F. Wesser, *Charles Evans Hughes: Politics and Reform in New York, 1905-1910* (Ithaca: Cornell University Press, 1967), p. 163.

Patterns in New York State Politics

GERALD BENJAMIN

Even though there have been more Democrats than Republicans enrolled in New York State in every year since World War II, Republican candidates have won virtually all the statewide elections. In 1971 there were 3,663,201 enrolled Democrats in the state and 2,891,716 Republicans; the Democratic enrollment margin exceeded three-quarters of a million voters. And yet, during the period since the war, the GOP has controlled the governorship and the state assembly for all but four years and has lost dominance of the state senate for only one year, as the result of the overwhelming Republican presidential defeat in 1964. During the last three decades, the state Democratic party has never controlled the executive and legislative branches concurrently, and, furthermore, has not produced a successful home-grown candidate for the United States Senate since Herbert Lehman, who last ran in 1950. The only consistent recent Democratic success for state office has been Arthur Levitt, the comptroller since 1955.

In fact, a recent study demonstrated that, on the basis of a combined measure of party success in governorship and state legislative races, New York was the seventh most Republican state in the nation between 1956 and 1970. Among the "megastates," the ten identified by journalist Neal Peirce as being the most important—politically, socially, and economically—in the United States, New York is the most Republican in its internal politics and among the least competitive, ranking behind only Texas and Florida.[1]

[1] Austin Ranney, "Parties in State Politics," in *Politics in the American States,*

Though this picture of the Empire State as a GOP bastion may be unfamiliar to observers used to making judgments about its politics from the pluralities it has generally produced for Democratic presidential aspirants, it is well known to participants in the state's political processes. Within New York, Republican successes are usually explained to be the result of a combination of three factors: the impact of dominant personalities (Dewey and Rockefeller), the GOP control of overwhelming financial resources (Rockefeller again), and the disarray of the state Democratic party. Though all of these are of major importance, there are other, less noticed, structural and political considerations that have a good deal of influence on the outcomes of state politics. These include the "surge and decline effect" evident in off-year elections, the higher turnout level of Republican as compared to Democratic voters, the greater strength of party loyalty among the state's Republicans as compared to its Democrats, the advantages of incumbency in the governorship and its impact on party organization and performance, the divisive effect that the primary system, established in 1966, has had on the state Democratic party, and the strategic role of strong third parties on the ballot.

Trends in the Electorate

One prime structural factor that works to Republican advantage in New York State elections is the fact that they are held in off years. Political scientists have long noted that voter turnout in the United States is much higher in presidential years than in off years. In New York a presidential election regularly attracts well over a million more voters to the polls than an election for governor. This increase in turnout always helps the Democratic candidate, even when he is relatively weak. In 1956, for example, Adlai Stevenson attracted over 450,000 more votes on the Democratic line than had Averell Harriman who won the gubernatorial race in 1954, and in 1972 George McGovern (D) garnered about 600,000 more votes than had Arthur Goldberg, the Democratic candidate for governor in 1970.

Republican presidential candidates may gain votes from this presidential year surge, but it is less helpful for Republicans than Democrats. In 1960 the surge brought Nixon 319,490 more votes for presi-

eds. Herbert Jacob and Kenneth Vines, 2d ed. (Boston: Little, Brown & Co., 1971), p. 87; Neal Peirce, The Megastates of America (New York: W. W. Norton & Co., 1972).

dent than Rockefeller had received for governor in 1958, but at the same time provided John F. Kennedy with 1,153,940 more than the Democratic candidate (Harriman) for governor in 1958. In 1964, Goldwater's Republican vote for the presidency was 838,028 less than Rockefeller's vote for governor in 1962. An extraordinarily popular Republican presidential candidate (Eisenhower) or a weak Democatic nominee (McGovern) can bring the relative advantage of the surge to the Republican column, but this is the exception, not the rule. The off-year state election shelters New York's GOP from a voting turnout phenomenon that must always help the Democrats but may only sometimes be significant for the Republicans.

The lower turnout of an off year is also an advantage for the Republicans because of the consistency of that party's voters. Voting research generally shows that persons of higher socioeconomic status are more likely to participate in nonpresidential years than those of lower status.[2] It is also true that persons of higher socioeconomic status are more likely to be Republicans. As a consequence, though there are fewer Republicans in New York, Republicans are more likely to vote than Democratic registrants in gubernatorial elections. This becomes evident by comparing enrollment with actual voting patterns in each party's areas of greatest strength.

Generally, party enrollment is a better predictor of the magnitude of the expected vote for the minority party in localities in New York than for the dominant party. People enroll in the dominant party—the Democrats in New York City or the Republicans in upstate Monroe County, to cite two examples—for any number of reasons that have little to do with their political convictions. To enroll in the minority party, however, is an indication of some intensity of commitment, since it is an act that entails forfeiting a voice in key majority party primaries, endangering access to local officials and the favors they might provide, and, in some jurisdictions, risking economic sanctions. Since political convictions have little to do with majority party enrollment in localities in which one party is overwhelmingly dominant, it would be expected that there would be a considerable drop-off in actual voting from enrollment figures for dominant parties in these areas. This is in fact the case.

An examination of the 1970 gubernatorial election illustrates this point nicely. In counties that were over 55 percent Republican in en-

[2] See Angus Campbell et al., *The American Voter* (New York: John Wiley & Sons, 1960).

TABLE 1

*Party Vote for Governor as a Percentage of
Enrolled Strength, 1950–70*

Party	Enrollment	1950	1954	1958	1962	1966	1970
Republican	Core Counties (55% or more R.)	89	90	91	83	72	74
	Swing Counties (45–55% R.)	106	99	100	84	85	100
	New York City (55% or more D.)	198	129	167	141	153	194
Democratic	Core Counties (55% or more R.)	122	137	128	115	118	95
	Swing Counties (45–55% R.)	118	119	98	92	82	79
	New York City (55% or more D.)	56	74	61	51	46	44

rollment in 1970, the Republican vote was 74 percent of enrolled strength (see table 1). In New York City, overwhelmingly Democratic in enrollment, the Democratic vote was 44 percent of enrolled strength.

Twenty-year trends show further that both parties have increasingly had the problem of keeping their partisans in mutual areas of strength. Republican votes as a percentage of enrolled strength declined 15 percent in GOP strongholds between 1950 and 1970, with greatest declines corresponding with the coming of age of the state Conservative party in 1966. In New York City, the Democratic vote as a percentage of party enrollment dropped 12 points during this period. Both parties are hurt by lack of turnout and voter switching in their areas of dominance, but in both absolute and relative terms Democrats have regularly suffered much more than Republicans.

It is also evident from table 1 that Republicans in New York State do better than Democrats in "swing counties," those with 45 to 55 percent enrolled Republicans in 1970. Since swing counties in party enrollment also tend to be those in which the percentage of nonenrolled voters exceeds the state average, Republican success here is also an indication of ability to attract the independent voter. The GOP vote exceeded party enrollment in two-thirds of the fifteen counties in which the percentage of nonenrolled voters exceeded the state average in 1970. In contrast, the Democratic vote exceeded its enrollment in only four of these counties.

Geographically, the "swing counties" identified in this analysis stretch in an almost unbroken line from the suburbs of New York City (Nassau, Suffolk, Westchester, Putnam, and Rockland), north along the Hudson (Ulster, Dutchess, Orange, Sullivan, and Columbia) to the city of Albany and its environs (Albany and Rensselaer), and then generally westward (Schoharie, Montgomery, Oneida, and Cayuga) in a broken line to the Buffalo area (Erie, Niagara, and Chatauqua). The only upstate county with less than 55 percent Republican enrollment and remote from this course is Clinton, in far northeastern New York. Generally, New York politics has been viewed as an upstate-downstate struggle or a battle to capture New York City and its suburbs. A focus on a group of swing counties broadens the analysis and accounts for the impact of the Rockefeller appeal over the past fifteen years in such former Democratic upstate strongholds as Erie and Albany counties.

One measure of the growing importance of the swing counties in New York politics emerges from a comparison of the vote for Dewey in 1950 with that for Rockefeller in 1970. In 1950 the Republican gubernatorial candidate received 40 percent of his total in New York City, 36 percent in the swing counties, and 24 percent in the core Republican counties. In 1970, 44 percent of Rockefeller's vote was from the twenty swing counties, 34 percent from New York City, and 22 percent from Republican dominated counties. In absolute numbers, the core Republican counties and the New York City vote remained almost exactly the same in these two party victories separated by two decades, but Rockefeller's total in the swing counties exceeded Dewey's by over 350,000. A future Republican gubernatorial candidate must still do well in New York City, but the center of the constituency that will determine his victory is in the suburbs of that city and its upstate sisters, and in the growing counties of the lower Hudson valley. And, it should be recalled, over half the state's nonenrolled voters can be found in these twenty counties.

When voting patterns among ethnic groups in the New York State electorate are examined for gubernatorial elections, what emerges as important is the capacity of the Rockefeller campaigns to make major inroads in areas of normally overwhelming Democratic strength. Thus, whereas the Republican vote in presidential years in New York among blacks is only about 5 percent, Jews about 12 percent, and Spanish-speaking voters about 15 percent, about 20 to 30 percent of these groups have voted for Rockefeller in gubernatorial elections. Among Italians, the largest ethnic group in New York State, Rockefeller's support in his worst year (1966) was 34 percent of the vote. In

1970 the combination of his direct appeal to the Italian community and a campaign by Goldberg that eschewed ethnic appeals produced a two to one Republican margin among Italian-Americans in New York. The Rockefeller campaign approach has been very sensitive to the ethnic factor in state politics. In 1970 there were thirty-one ethnic and nationality committees, largely letterhead organizations, that supported the governor's candidacy.[3]

When measured against the total vote for other offices, the statewide Rockefeller vote over the past four elections seems three tiered (table 2). At the center was the straight-ticket Republican voter group. The size of this vote was about 1.85 million, as measured by the Republican total for comptroller in 1966 and 1970. To this was added another half-million usual GOP voters, measured by party totals for state senate candidates. Finally, the clear margin of victory was provided by voters numbering 300,000 and 600,000, depending upon the conditions of the particular election, who were attracted to the top of the ticket by Rockefeller himself. The statistics of congressional and state senate vote totals for gubernatorial election years showed a decline in the usual Republican vote in 1966 and a further decline in 1970, but it was partially masked by an increase in the Rockefeller total among switchers at the top of the ticket. The decline can be attributed to the emergence and growth of the Conservative party in New York State.

For the Democrats, what emerges from a multioffice comparison is a picture of almost constant attrition over the past fifteen years. Demo-

TABLE 2

Major Party Vote Totals for Major Offices, 1958-70

Year	Governor	Comptroller	Attorney General	Congress	State Senate
			Republican		
1958	3,126,929	2,763,895	2,915,657	2,699,291	2,703,309
1962	3,081,587	2,363,102	3,111,072	2,686,099	2,704,786
1966	2,690,626	1,861,450	3,062,355	2,375,609	2,416,756
1970	3,105,220	1,853,142	2,891,969	2,216,721	2,339,109
			Democratic		
1958	2,269,969	2,484,171	2,353,374	2,525,165	2,496,280
1962	2,309,743	2,883,064	2,194,584	2,613,346	2,534,378
1966	2,298,363	3,084,981	2,033,981	2,544,838	2,363,764
1970	2,158,355	2,881,642	1,886,631	2,396,178	2,193,967

Source: *Legislative Manuals*, New York State.

[3] Mark K. Levy and Michael S. Kramer, *The Ethnic Factor*, 2d ed. (New York: Simon & Schuster, 1972).

cratic gubernatorial candidates regularly run behind their counterparts in the statewide totals for the state senate and well behind totals for the House of Representatives. This is another indication that much of the switching from normal party loyalties in New York State favors the Republicans. In order of magnitude, the usual Democratic gubernatorial vote is now about 2.3 million, a figure very close to that of the GOP. The natural question is why the Republicans have been able to build upon their usual vote, while the Democrats have failed.

Republican Resources and Techniques

The key resources that have shaped the Republican party's continued dominance in New York include powerful statewide candidates, a strong organization able to subsume personal and ideological differences toward the goal of winning, and differential access to campaign funds. These resources in turn have been buttressed by the power of incumbency and the credible nature of the Democratic challenge.

During the Rockefeller years there have been many more Republican than Democratic dollars in New York State politics. In his first race, in 1958, the governor reported spending $1,786,000, about one-third more than Harriman. In 1962 and 1970 the Rockefeller gubernatorial campaign spent five times more than the Democratic opposition and ten times more in 1966. The total reported spending for "Rockefeller for Governor" in the 1970 election was $6,900,000, about four times what the 1958 campaign had cost. Much of this money was raised from Rockefeller's personal and family resources. The Rockefeller name also smoothed the way for short-term bank loans not usually available to political candidates: $800,000 in 1958, $600,000 in 1962, $350,000 in 1966, and $800,000 in 1970.

But the governor's victories have not been simply the result of burying the opposition under an avalanche of money. Rockefeller was an appealing and energetic campaigner. His capacity for blintzes and pizza seemed almost limitless, at least during election years, and he was at his best in the give and take of person to person encounters. One indicator of the governor's continued energy was the number of speeches he gave while running for office. In 1970 the number was 321. As the campaign peaked that year, Rockefeller was delivering three or more addresses a day.

Rockefeller's campaigns began early, fifteen to eighteen months in advance of the election. A campaign director was appointed and preliminary planning and organization were coordinated by him. As the election drew closer, campaign policy decisions were discussed by a strategy board that included the governor and some of his most trusted and experienced aides and advisers, such as R. Burdell Bixby, William Ronan, Malcolm Wilson, Hugh Morrow, George Hinman, William Pfeiffer, and Norman Hurd. The party organization was well integrated into the effort. Campaign targets such as population groups, issue areas, and geographic objectives were identified early and resources were focused on them, not squandered in an undirected way. Excellent staff work and a good political intelligence system allowed the candidate to tailor his appeal to the various interests of his changing audience as he barnstormed through the state.

Two major tools used well by Rockefeller in recent gubernatorial campaigns have been opinion polls and media advertising. Polls were used to identify the governor's strengths and weaknesses in the electorate on image and policy issues and to measure these against the attributes of potential opponents. They provided a series of snapshots of the electorate as the campaign progressed. For the 1970 election five of these were done. In that year polls were designed to identify pivotal voters (those who were undecided or who favored Rockefeller's opponents but gave the governor a fairly good rating on a scale of 0-10 on his personal or political attributes), to locate these voters geographically, and to pinpoint their concerns. Television and radio advertising was then used to address these concerns. The 1970 media budget was $3.2 million. It was estimated that this effort reached 95 percent of the television homes in the state and that the average New York City family saw 9.4 Rockefeller television commercials in that year.

Incumbency gave the Republican statewide political effort a great advantage. It allowed the governor to keep his team together, in various positions in the state government, when he was not running. It gave him the opportunity to plan ahead without having to worry about winning the nomination and thus the ability to focus all efforts on one goal. It provided the resources of patronage and preferment, the glue that held the party together, and kept it responsive to Rockefeller's priorities. It facilitated fund raising. In 1970 the Governor's Club attracted $386,000 in contributions of $100 to $500, the equivalent of 25 percent of the Democratic campaign fund for governor in that year.

It is important to note, too, that between 1958 and 1973 the Republicans enjoyed not simply incumbency in the governorship, but the incumbency of one man. Rockefeller's long tenure produced an enormous reservoir of personal loyalty among party leaders throughout the state. There was probably no Republican of any stature in New York for whom the governor had not done a favor. As journalist Richard Reeves has commented, "Governor Rockefeller has skillfully used the power of his office, the power of his personality, and his wealth to make the Republican party . . . [in New York] . . . an extension of himself."

Republican cohesion was reinforced, too, by the credible potential for a Democratic victory. There were, after all, a great many more enrolled Democrats than Republicans in the state. Republican leaders played on this fact, urging party members to hang together lest they hang separately. The real potential of a Democratic victory made the Republican effort in New York less ideological than it otherwise might have been and more oriented toward internal compromise to assure continued control of the state government. The governor, the state chairman, and other political leaders continually stressed the unity theme, especially outside New York City, where a Democratic victory was pictured as having the consequence of state control by a "Manhattan monopoly."

Democratic Weakness

Whereas success has bred success for New York Republicans, failure has contributed to further failure for the Democrats. Having held the governorship for only four years in the last thirty, and then by virtue of an alliance with the Liberal party, the Democrats have not enjoyed the advantages of incumbency, and, as Robert Kennedy remarked upon becoming United States senator from New York in 1964, no other office has enough influence to unite effectively the party around it. In addition, tensions between regular and reform elements in the state Democratic party have torn it asunder. And, unlike the case for the Republicans, threats in the party's area of strength or even victories (John Lindsay), have not provided the impetus for effective internal compromise.

The nominating procedure for statewide office has contributed to Democratic division. Under the convention system, used in the state until 1966, New York City party leaders were dominant, and upstate leaders, representing a growing proportion of the statewide party vote, were insurgent. After 1954, party leaders outside the city were increasingly united against downstate control, and by 1962 they were making progress toward gaining a major voice in statewide candidate selection and thus, possibly, toward more electable statewide tickets.

In 1966, however, under pressure from Democratic legislative leadership, the nominating procedure was changed. Statewide candidates are now selected by designation of the state committee, but a primary challenge is possible by a candidate who receives at least 25 percent of the votes in the committee or who might reach the ballot by filing designating petitions.[4]

The new nominating system, supported by the Democratic leadership, has added to party difficulties. It has made the choice of a balanced ticket almost impossible, and, if a primary is forced, leaves the selection of statewide nominees in the hands of those few voters who will participate in the primary. These voters tend to be unrepresentative, both ethnically and geographically, of the enrolled Democrats in the state. Moreover, the 1966 law leaves the annual selection of the date of the primary to the Republican legislature and the governor. The Republicans have used this tool to their own advantage. By setting late primary dates, they have left the Democrats little time to mend wounds before the general election. It is ironic that one of the reform proposals made in 1969 by a committee appointed by John Burns, Democratic state chairman, and chaired by Theodore Sorensen was a direct primary system to replace the designation of nominees by the state committee. It would seem that such a change would make the selection of a winning statewide ticket even more difficult than it is now.

Daniel P. Moynihan has traced the current split in Democratic ranks back to differences between the Smith and Roosevelt wings of the party in the mid-1930s.[5] Certainly the early reform leaders, Herbert Lehman, Thomas K. Finletter, and Eleanor Roosevelt, had their roots in the FDR tradition, and their national standard bearer in the 1950s, Adlai Stevenson, was anathema to the more conservative Irish and Italian Catholic regular party leadership in New York. James Farley, for example, already by then a grand old man of the New York party, was heard to remark that sending Stevenson, the two-time Democratic presidential nominee, to negotiate with Khrushchev was "like sending the cabbage patch to the goat."

However, differences between the reform and regular factions extend beyond leadership squabbles to basic matters of ethnicity, class, and political ethos. Regular party leaders tend to be older, Catholic (increasingly Italian rather than Irish), from the lower class or lower-mid-

---

[4] See Judson James, "The Loaves and The Fishes" (Ph.D. diss., Columbia University, 1966), pp. 42-47.

[5] Daniel P. Moynihan, "Bosses and Reformers: A Profile of New York Democrats," *Commentary*, June 1961, pp. 461-70.

dle class, and "job oriented" in their politics. Reformers tend to be younger, from the middle or upper-middle class, Jewish, and "issue oriented" in their politics. Regulars seek power for its perquisites; for them issues and the necessity to take positions on them are an omnipresent but unpleasant aspect of political life. Reformers seek power in order to implement programs. Issues and positions on them are central to their political perceptions.[6]

Internal differences of style and substance have kept New York's Democrats from uniting to capture high state offices. These differences have often centered around the control of the party machinery and designation of candidates for major offices and, since New York is so central to the national party, have often been affected by influences external to the state. In the late 1950s, Carmine DeSapio, de facto party boss during the Harriman administration, became a particular reform target because of his role in forcing the nomination Frank Hogan, rather than Thomas Finletter, for the United States Senate in 1958. DeSapio added to his difficulties by attempting to keep Herbert Lehman, senator emeritus, off of the 1960 national convention delegation, and, with State Chairman Michael Pendergast, by secretly backing Stuart Symington rather than John F. Kennedy for the presidential nomination. Before reformers unseated DeSapio in a 1962 primary in his own district, President Kennedy attempted to undermine him by channeling federal patronage through Mayor Robert Wagner in New York City. Wagner, a former ally of DeSapio's, broke with him in 1961 and, in effect, ran as a reform backed mayoral candidate against his own eight year record. Later, with Wagner growing too powerful, Kennedy began to rely on the new state chairman, William H. McKeon, as his patronage referee. Little wonder that the *Reporter* magazine in 1963 compared New York Democratic politics to those of a tribal society.[7]

In 1964 the almost unprecedented Democratic victory in both houses of the state legislature led to a major battle between the Wagner forces, which were led in the legislature by Anthony Travia, and those of Stanley Steingut for control of the assembly. The battle was not settled until Governor Rockefeller provided Wagner and Travia with Republican votes to make up their majority. The election of Robert Kennedy in 1964 provided Wagner with a major intraparty rival, but from his Senate seat in Washington Kennedy was not able to bring

[6] James Q. Wilson, *The Amateur Democrat* (Chicago: University of Chicago Press, 1962).

[7] "The Reporter's Notes," *Reporter*, October 16, 1963, p. 20.

unity to the state's Democrats after the mayor stepped down. Evidence of this was the divisive mayoral primary in New York City in 1965, which contributed to the Lindsay victory, and the losing 1966 gubernatorial campaign. Differences between Senator Kennedy and President Johnson, on a whole host of matters, especially Vietnam, also led to internal party tensions.

With Robert Kennedy's assassination in 1968, whatever hope there was for Democratic party unity in New York vanished. Another bitter New York City primary in 1969 contributed to a second Lindsay victory. In 1970, in the wake of another crushing gubernatorial defeat, party leaders told a *New York Times* reporter: "There is no Democratic party in New York." The McGovern presidential nomination reinforced division in the state party, and the loss to Nixon, the first such presidential year loss for the Democrats since 1956, seemed to confirm this 1970 observation.

Democratic divisiveness has had great impact on party fortunes in statewide races. It has led to the running of little known (Morgenthau), untried (Goldberg), or underfinanced (O'Connor) gubernatorial candidates, often with the backing of only a fraction of the party. It has led to the expenditure of time, energy, and money, which are all in short supply for the challenging party in pursuit of the nomination, well before the general election. It has produced intraparty bickering at the height of campaigns, such as Arthur Goldberg's. Finally, it has often resulted in the violation of elemental rules of racial, ethnic, and geographic balance on the ticket, rules still fundamental for victory in heterogeneous New York. In 1970, for example, the Democrats ran four New York City men for statewide office, three Jewish and one black.

Third Parties

Because the New York election law permits a candidate to run on more than one ticket and to have his votes on all lines counted in a grand total for the purpose of determining a victor, third parties have come to play a pivotal role in state politics. The role of these parties is further enhanced by a psychological factor, the politician's belief that it is better to be safe than sorry. This makes the third party's line on the ballot, with its habitual adherents, an especially attractive form of political insurance. The extent of the contemporary strength of the Liberal and Conservative parties is reflected in some recent statistics. In 1970 there were 109,311 Liberals enrolled in the state and 107,372 Conservatives, but both of these parties attracted many more voters than they had registrants. In the 1970 election for governor, the Liberal line on the ballot delivered 263,070 votes to Arthur Goldberg. The Conservative candidate, Paul L. Adams, attracted 422,514 votes.

Enrolled Conservative strength is about evenly balanced between New York City and the rest of the state, though most of the actual Conservative voters reside outside the city, many of them in swing counties. Conservatives in 1970 received three votes outside the city for governor for every one they received in it. In contrast, Liberal party voting mirrors party registration. About seven of every ten Liberal party members in 1970 lived in New York City, and about two-thirds of those who voted Liberal resided in the metropolis.

During the last two decades the Liberal party has sought to play a balance-of-power role in state politics by either endorsing or withholding endorsement from major-party candidates. For gubernatorial races this tactic has worked only once in the last six elections. It has been more effective at other levels, such as the New York City mayoralty race, some state legislature races, and for the Appellate Court judgeships. Because of its occasional success the Liberal party retains statewide credibility. Any Republican gubernatorial candidate would breathe a bit easier knowing that the Liberals were running their own man rather than backing his Democratic opponent. The hard fact is, however, that constant opposition by this party has failed to undermine Republican control of the statehouse.

The Conservative party, organized in 1962 to oppose "liberal Republicanism" in New York, came of age with the victory of its United States Senate candidate, James Buckley, in a three-way race in 1970. Because of their ideological origins, the Conservatives have worked at the state level only half of the Liberal party balance-of-power equation. They have functioned to deny votes to the major parties, but have not tried to add their strength to one or the other of them in statewide races. However, in lesser jurisdictions, such as legislative districts, major party candidates have received Conservative endorsement.

Since the entry of the Conservative party into New York politics, the Republican base has been cut by about 300,000 votes. As a consequence, Rockefeller and other Republican statewide candidates have grown increasingly dependent on Democratic switchers and non-enrolled voters. However, because of the inability of Democrats to capitalize on the opportunity presented them by upstate Conservative inroads, the meteoric rise of this party in the last decade has not been successful in unseating the Republican administration in Albany.

Conclusion

The lessons of this analysis are clear. New York's Democrats will have their best opportunity for victory in a year when they do not face an incumbent governor. Their best candidate would probably be from a swing county, well known in New York City but not from this city, popular among ethnic group voters but not himself a member of any one group. It is important that the ticket be balanced, perhaps with an Italian-American candidate for the lieutenant governorship to reverse Republican inroads into that major group's voting population. Liberal endorsement is essential to a Democratic hopeful. It is important, too, that any Conservative endorsement of the statewide Republican ticket be blocked. Finally, a division within the party should be avoided to assure a strong effort to capture the governorship and adequate financing of such an effort. The likelihood of a primary makes both the avoidance of division and the selection of a balanced ticket very difficult tasks.

Major Republican difficulties may well result from Nelson Rockefeller's resignation from the governorship. The advantages of incumbency and the unifying force of Rockefeller's personality and web of relationships will be lost, finances may be much more limited, and internal battling for statewide nominations will be much more likely. Without Rockefeller on the ticket, Republican candidates may well seek an accommodation with the Conservative party, similar to the 1972 joint designation of electors for Nixon-Agnew, in order to restore that portion of the Republican base that has been lost since 1966. Such a move, however, would be strongly opposed by Republican county leaders, many of whom have attempted to guard their power by trying to block dual endorsements of local and legislative candidates. The Republican gubernatorial candidate would be helped, too, by a Liberal nominee for the statehouse running independently of the Democratic candidate.

Like the Democrats, New York's Republicans might be well advised to seek an attractive Italian-American for the lieutenant governorship in an effort to institutionalize the support given by this group to Republican candidates in 1970 and 1972. The impact of the nominating system on the Republican party has not yet been tested; party leaders should work hard to prevent it from becoming an instrument of division and, as a consequence, defeat.

Modernization of the Legislature

STUART K. WITT

Though New York has always had a strong governor, the powers of the state legislature in the eighteenth and nineteenth centuries were greater, relative to those of the executive branch, than in the twentieth century. The legislature selected United States senators, appointed many executive officers, controlled expenditure and revenue policies, chartered individual corporations, and involved itself deeply in the affairs of local government. Those powers have been displaced or diluted by direct election, gubernatorial appointment, the executive budget, general incorporation laws, and home rule. In addition, the legislature has delegated extensive law-making authority to the state bureaucracy and has had its remaining authority limited by an increasingly detailed state constitution, by the expansion of the powers of the national government, and by the policies of the federal courts.

Thus the evolution of the legislature has involved a diminution of its external social significance. It has also involved a process of institutionalization that has reflected the bureaucratization of the society around it. The legislature's annual operating expenditures have nearly tripled in the last decade and are currently over $27 million, an amount greater than the entire state budget at the turn of the century. Legislators and leaders stay in office much longer than they did a century ago, giving the legislature greater institutional continuity. Other marks of change include an increase of specialized staffs, a tightening of physical security, a new legislative office building, higher legislative salaries and expense allowances, and a modern image-oriented public relations emphasis. Amid these changes, however, are substantial continuities that have determined the political character of the legislature in the twentieth century. These include the concentration of formal powers of the organizational and parliamentary control in the hands of the leader of the majority party in each house, the interdependence of the legislator and his political party in an exclusive two-party system, and the dependence of the legislature upon executive initiative.

The contemporary legislature shares law-making authority with the governor in a manner that depends on the character of the issues involved, the partisan alignment in each house, and the personal leadership characteristics of the governor and the two principal legislative leaders. It also depends upon the more durable provisions of the state constitution, which grant formidable legislative powers to the governor, and upon the organization of the two houses of the legislature.

The Legislative Powers of the Governor

The single most important legislative power of the governor is the veto. While qualified in law, in actual practice it has come to have the effect of an absolute veto. During the legislative session the governor has ten days to approve or veto a bill after it reaches him. If he fails to act within this time, the bill becomes law without his signature unless the legislature has adjourned. If adjournment has occurred, the governor must then act within thirty days; his inaction kills the bill. Bills vetoed during the session are returned to the legislature, where the veto may be overridden by a two-thirds vote in each house. Although in this century roughly one out of every four bills reaching the governor has been vetoed, the legislature has not overridden a single veto of the governor and has attempted to do so only once.

The implication of the veto power for the legislature is simply that the leaders must obtain the promise of the governor to accept a bill before it is passed if they want to be sure that it will become a law. In practice there is often much discussion between the governor and the leaders during the drafting of important legislation. The character of that discussion ranges from conflict, through bargaining, to cooperation. The name of the game is power politics and public policy; the ethic is survival and compromise. The veto gives the governor the last word in legislative matters. Other powers give him the first word as well.

The most important bills considered by the legislature every year include those that appropriate money for the support of the government. For nearly fifty years it has been the governor's responsibility, exercised through the Division of the Budget, to prepare an executive budget for submission to the legislature. The legislature may delete or reduce items in the budget, and it may add items subject to an "item veto," but it may not increase any item of appropriation included by the governor.

The budget bills and supporting materials from the state agencies are referred to the Assembly Ways and Means Committee and the Senate Finance Committee and are reviewed by the fiscal staffs. While the quality of the staff review has improved over the past decade (better arming the leaders for their long bargaining sessions with the governor), the legislature has remained heavily dependent upon information selected by the executive. In 1966 the legislature sought some independent information by beginning to hold hearings on selected agency budgets. More recently the new Legislative Commission on Expenditure Review, modeled in part on the General Accounting Office, has produced a few studies of state programs. However, this office is not yet very important to legislative budget review.

Most members of the legislature, including members of the fiscal committees, have only a cursory understanding of state finance. Their interest tends to be limited to particular programs, to the general level of state aid to their local governments, and to the amount of money available to themselves (an amount over which the legislature has exclusive control). Supported by the arguments of legislative reformers that well-paid legislators produce better legislatures, the New York State Legislature has been very good to itself in the last few years. No one has yet suggested that if they took vows of poverty they might be more incorruptible and more understanding of the needs of the poor.

In addition to his veto and budget powers, the governor is obligated by the constitution to present the legislature with annual recommendations for legislation. These are given in general form in his State of the State address at the opening of the legislature in early January and in special messages on particular topics throughout the early part of the session. The bills that embody his recommendations are drafted in his counsel's office and are later delivered to the speaker and the senate majority leader. The governor's "program bills" receive special attention in the legislature and become important elements in the ongoing negotiations between him and the two leaders. Of less importance, but still receiving special attention, are the hundreds of bills initiated by the dozens of state departments and agencies. They are typically drafted by agency counsel under the supervision of the agency head, screened by the governor's counsel, and transmitted by the governor's legislative secretary to the leaders' offices for introduction by members selected by the leaders.

When the Democrats controlled the legislature in 1965, the leaders kept the bills they liked for their members and gave the rest to the Republicans. Under Republican control the leaders have given them exclusively to Republican members for introduction. Bills are a kind of currency in the legislature; it looks good to the public for a member to have sponsored bills that were enacted into law. Administration bills have a greater chance of enactment than most others. Of the thousand or so bills passed every year—a roughly constant figure in recent decades—about a third originate in the executive branch. Nearly as many come from local governments and the rest from organized interest groups and the legislators themselves.

The annual legislative session lasts for about four or five months at the beginning of the year. After adjournment the legislature, powerless to call itself back into session, is nevertheless subject to the governor's power to convene an extraordinary session, at which the only subjects that may be acted upon are those recommended by the governor. Extraordinary sessions are relatively common occurrences; there has been about one every two years over the last half-century.

According to the constitution, bills must be on the desks of the members for three days before they can be passed, but the governor is granted the power to make exceptions to that rule by delivering a Special Message of Necessity to the legislature. In the typical session the great bulk of legislation, often as many as a hundred bills in a single day, is passed in the closing weeks. Scores of bills never before seen by the legislators are rushed through with a Message of Necessity, often irritating the members and arousing the criticism of reformers. The last minute rush has been a traditional legislative practice since the nineteenth century, as has been the annual *New York Times* editorial on the subject. The leaders have often talked about limiting the use of the Message of Necessity, but it continues to be abused.

The adjournment log jam needs to be understood in relation to the manner in which the business of the legislature is organized. Business is carried forward on a session basis and dominated by negotiations of the governor, the state majority leader, and the speaker of the assembly. Until the legislature adjourns, there is still time for bargaining. The governor can still threaten to use his veto against a leader unless he gets one of his program bills passed, and the leaders can threaten to kill a program bill unless the governor goes along on a new appropria-tion. Since adjournment ends the process, the participants are forced to make the best deals they can before the crucial date is reached, but the date is often uncertain and is itself an element of the game. In 1973, both houses agreed by resolution to five different adjournment dates before it was all over.

Late night bargaining at the end of a session leads to last minute deals, and the Message of Necessity is used as a means of consummat-ing them. When the hour of adjournment is finally approached—mid-night is a hopeful hour often written into the resolutions—the clocks in the two chambers are stopped as the members wearily proceed to ratify or occasionally reject the decisions reached by the leaders. At the final fall of the gavel, the general feeling is one of exhaustion and relief.

The Legislative Leaders

It is useful to think of the legislative process in New York as organ-ized around the three-person game played by the governor, the speak-er of the assembly, and the senate majority leader. In that game the two legislative leaders have much more in common with each other than with the governor. Each leader faces not only the other and the governor but is also involved with the members of his house, upon whom he is dependent for his office in the first place and also for con-tinued support in his negotiations with the governor. The speaker and the senate majority leader are elected by majority vote at the begin-ning of each session. This vote ratifies the decision reached earlier by the members of the majority party in their secret party conference. The members of the minority party elect their minority leader in the same way.

Control of the organization of the 60-member senate and the 150-member assembly is firmly established by the rules and by tradition in the offices of the senate majority leader and the speaker of the as-sembly. The leaders' powers are similar and quite extensive. Each ap-points the members of standing committees and interim joint legis-lative committees in his house (minority members on the recommen-dation of the minority leader) and selects committee chairmen (often on the convenient basis of seniority). Each has final control over the appointment and salaries of the hundreds of legislative employees (a small portion of this patronage is traditionally allocated to the minor-ity leaders). Each supervises the auxiliary offices and controls the physical space of his house. As chairman of the Rules Committee, a leadership committee lopsided with loyal majority party members, the leader controls whatever bills he chooses to refer to the committee throughout the session, has the power to expedite the consideration of bills on the floor, controls the flow of bills coming from the other house, and regulates the flow of bills to the floor during the important closing weeks of the session. Leadership control of the Rules Committee is especially important in the assembly when the other committees have stopped functioning in the waning days of the legislative session. In the assembly the speaker is the presiding officer as well. In the senate the lieutenant governor presides.

The leaders' powers are exercised with the assistance of loyal staffs personally accountable to them. The most important of these are the counsels, the fiscal staff, the administrative staff, and the public relations staff. Counsels advise them on the substantive content of bills, on the referral of bills to committee, on the parliamentary status of bills, and on political implications of legislation. They supervise the activities of the standing committees, especially in the senate where bills are normally cleared with them before being reported out; they put the calendar together; and they coordinate the flow of bills to and from the other house and the governor's office.

The fiscal staffs are attached to the Senate Finance Committee and the Assembly Ways and Means Committee, but the important position of secretary to each of these committees is filled by personal appointment of the leader, not by the chairman of the committees. The role of the chairmen seems to depend upon their personal relationship with the leader, their ability, and their willingness to involve themselves in the intricacies of budgetary policy. In recent years chairmen of the Senate Finance Committee have been more deeply involved than chairmen of the Assembly Ways and Means Committee.

The administrative staff coordinates the many housekeeping activities. In the senate much of this responsibility is in the hands of the secretary of the senate. In the assembly the administrative staff of the speaker has recently become a more specialized operation, modeled on modern management practices.

Finally, in the last decade, the leaders of the two houses have come to rely more and more upon professional public relations staffs to promote and protect the public image of the legislature and its leaders. No nineteenth century speaker or senate majority leader had anything like the organizational resources of the modern legislative leaders.

Every year over ten thousand bills are introduced into each house of the legislature and are referred by the leader to a standing committee. The number of committees in each house has recently been reduced from over thirty to twenty-one. The most important, besides the Rules Committee, are Senate Finance and Assembly Ways and Means, Codes, and Judiciary committees. They are likely to process the more important bills enacted into law, important in terms of general state policy and in terms of their political implications.

All committee chairmen owe a measure of loyalty to the leader who appoints them and who can remove them. Their control of their committees normally takes that fact into account. In the senate, the majority leader's counsel closely supervises the work of the committees, often to the extent of controlling an individual committee's agenda. In the assembly under Speaker Perry Duryea the standing committees have gradually been given greater independence, at least with respect to the less important legislation, and a newly created central staff provides them with informational resources that they have traditionally lacked. Yet it remains a central fact that the leader retains control of the most important bills in each house, a control that he keeps to himself or shares in a collegial fashion with others, depending on his style and on his relations with the members of his party.

The Members of the Legislature

In each house the leader is limited in the exercise of his powers by his desire to retain his position, which depends upon the support of the members of his party. The effectiveness of his leadership is a function of his ability to sense the needs of the members, to anticipate their dissatisfaction, and to keep them relatively happy and comfortable. In an earlier day when the members and the leaders served only for a year or two and party leaders outside the legislature had greater control over the legislation, that requirement was not as important as it has become in recent years. While external party influence remains important today, the legislative party organizations have become more durable and more independent political structures.

The leader needs the member's vote for his dealings with the governor, and he needs the member's loyalty and reelection for his continuance in office. Members need the leader's blessing for advancement to and maintenance of positions of rank in the legislature and for assistance in passing bills, and they need the leader's understanding for their particular constituency problems when they feel they must oppose a leadership position on a matter.

In New York State the legislative career typically begins within the dominant local party organization, where the prospective legislator learns the value of party loyalty, gets to know people with a reputation for influence, occupies minor elective and appointive offices, and pleases the local party organization sufficiently to be selected as a candidate for the assembly, usually without a primary election contest. In most districts the candidate of the dominant party organization is assured that he will not have much trouble winning if he runs a respectable campaign, unless important national issues affect the vote as in 1964.

As soon as the prospective legislator is nominated by his local party, the leader of his party in the legislature begins to take an interest in him by writing letters of congratulation; sending packets of information, including summaries of legislation and the roll-call votes of any incumbent opponent; and inviting him to campaign seminars to be educated on state finance and current issues, and to be instructed in the organization of the legislature and the importance of party loyalty and party leadership. If the candidate has a chance to win and needs help, the leader may even spend a day campaigning with him. The legislative career is normally confined to one political party, but to a party with separate though intersecting local and legislative organizations.

Members of the legislature are elected by plurality rule from single-member districts, a scheme that is biased in favor of the Republican and Democratic parties, both of which have traditionally agreed on the desirability of a *two*-party system. Independent third parties have little chance for representation unless their strength is extremely concentrated in one locality. But third parties have usually been active in legislative elections, having their effect through endorsement of major party candidates or through taking votes away from the most ideologically compatible major party candidate. In 1921 five Socialists elected to the assembly were kept from taking their seats by a vote of both major parties. In 1935 the legislature acted to curtail the Communist party, and in 1947 the Wilson-Pakula Law was passed in order to exclude the American Labor party. The legislature remains committed to an exclusive two-party system, although that commitment is not quite as strong as it was fifty years ago.

The distribution of Republicans and Democrats in the electorate has been characterized by an upstate-New York City division for over a century. The effect of the single-member district, plurality rule method of election has been to produce legislative party organizations that are more biased in favor of one area or the other than are the two state party organizations. That is, the proportion of upstate Republican seats in the legislature is much greater than the proportion of upstate Republican votes, and the proportion of New York City seats in the legislature is much greater than the proportion of New York City Democratic votes. Since the legislative leader's immediate constituency is made up of the members of his party, he will reflect that bias in policy matters. The governor's partisan constituency is more broadly based in the electorate. If a Republican, he will ordinarily be more responsive to the needs of New York City than the Republican leaders in the legislature. If a Democrat, he will ordinarily be more responsive to the needs of upstate New York than the Democratic leaders in the legislature.

The system of representation in New York has changed in the past decade. Prior to the federal court-ordered reapportionments beginning in 1964, the Republicans enjoyed an advantage in the assembly that gave them roughly 10 percent more seats than their proportion of the total statewide vote would indicate. Reapportionment on the basis of one man, one vote has shifted representation away from the traditionally Republican rural areas toward the more politically volatile suburbs of New York City. More recently, the courts have begun to examine the question of discrimination against ethnic minorities through the traditional practice of gerrymandering.

The newly elected, or reelected member, most likely a lawyer, joins the other members of his party in his house for a presession party conference, where the party leader is elected. The individual member's influence on this question is normally vitiated by the durability of the incumbent leadership. The last major leadership battles occurred in 1965, when the Democrats won control of both houses for the first time in thirty years, and in 1966, when Republican Perry Duryea successfully challenged George Ingalls for the position of assembly minority leader.

If the member's vote on the leadership question is rendered insignificant by the absence of a contest, his vote on legislation during the session is his single most precious resource. With it he seeks to protect his electoral position and to protect and promote his status in the legislature—in that order of priority when there is a conflict. At the same time, his party leader, whose control over the member's status in the legislature is normally greater than his ability to affect the member's electoral position, has an interest in controlling the member's vote on critical roll calls, in maintaining the member's support of his leadership, and in retaining his party's members in office. The greatest tension and excitement in the legislature appear when a member or large numbers of members are caught in a conflict between their loyalties to their leader and to their electorate. When issues of conscience are involved, as in the recent debate on abortion law reform, the strain can be agonizing.

Communication between the members of a party and their leader, through which mutual needs and desires are made known, is normally secret. The party conference meets periodically throughout the session and is the most "public" arena, but only in the sense that all members are in the presence of the leader together at the same time. Others are excluded, except when "experts" are invited to explain the complexities of some matter of policy. On the floor of the house a member rarely explains the political reasons for his vote, the language of justification being rhetorical; but in the party conference, discussions of the political implications for the members are more forthcoming. Most of the member's communication with the leader takes place through private meetings or phone conversations with him or a member of his staff. Personal face-to-face communications are the cement that gives structure to the legislative party organization. Some of the members are better situated than others in the system. Chairmen of the more important committees and assistant leaders in the majority party (assembly majority leader and the newly created deputy majority leader of the senate, for example) sit with the leader on the Rules Committee. Others have his ear depending on their personal associations, their political influence, and their policy expertise.

In their initial selection of the leader and through their contacts with him, members give definition to and establish vague limits for the leadership. However, the acceptance of strong leadership has been a traditional characteristic of the legislature throughout most of this century.

Modernization of the New York Legislature

In the last decade the legislature, like the rest of the world, has gone through some significant changes. The revolutionary 1960s ushered in a period of middle-class reform comparable to that of the early part of the twentieth century. The climate of legislative reform has been prepared by the Supreme Court's apportionment decisions, the American Assembly, the Citizens Conference on State Legislatures, the Ford and Carnegie foundations, the National Municipal League, the National Conference of State Legislative Leaders, the Eagleton Institute, and the press. "Good government" once again has become good politics. In the legislature the lead has been taken in the assembly, the senate sticking to the traditional patterns throughout Earl Brydges's leadership, which ended in 1972. The new majority leader, Warren Anderson, currently seems to be adopting a posture of reform.

Perry Duryea became speaker in 1969, following Democrat Anthony Travia's one-man show of 1965-68. Travia, at once the benevolent despot and the tyrannical dictator, had the style of the baronial Brooklyn Democratic district leader. Duryea, more the benign Rotarian and the tough-minded pragmatist, is reminiscent of a collegial corporation manager. Travia ran the speaker's office much the way he ran his political clubhouse, always willing to get up early and stay late at night to meet with a steady stream of petitioners. Duryea put a receptionist outside his office, erected new doors, and made himself less accessible. At the same time he hired administrative assistants and a public relations staff to insulate himself further, and he began to delegate a little more policy-making responsibility to the standing committees. Leadership styles are not simply random or independent variables but should be understood in some measure as having been selected by the members.

The most important changes brought about under Speaker Duryea have been the expansion of staff resources and the modification of the committee system. Two new staffs have been added, the Legislative Commission on Expenditure Review, which conducts selected studies of the operations and finances of individual state agencies or programs from an office up the street from the capitol, and the central staff, which provides research information to the standing committees. Under Duryea the standing committees have looked a little less like structures without functions, except for the function of patronage.

In 1969 the number of standing committees was reduced from thirty-four to twenty (Ethics and Guidance, which does not have regular legislative responsibilities, was added in 1970). At the same time a feature was added that proved immensely popular; each chairman and ranking minority member was provided with a "lulu," as were the members assigned to the titular positions of deputy leader, conference chairman, vice chairman, and secretary in both parties. The year before, the fictitious majority and minority committee coordinators were given lulus. A "lulu" is money "in lieu of expenses." The speaker gets $21,000 in addition to his annual salary of $15,000 and the $5,000 lulu that all members receive. Chairmen of the less important committees receive $5,000, and ranking minority members $3,500. In

1968, seventeen assemblymen received extra lulus. In 1969, fifty-five received them. Beginning in 1975, the members will each receive $23,500 plus $40 a day instead of a lulu. Reducing the number of committees did not deprive anyone of anything except a title, but it did put extra cash into the pockets of many. (New subcommittees have provided new titles.)

The distribution of bills among the committees is less skewed than it used to be. The committees now meet more often, the members are taking a greater interest in their activities than before, and the speaker has interfered with them less than his predecessor. The system seems to have shifted somewhat away from anticipation and toward greater participation. The committees are beginning to hold a few open meetings and public hearings, and some of them are conducting hearings and investigations between sessions with assistance from the central staff.

These changes have been brought about without diminishing the powers of the speaker. They have enhanced his own image and that of the assembly, but the essential powers of leadership remain, and the essential game with the governor continues to be played according to the same basic rules. A new governor, who served in the assembly for twenty years and presided over the senate for fifteen years, has been introduced into the picture, for one session at least, but he still has the veto, the budget initative, and the other legislative powers of his strong-willed predecessor.

Much of what passes for reform can be written off with the words of Henry Jones Ford, who testified before a New York legislative committee in 1910: "All these tricky expedients, all these fallacious nostrums, all these humbug reforms are never going to help you out. Simply, the situation requires radical treatment."

If legislative modernization is to have some meaning other than tinkering and bureaucratization, a good place to begin might be with the system of representation. Republicans fought against the equitable apportionment decisions of the mid-1960s, both parties have used the gerrymander in drawing district lines, and both parties have treated the election law in a manner that discriminates against third parties. The legitimacy of a majority vote in either house is, at best, suspect. Fewer than half the eligible electorate bothered to vote at all in the 1970 legislative elections. Fewer than half of those who did vote selected the party that ended up with a majority in each house, and one out of seven voted on third party lines. Yet every bill passed in the legislature continues to echo the Lockean myth of the Glorious Revolution:

"The People of the State of New York, represented in Senate and Assembly, do enact as follows...." The senate and assembly, fearful of the people, now have uniformed armed guards patrolling the halls of the capitol and have erected shields around their galleries that are about as transparent as shower glass. These are signs of governmental failure. A system of proportional representation might be worth thinking about.

Greater openness and better press reporting would be welcome. Each house has indicated that it intends to open committee meetings, to have them hold more public hearings, and to make public the record of votes taken within committee. Only the press can make them keep their word. The danger that the press faces, however, is co-optation. Life can become too comfortable for legislative correspondents and their publishers. They are on the receiving end of legislative public relations and need to be able to discern what is important independently of what they are told by the legislative image makers. Their job is difficult, though, because there is something seductive about the flattery that accompanies deceit and the false humility that conceals hypocrisy. The mistake is often made of paying too much attention to pretentious reforms.

The Administration of Justice and Court Reform

BARRY MAHONEY

During 1971 and 1972, a blue-ribbon commission composed of eleven citizens selected by Governor Rockefeller and the leaders of the legislature conducted an extensive inquiry into the administration of justice in the courts of New York. According to its chairman, D. Clinton Dominick, the commission found a court system that was in grievous need of reform:

> Administrative responsibility is fragmented. Criminal and civil case backlogs are too large. The need to resort to plea bargaining is too prevalent. Judges and other court personnel are allocated unevenly. Coordination with court related agencies is insufficient. Long-range planning and the collection and analysis of data are deficient. The cost of the courts and court-related agencies is dispersed inequitably among the state and its municipalities, and there is no uniform budget for the entire court system. Court facilities are inadequate. The procedure for disciplining judges is cumbersome and lacks flexibility and public understanding. The bail system discriminates against the poor. The grand jury and preliminary hearing procedures have unnecessarily duplicate steps.[1]

Other items could be added to the list, but even as it stands this enumeration of defects comprises a substantial agenda for court reform. Yet these defects have not appeared for the first time only in recent years; on the contrary, they have been plaguing the New York courts for decades. Most of them have been targets of previous court reform efforts, and in order to gauge prospects for successfully ad-

[1] Temporary Commission on the State Court System, Final Report of, ... And Justice for All (Albany, 1973), Part I, p. 4.

dressing them in the near future, it may be useful to begin by briefly examining the recent history of court reform in New York.

The Court Reforms of 1962

The modern history of court reform in New York can be dated from the creation in 1953 of a temporary commission on the courts chaired by Harrison Tweed, a senior partner in a leading Wall Street law firm. Established by the legislature at the urging of Governor Dewey, the Tweed commission spent five years reviewing all facets of the operations of the state courts. At an early point, most of its members came to conclusions essentially similar to those reached by the Dominick commission in the 1970s regarding the principal problems: there were too many courts, most of the courts were poorly managed, there was no effective supervision over the system as a whole, and fiscal responsibility for court operations was badly fragmented. The Tweed commission's initial proposal for addressing these problems, advanced "tentatively" in June of 1955, called for creating a greatly simplified judicial structure in which many of the specialized courts established over the years would be eliminated as separate entities, as would town and village courts. The proposal also called for a unified budget for all of the state courts, for free assignability of judges anywhere in the state in order to cope with unusually heavy workloads in particular localities, and for the establishment of a single entity that would have "general administrative authority" over the courts.

This early proposal of the Tweed commission incorporated virtually all of the major elements of streamlined structure and modernized administration that court reformers led by Roscoe Pound had advocated for half a century. Not surprisingly, it met with a storm of criticism from judges, party leaders, and local elected officials, and from their allies in the state legislature. The proposed abolition of town and village courts particularly disturbed officials and legislators from upstate areas, where the local courts were deeply embedded in the political and social fabric of the communities and where there was an especially strong feeling that courts ought to be "close to the people." The recommended creation of a central administrative entity also engendered considerable opposition. Party leaders and local officials were concerned about the effects that establishment of such an entity would have on traditional patronage practices, since many positions (e.g., "confidential attendants" and law secretaries for judges) were normally filled by persons recruited through local political organizations. In addition, many judges were fearful of losing some of their traditional prerogatives to a central administrative office and of being subjected to assignments that would take them to distant areas of the state.

Later proposals of the Tweed commission, the last of which was put forward in 1958, reflected a heightened sensitivity to the political opposition with which its initial "tentative" proposal was met. The commission ended up completely abandoning plans for sweeping structural reorganization, recommending instead only some relatively minor restructuring such as the merger of the former Domestic Relations Court and Children's Court in New York City into a single Family Court. The idea of a centralized administrative entity with statewide responsibilities was retained, but that entity would be a collective body—the Judicial Conference—dominated by the appellate divisions and lower court judges. Moreover, significant administrative powers would be left with the appellate divisions, which had traditionally been the principal focal points of administrative authority over the lower courts.

The Tweed commission's 1958 proposals were closely paralleled by a series of recommendations made in the same year by the state's Judicial Conference. Together, these sets of plans formed the basis for fresh court reorganization proposals submitted to the legislature in 1959 by Nelson A. Rockefeller, the state's newly elected governor. During the mid-1950s, Rockefeller had been chairman of the Commission on Revision and Simplification of the State Constitution, and in the course of his work with that commission he had developed an active interest in court reform. Rockefeller's natural inclinations were toward a restructuring that would vest major responsibility for the operations of the system in a single strong administrator, but in 1959 he was prepared to settle for much less sweeping reform. Responsibility for formulating a viable program was given to the office of the governor's counsel, where it fell principally to then Assistant Counsel Robert MacCrate.

The compromise that ultimately emerged from numerous negotiating and drafting sessions in MacCrate's office made some significant concessions to Republican legislators and party leaders, who were naturally skeptical about proposals that might reduce the traditional autonomy of the courts and cut into important sources of party patronage at the local level. Thus, for example, procedures for selection of judges (an area in which party leaders have long played a leading role) were left unchanged, replacement of town and village courts by district courts was made contingent upon voter approval in the affected localities, the court of claims and surrogates courts remained as independent courts, and there were virtually no significant changes in court structure outside of New York City. There was, however, a considerable amount of restructuring of courts within New York City, where problems of congestion had been getting increasingly serious and where there had been some serious charges of maladministration. In addition, an important stride was made toward centralized administrative oversight of all the courts in the state through the creation of a new entity, the Administrative Board of the Judicial Conference. This new body, composed of the chief judge of the court of appeals and the presiding justices of the four appellate divisions, was vested with "the authority and responsibility for the administrative supervision of the unified court system for the state." The Administrative Board was a smaller group than the old Judicial Conference (which had included a number of lower court judges) and was expected to take a somewhat less parochial attitude toward administrative reforms. Under the leadership of a strong chief judge and with the aid of a capable staff in the new Office of the State Administrator of the Courts, it could be a significant force in improving the efficiency of court operations throughout the state. However, there was also considerable potential for discord and stalemate—other provisions of the constitution made grants of administrative authority to the appellate divisions, and the presiding justices could not be expected to lightly relinquish their prerogatives to the Administrative Board or to the board's staff. Moreover, the financing of all courts except for the Court of Appeals and the Court of Claims was left wholly or partly in the hands of local governments, which meant that the Administrative Board would be severely limited in implementing significant reforms.

Despite the potential for stalemate over initiation of new policies, the proposed constitutional amendment embodying the basic structural elements of the reform package was endorsed warmly by elite groups within the bar, various good government groups such as the Citizens Union and the League of Women Voters, and influential segments of the press (notably the *New York Times*), all of which had long been advocating court reform. By the time of the referendum on the amendment in November 1961, a wide range of interest groups and political leaders had come out in support of it, and it passed overwhelmingly, 2,303,446 to 507,211. The following April, Governor Rockefeller signed into law twenty-two implementing bills, completing the revamping of the court system. A *New York Times* article published on the day the reorganization went into effect observed that the state was "beginning an era in the administration of justice that many hope will someday bring an end to the crisis in the state's courts."[2] It was a hope that would prove sadly illusory.

The Pressures of the 1960s

The decade of the 1960s saw American courts hit with the full force of what Harry W. Jones has aptly termed the "mid-century law explosion."[3] The era since the close of World War II has been one of rising population, growing affluence (and concomitant rise in automobile purchase, usage, and accidents), increased complexity of the socio-economic system, new demands for social justice, and frequent demands for recognition of legal rights not previously acknowledged by the courts. The law explosion reached its peak during the 1960s, a decade of rapid social change during which courts throughout the nation, like many other institutions in the society, were placed under unprecedented strains.

In New York, the strains placed on the court system were caused in part by a marked increased volume of cases entering the courts and were reflected most obviously in longer and longer delays in the disposition of cases by the courts. The volume of cases entering the courts had been increasing throughout the 1950s, and continued to rise throughout the 1960s. In 1960-61, for example, the total number of civil cases coming into the states supreme court was 58,633; in 1970-71 it was 75,809. Automobile accident cases accounted for a very high proportion of the cases on the dockets of the state's civil courts, and they also tended to be the most troublesome, time-consuming cases to litigate or to settle.

The fact that automobile accident cases required so much court time had another effect that began to become widely apparent only relatively recently: courtrooms and judges were not available for the handling of criminal cases. Until recent years, the processing of criminal cases by the courts had seldom received much attention from either the bar or the general public, with the exception of the few spectacular cases that attracted media attention. Indeed, the area had been one of such low visibility (and, for most leaders in the court reform movement, low priority) that the courts themselves had kept only sketchy sta-

[2] Leonard E. Ryan, "Crisis Confronts New Court Set-up," *New York Times*, September 4, 1963.
[3] Harry W. Jones, "Introduction," in *The Courts, the Public and the Law Explosion*, ed. Harry W. Jones (Englewood Cliffs, New Jersey: Prentice-Hall, 1965), p. 2.

tistics regarding volume, backlogs, dispositions, and delays. During the 1960s, however, a combination of circumstances led to a dramatic rise in interest in criminal law and to greatly increased pressures for criminal justice reform that were felt by the judicial systems of all the states.

Crime rates, which had been rising throughout the 1950s, began to climb steeply during the 1960s. So did arrest rates, with the inevitable result that more people were brought before the courts charged with felonies or misdemeanors. Table 1, showing the numbers of arraignments of defendants in Criminal Court in New York City over a fifteen year period, illustrates the rise.

While the volume of cases was increasing, the cases themselves were becoming more procedurally complex. During the early and mid-1960s, the United States Supreme Court decided a number of cases that had the effect of significantly expanding the procedural due process rights of defendants in criminal cases. The litany of case names —Mapp, Gideon, Noia, Escobedo, Miranda, Wade—is a familiar one, and the rulings in virtually all of these cases required courts to establish new procedures designed to permit consideration of new constitutional claims asserted by defendants in criminal cases. Before the early 1960s, pretrial hearings on motions for suppression of evidence on constitutional grounds had been almost unknown; by the end of the decade they had become commonplace. Similarly, there has been a great proliferation in the number of postconviction hearings held, in both federal and state courts, in response to prisoners' claims that there had been errors of constitutional construction in the proceedings leading to their convictions.

Public interest in the courts' handling of criminal defendants

TABLE 1

Arraignments of Defendants in Criminal Court in New York City

	Felonies Excluding Traffic Felonies	Misdemeanors Excluding Traffic Misdemeanors	Violations	Traffic Cases Including Traffic Felonies, Misdeameanors, and Infractions	Total
1954	20,646	85,526	172,273	1,462,813	1,741,258
1959	28,966	108,931	241,736	2,118,808	2,498,441
1964	46,610	126,120	250,229	3,109,007	3,531,966
1969	63,842	134,108	244,890	4,600,191	5,043,031

Source: Sixteenth Annual Report of the Administrative Board of the Judicial Conference of the State of New York.

heightened considerably during the 1960s. As the crime problem became a subject of serious public concern, the role of the courts in handling criminal cases began to receive greatly increased attention from the media and from political leaders at every level of government. Often the judgment of the courts' work was negative. Perhaps the most serious criticism of all came in a report made public by the highly respected Economic Development Council of New York (EDC) during the summer of 1972. An extensive study undertaken by EDC pinpointed a number of serious problems in the administration of the courts in New York City and included the finding that judges in the criminal division of the supreme court in the city spent an average of less than three and a half hours per working day actually on the bench.

With the enactment of the federal Omnibus Crime Control and Safe Streets Act of 1968, federal funds became available for use by the states to improve their criminal justice "systems." When the Safe Streets program first began, the focus of attention was principally on police work, but it was not long before the new cadre of state and city criminal justice planners started to give close attention to the functioning of the criminal courts. In New York, the state agency responsible for administering the federal funds made available under the Safe Streets Act is the Division of Criminal Justice Services, which has been a part of the Executive Department throughout its five years of existence. The agency has consistently placed a high priority on improving the administration of the state's criminal courts and attacking problems of congestion and delay in the processing of criminal cases. During the first five years of the Safe Streets program, its top officials played an active role in shaping programs aimed at upgrading the courts' management planning capabilities. This was done partly through the funding of specific projects (e.g., studies of the operations of particular courts, establishment of a network of "court planners," development of computer-based management information systems) and partly through joint planning sessions with the office of the governor's counsel and with various court officials. The general thrust of the agency's efforts has been toward strengthened central administration of the courts and better management at every level of the judicial hierarchy.

The pressures on the court system that grew out of increased civil and criminal caseloads, growing interest of the media and the public, and active involvement in court operations by executive branch agencies such as the Division of Criminal Justice Services, can be regarded as external pressures. There have also been some internal pressures on the courts by those working within the system. Judges, court clerks, court attendants, and other "nonjudicial personnel" who are essential to the operation of the courts all have their own interests and objectives. Like other civil servants, they want higher wages, better working conditions, long vacations, and influence over the aspects of governmental policy making (especially personnel policies) in which they are involved. Nonjudicial personnel in the courts have unions of their own and have demonstrated their readiness to resist the development of innovative reform programs that they fear might jeopardize their own interests. To a significant degree, these internal pressures run counter to the reformers' orientation toward innovation and toward strong central administration.

However, there have also been some significant internal pressures favoring reform. A number of judges within the system have been sensitive to the mushrooming problems of the courts and have been vigorous proponents of changes in long-established practices. The pressures they have generated have contributed significantly to the revived court reform movement that now seems to be underway in New York. In 1971, for example, the judges on the Administrative Board of the Judicial Conference took the initiative in addressing the problem of delay in criminal cases by promulgating a "speedy trial rule" for criminal prosecutions. Although the impact of the rule was softened by legislation passed before it took effect, the board's action forced all branches of government to examine a problem that previously had not been on the state's political agenda at all.

Responding to the Pressures: Halting Steps Toward Future Reforms

During the early 1960s, the principal concern of the Administrative Board (and of its staff agency, the Office of the State Administrator of the Courts) was to establish uniform personnel standards and regulations. Prior to the 1962 court reorganization, the different fiscal authorities that funded the individual courts had prescribed job categories, wage scales, working conditions, and most other personnel policies. After 1962 it became the Administrative Board's responsibility to establish statewide standards concerning qualifications, appointment, promotion, and removal of nonjudicial personnel throughout the state's court systems. Since local authorities remained responsible for financing the operations of most of these courts, the effect of the 1962 reforms was to create a series of tripartite bargaining relationships involving the board (represented by staff from the State Administrator's office), the local fiscal authorities, and the court employee organizations. By the mid-1960s, career service rules and a job classification structure had been established, and the board had become a party to numerous collective bargaining contracts.

The board's efforts in establishing a statewide career service system and in bringing some order into what had been a totally chaotic personnel situation were significant steps forward. However, the establishment of a rigid job classification structure that essentially parallels the existing court structure has also had some unfortunate consequences. Among other things it has made it difficult to use nonjudicial personnel in a flexible manner. All too often, the "lower" courts in the hierarchy, where much of the most difficult work of the judiciary is done and where well-trained clerks and court attendants are essential, have inexperienced personnel, because seniority and experience are rewarded by promotion to better paying (though often less demanding) positions in the "higher" courts.

Another consequence of the Administrative Board's emphasis on establishing job classification structures and dealing with other pressing employee relations problems was that it largely neglected long-range planning. There is little evidence that, prior to 1971, there had been much in the way of innovative thinking about what the problems of the courts were and would be for the next ten to twenty years, what the needs would be, what sort of data should be gathered in order to adequately analyze problems and needs, or how the planning ought to be done. Although some imaginative work had been done on a local or regional basis (notably in the state's Fourth Judicial Department, where the presiding justice of the appellate division, Harry Goldman, had taken the lead in developing regional court planning capability and in pushing through new court rules and other programs that led to marked reductions of case backlogs in metropolitan centers such as Buffalo and Rochester), little had been accomplished on a statewide basis. It was not until the 1971-72 period, however, that the full implications of the board's lack of a true planning capability began to become apparent and that the first steps toward strengthening its staff arm and overcoming the systemic fragmentation that still exists were taken.

The precipitating factor was the board's own decision, made in April 1971, to establish a "speedy trial rule" to govern the prosecution of criminal cases. The rule, which was scheduled to go into effect on May 1, 1972, would have applied to all cases except those involving

homicides and provided in essence that (a) a defendant who was being held in jail pending trial would have to be released on bail or
on his own recognizance unless brought to trial within ninety days of
the date of his arrest; and (b) a prosecution against a defendant would
have to be dismissed if the defendant was not brought to trial within
six months of the date of his arrest. The promulgation of the rule was a
bold step on the part of the board, which theretofore had done very
little with respect to problems of criminal justice administration, although several of its members—notably Chief Judge Stanley H.
Fuld—had been leaders in reexamining old precedents in individual
cases involving points of criminal procedure. Unfortunately, however,
the step was apparently taken with little realization of the nature or
full extent of the delay problem in the metropolitan courts of the state
or of the political opposition that it would engender.

As the months passed and the effective date of the rule grew closer,
the opposition to it mounted. Efforts to delay or soften the impact of
the rule were led by the state's District Attorneys Association, whose
leaders insisted that allowing the rule to stand would result in a general jail delivery. The board could not effectively refute these claims,
since it had little in the way of data necessary to analyze the problem.
Although the Office of the State Administrator of the Courts had been
responsible for collecting court statistics ever since the reorganization
of 1962, it had concentrated mainly on civil cases. Problems of volume, case flow, backlogs, and time delays in criminal cases had never
been explored, and meaningful statistics were nonexistent. When a
hasty survey of the delay problem was undertaken in the fall and win-
ter of 1971-72, the results were shocking. In the four largest counties
of New York City—New York, Kings, Queens, and the Bronx—the
data indicated that approximately 40 percent of the cases in which
defendants had been indicted by a grand jury took more than six
months to go from the date of arrest to the date of disposition. Cases
involving jailed defendants moved somewhat more rapidly than others, yet only about 35 percent were concluded within ninety days.
Neither the Administrative Board nor any of the agencies involved in
the actual handling of criminal cases could state with assurance just
what would be needed in the way of additional resources (including
new judges, court clerks, prosecutors, defense attorneys, and probation officers, as well as additional space for courtrooms and officer and
detention facilities) in order to meet the requirements of the rule.

It was at this point, near the start of the 1972 legislative session,
that the governor's office began to get deeply involved in both the

controversy over the speedy trial rule and—for the first time since the 1959-61 period—the larger but closely related problems of court administration. During 1972 and 1973 Governor Rockefeller was in the forefront during a series of battles over court structure, financing, and administration. Several of his efforts warrant particular mention.

In an effort to resolve the dispute over the impact of the Administrative Board's speedy trial rule, the governor urged a compromise that was adopted by the legislature in 1972: a statute requiring district attorneys to be ready to proceed to trial in any felony case within six months of the date of the defendant's arrest. Since this "ready rule" legislation did not require dismissal of a prosecution if no judge or courtroom was available to try the case, it was obviously less severe than the Administrative Board's rule, which it superseded. Passage of the statute removed some of the urgency from efforts to attack backlog and delay problems, though it may at least have had the salutary effect of requiring district attorneys to keep close track of the progress of cases through the courts.

Late in the 1972 legislative session, Rockefeller proposed the establishment of an "emergency felony case processing program" to attack the problem of criminal case backlogs in New York City and other metropolitan areas. The program contemplated the establishment of new court "parts" to hear felony cases and was structured to require joint planning by the Office of the State Administrator of the Courts and the Division of Criminal Justice Services. As approved by the legislature, it called for relatively modest first-year funding ($3.0 million in new state funds, $3.7 million in city funds), but it marked the first time a concerted attack was undertaken on problems of congestion and delay in the criminal courts of the state.

At the same time the legislature passed the emergency felony case processing program, it also approved legislation recommended by the governor that markedly expanded the powers of the state administrator of the courts and made the directors of administration in the four appellate divisions subordinates of the state administrator. Although state constitutional provisions still left the appellate divisions with a claim to substantial authority over the administration of the courts within their respective judicial departments, the legislation was a major step toward centralized administration.

During the fall of 1972, in response to allegations of corruption said to involve policemen, lawyers, and judges in New York City, the governor appointed a special prosecutor, Maurice Nadjari, to investigate such charges and bring prosecutions in appropriate cases. After more than a year in operation, Nadjari's office has succeeded in obtaining several indictments, but it is too early to tell whether he will be able to produce evidence of widespread corruption.

Early in its 1973 session, the legislature passed a no-fault automobile insurance bill, over the bitter opposition of many trial lawyers in the state who feared a loss of business. Rockefeller had been strongly urging enactment of such a bill for two years, principally on the grounds that it would remove from the courts a high percentage of the automobile accident cases which for years had been contributing so heavily to congestion and delay in the handling of civil cases. By the governor's estimate, the time of approximately 125 New York judges had been occupied with hearing automobile accident cases. The no-fault legislation, which took effect on February 1, 1974, should enable them to spend much of their time handling criminal cases.

Rockefeller successfully pressed during 1973 for the adoption of an emergency program to deal with the seemingly intractable problem of narcotics abuse. The most controversial element in the program was legislation imposing severe penalties (up to life imprisonment) for persons convicted of trafficking in drugs and sharply restricting plea bargaining in such cases. Since heavy sentences and an end to plea bargaining in narcotics cases would necessarily mean that many more trials would have to be held, Rockefeller also sought a major expansion in the number of judges in the state. The program ultimately passed by the legislature included authorization of 100 new judgeships, including 68 in the Court of Claims, to which appointments are made directly by the governor with the consent of the senate. It also provided an appropriation of $66.3 million to implement the program, using the joint planning process (involving the Division of Criminal Justice Services and the Administrative Board of the Judicial Conference) that had been put into operation the year before as part of the emergency felony case processing program of 1972. The program was strenuously resisted by most of the "criminal justice establishment"—judges, prosecutors, defense attorneys, police officials, and criminal justice planners—mainly because of a fear that even a greatly expanded court system would not be able to handle the expected sharp increase in the number of trials. Whatever the outcome, it is an experiment that is likely to have important repercussions in New York and nationally in the years ahead.

Prospects for the Future

Early in 1973 the temporary commission on the courts chaired by D. Clinton Dominick submitted its report to the governor and the legislature, detailing the problems outlined at the start of this essay and making 180 specific recommendations. Most of the recommendations were designed to implement a few basic ideas similar to those advanced by the Tweed commission in the 1950s: simplification of the court structure, improved central administration of the courts, state financing of virtually all the courts in the system, new machinery for the disciplining and removal of judges, and abolition of the bail system.

The proposals relating to court structure, administration, and financing have one important element in common: they tend to move the center of decision making with respect to the administration of justice out of local political arenas and into the larger statewide arena. Such a move has obvious implications for the kinds of decisions that will be made. The decision makers will be different and their constituencies will be different. In a centralized administrative office with budget-making power over the courts in the state, for example, local patronage considerations are likely to be subordinated to consideration of efficiency and the setting of priorities on a statewide basis. Since the influence of local political organizations over the operations of the courts would be reduced by the adoption of such proposals, local party leaders and others who stand to benefit from localized financing and administration can be expected to resist them.

Nevertheless, there now seems to be a strong current of reform sentiment running in the state. Indeed, in a survey conducted by the Citizens Union among members of the legislature, court reform was ranked as the most important issue on the state's political agenda for 1974. Bar associations and good government groups seem prepared to press vigorously for changes along the lines suggested by the Dominick commission. And the new chief judge of the state's Court of Appeals, Charles D. Breitel, has indicated his own commitment to such reforms both in public statements and in his appointment of Richard J. Bartlett to the newly created post of state administrative judge. Bartlett has been delegated broad authority by the presiding justices of four appellate divisions, who, together with Chief Judge Breitel, make up the Administrative Board of the Judicial Conference. For the first time, a single individual will be accountable for the performance of the court system on a statewide basis and will have significant administrative authority to achieve program goals.

Bartlett's appointment reflects a commitment by the leading figures in the state's judiciary to the concept of a cohesive, statewide court system. But if the long-existing fragmentation is really going to be overcome, legislation providing for state financing of the costs of major courts will be necessary. Governor Rockefeller's past proposals for state assumption of court costs were tied to a reduction in general state aid to localities and was successfully resisted by local officials on the ground that the localities would suffer a net financial loss. It remains to be seen whether Rockefeller's successor as governor, Malcolm Wilson, will take the lead in devising a workable formula for state assumption of these costs. If he does, the prospects for truly significant court reform would seem to be quite good.

Historically, court reform efforts in New York have been characterized by slow and sporadic movement toward increased centralization and simplification of court structure, with most "reforms" taking the form of compromises that did not greatly disturb the equilibrium of the existing system.[4] That trend seems likely to continue, somewhat accelerated now by the pressures introduced by the narcotics problem, the general rise in crime during recent years, and the growing awareness—both within and outside the judiciary—that modern management techniques can be productively used in addressing many of the problems of the courts. Strong central administration and state financing of major courts seem fairly close to becoming realities. Other items traditionally on the agenda of court reformers, such as the abolition of town and village courts and the appointment (instead of election) of judges, have always been strenuously resisted in New York, and there is little in recent history to suggest that significant changes will be made in these areas. A 1973 proposal by Governor Rockefeller that would have provided for gubernatorial appointment of future supreme court justices, for example, was quietly buried by the legislators. History suggests that as trade-offs are made in the politics of court reform in the future, it is less probable that legislators and party leaders will yield to reformist pressures in the area of judicial selection than in the area of financing and administration.

---

[4] Arthur L. Galub, "The Politics of Court Reorganization in New York State" (Ph.D. diss., Columbia University, 1968). Galub's study provides an excellent historical overview and analysis of court reform efforts in New York, focusing particularly on the events leading to the court reorganization of 1962.

Finally, it should be noted that problems in the administration of justice in New York are by no means limited to the structural and administrative problems that have been principal topics of the foregoing discussion. There is a myriad of difficult issues, ranging from where and how to obtain capital resources necessary to provide adequate physical facilities for the courts, to how to assure equality of access to counsel and to the courts for poor and middle income people, to how courts should handle problems of juvenile delinquency. It will be a long time, if ever, before they are all resolved. It is encouraging, though, that there seems to be a far broader interest in the administration of justice today, on the part of both members of the bar and the general public, than there has ever been before.

The Changing Role of the States
in the Federal System

WILLIAM G. COLMAN

The last half-century has been a turbulent one for mankind; it has been no less so for testing the fabric of the American governmental system. The post-World War I period was a time of crisis and change for the concept of federalism—the major unique contribution of this country to the art of government. Conceived and articulated in 1787 in an attempt to combine the twin goals of unity and diversity, the United States Constitution delegated power from the new states to the central government to provide it with the capacity for national leadership and interstate coordination domestically and for economic and military security from events beyond the seas. Legally, as well as philosophically, the new nation was a union of states.

The conception of American federalism has swung like a pendulum from decentralization to centralization and back again. Despite the prominent attention given to urban affairs, the crisis of the cities over the last decade, and the varying degrees of direct federal-local relationships since 1935, the structure of federalism in the United States has essentially been one of federal-state relations, and it is toward that arena of intergovernmental affairs that this paper is mainly directed.

The Founding Fathers intended important roles for the state governments in the federal system. They were to be repositories of most domestic governmental functions as well as political laboratories in which new theories and initiatives of government could be tested in the crucible of practical experience, with failures noted and successes adopted in other states and, after further improvement, adopted by the nation as a whole. The states were to be sturdy buffers in a represen-

tative democracy against what Alexander Hamilton and others feared
might be the excesses of the popular will. Originally, for example,
United States senators were not elected directly but selected by the
state legislatures. Finally, the states were to be equals in proposing
amendments to the national Constitution. This last role was one of the
few examples of fuzzy conceptualizing on the part of the drafters,
and confusion still prevails as to the nature and scope of a national
constitutional convention that would be established by the action of
thirty-four state legislatures. With some resistance, these early concepts prevailed until 1861-65 when a wide swing of the pendulum established the primacy of unity over diversity within federalism.

Restricting the Role of State and Local Governments

Determined to halt the epidemic of economic plundering in which
state officials and predatory private interests were engaged and further
determined to bring the surging tides of corruption engulfing city
governments under control, delegates to state constitutional conven-
tions set about to curb the power of state and local governments in the
fifty years following the Civil War. New restrictions were designed to
halt corruption and foolish spending through such provisions as those
forbidding the commingling of private and public funds for railroad
building. Similarly, strict limits were placed upon the size of the public
debt and the manner in which it could be incurred by the states and by
local governments. Only in the last decade has New York State succeeded in amending the restriction against mixing public and private
funds so that enterprises such as the Urban Development Corporation
could proceed. Other provisions were also designed to curb the power
of government. In many states, for example, governors were prevented
from succeeding themselves, and in a considerable numbers of other
states the governor's term was set at two years. The legislative session
was restricted to a few days each biennium in practically all states.
Frequently, a sixty-day period was chosen for this purpose. Some
people said that instead of sixty days every two years, it ought to be
two days every sixty years!

In contrast with the exclusive executive power conferred upon the
president by the national Constitution, the governor in all states was
forced to share executive power with several other directly elected
officials, sometimes a dozen or more. Finally, nearly all of the states
rigidly and narrowly proscribed the powers and functions of local
government. Legislative abuses in awarding city charters caused gov-

ernment reformers in the early part of the twentieth century to unfurl the banner of municipal home rule, a development that was to proceed apace in the years that followed.

In short, the actions taken by citizens during and following Reconstruction greatly hampered the powers of initiative and response of state and local governments for many decades to come. The effects continue through to the present. Once embedded in the state constitutions, these restrictions were extremely difficult to modify because political leaders recommending change were placed in an unavoidable posture of self-seeking. Ultraconservative and special-interest groups have always been able to frighten many voters into believing that easing restrictions was a sure prelude to raising taxes. When consideration was given to modifying state and local debt limits in New York and other states, for example, counsel for bondholders were quick to predict fiscal chaos, higher interest costs, and higher taxes. Of course, strict limits make more legal work for lawyers skilled in charting courses around them. More often than not, the proposed solutions result in a host of special authorities and districts which make responsive and accountable state and local government harder than ever to achieve.

Stewardship of the States in Providing Domestic Government

Prior to the Civil War, the states generally performed quite well in keeping with the original concepts of being repositories of most day to day domestic government and in serving as political laboratories, though in the latter role there were considerably more observers than performers. The national government had not found it necessary to move much beyond the areas of international security and the promotion of the free flow of interstate commerce, including road and river improvement and a postal service.

But the emergence of the Industrial Revolution during the Reconstruction period and economic and social changes in later decades began to put severe strains upon state governments. They were so weakened by restrictions that they found it increasingly difficult to respond in newly emergent areas of public policy. For most of the twentieth century a majority of the states defaulted upon the ideals of the national Constitution and shortchanged their own citizens in the process. In brief, through the 1950s most of the nation's state governments stood aside while the system of local government became increasingly impotent and anarchical. The Congress, the president, and the Supreme Court time after time had to step into the breach of state nonfeasance and malfeasance.

The record of most states during this half-century was deplorable. They largely ignored deteriorating conditions in the cities and the escalating aspirations of the urban poor. They countenanced widespread abuses of zoning and building code powers. These powers, inherent in the states, had long ago been delegated, without strings, to localities. The property tax, which was the revenue mainstay of local government, was allowed by the states to lapse into serious disrepair until it was marked by ineffective yields and inequitable administration. Moreover, state legislatures helped the process along by mandating property-tax exemptions with hardly a thought of replacing the lost revenue. Finally, to their everlasting discredit, states for years deprived urban residents of their rightful representation in the legislature, until federal courts found it necessary to intervene to require reapportionment.

Among many state legislative leaders a bias against the big city was a badge proudly worn, and, in the formulation of state aid programs, cities were miserably shortchanged. It is small wonder that after a century of maltreatment city mayors as a group became highly suspicious of state government and wanted as little to do with it as possible. It is small wonder that minority groups everywhere, and in the South in particular, cannot yet find it possible to place much confidence in either the ability or the willingness of state government to afford equitable treatment to all socioeconomic groups, since many state governments served consistently from 1865 onward as an instrument of racial oppression and discrimination.

The 1960s saw a reversal of this trend, however, and following the reapportionment decisions of 1962 and 1964 state legislatures began to come alive. This reversal complemented gubernatorial initiative where it already existed and sparked it elsewhere. The few states that had stood out as islands of leadership and excellence in a sea of apathy and mediocrity (New York, Wisconsin, Oregon, Massachusetts, and California) were joined by a growing list of others beginning to seize initiative. Some examples of state constitutional and legislative change in 1972-73 illustrate the point. Ohio enacted a personal income tax. Minnesota, Montana, and Wyoming authorized annual sessions of the legislature. Before 1960, annual sessions were the exception; since 1970 they have been the rule. Forty states took action to improve their judicial systems. Twelve states modernized their correctional systems. Twenty states considered the new uniform residential landlord-tenant code adopted by the National Commission on Uniform State Laws, and some passed appropriate legislation.

By 1973, twenty-five states including New York had created housing finance agencies and another twelve had similar plans under consideration. Thirty-one states had enacted fair housing laws, and forty had enacted "circuit breaker" or other property tax legislation designed to mitigate the impact of the tax on low and moderate income owners or renters. Nine southern states moved ahead in 1972 to lay out a work program for the Southern Growth Policies Board.

California adopted legislation for the control and management of coastal land through the initiative process. New York passed legislation making the Adirondack preserve the largest land area in the country under comprehensive land use control. Forty-two states began to provide financial assistance for the construction of local sewage-treatment plants. New York even arranged to pay in advance the federal funds to which localities were entitled. Many of these programs were backed up with bond issues approved by voters. Twenty states began to provide financial assistance to local governments for public transportation. Several states overhauled their system of school finance. Forty-eight states established at least one agency or charged an official by law or gubernatorial order with responsibility for some aspects of consumer protection. Several states considered and enacted various forms of no-fault automobile insurance, a program conceived by Massachusetts, not the United States Senate.

Essentially, the states in 1973 continued to bear the major burden of domestic governance in the United States. They paid with state tax dollars over half of all the bills for such vital services as higher education, transportation, health, criminal justice, and consumer protection. Furthermore, they had emerged anew as political laboratories for the testing of innovative governmental approaches to cope with the burgeoning problems that accompany population growth and technological advance. State financial aid and technical assistance to local governments continued to grow in breadth and scope. It nearly equalled the total amount of federal aid to both state and local governments. State activity in housing was also widespread, especially in finance, building codes, landlord-tenant relations, and property tax relief. Economic development, protection of the environment, and formulation of better balanced patterns of population settlement were three more areas of overriding concern. Finally, the human resources area witnessed a major shift of intergovernmental responsibilities and methods from specifically and sometimes microscopically designed and mandated federal project grant programs toward broader functional formula bloc grants and greater emphasis on income maintenance instead of service provision.

Meanwhile, governors and legislatures moved ahead to reshape financing and administration of elementary and secondary education, finding new and viable methods for dealing with the desperate plight of the inner city schools. Several states began to deal with the problem of equal opportunity in education for every child by assuming local educational costs. More must be done in this area, however, without the loss of local policy control. State governments also established a more meaningful role in manpower training for the unemployed and hard to employ, decentralized and improved the treatment of the mentally ill, held down costs and provided better health faciities and personnel, and undertook a variety of new initiatives in consumer protection.

In revitalizing the basic institutions of state government itself—the executive branches, the legislatures, the courts, and the system of criminal justice—dramatic progress has been and continues to be made. Forty-six states have undertaken major reorganizations in the last five years, eliminating the major shackles on the power of the governor. Legislative modernization and reform of state court systems have been nearly universal.

The Unfinished Agenda

An awesome collection of difficult problems remains to confront state governments. One need only look at finance, governmental structure, and urban growth policy to be convinced that the hardest tasks lie ahead.

Several aspects of state finance require reform. States must find ways to reform the property tax so that it may continue to be a substantial source of local revenue. They must develop a local revenue structure that is equitable, administrable, and provides an optimal mix among taxes, user charges, and other revenue sources. Finally, greater efforts must be made to assure an adequate market for local bond issues.

Financial reform inevitably involves other areas of government responsibility. States, for example, must find a way to assure an equal range of municipal services to neighborhoods, with administrative and financial structures appropriate to each, while avoiding the straitjacket of one-man, one-dollar egalitarianism portended by some judicial decisions. At the same time, states must avoid raising public expectations for services far beyond the ability of taxpayers to provide. The growing pressures of public employee unions and associate factors such as rising unfunded pension system liability and declining employee productivity are playing havoc with local budgeting and revenue raising, and thus may be considered as aspects of state financial problems.

Many other aspects of the financial plight of state governments could be mentioned in this paper, if only briefly. There is growing agreement across the political spectrum that federal revenues will continue to be shared and that welfare should and must be federalized. The survival of the inner cities poses the basic question of whether to undertake massive reconstruction or to adopt a people-oriented approach of assisted depopulation and resettlement coupled with planned economic disinvestment in core areas. Both plans would cost many billions of dollars.

The second set of reforms that are greatly needed would entail the modernization of the structure of local government. County, town, and city governments often have overlapping jurisdictions, and to bring about equity between city and suburban taxpayers is a major problem on the unfinished agenda. New York is far behind several other states in dealing effectively with the joint problems of several counties or other regions. One problem related to the achievement of a rational relationship between special districts, local or state-created, and general local government is the use and control of extraterritorial land in a do-nothing county or town.

Environmental concerns are forcing state governments to exercise some of their long-neglected responsibilities regarding urban growth policy and land use regulation. The state is responsible both for coping with existing urban problems and for planning for the urbanization to come. In many states the attitude toward urbanization has been to stress quantity rather than quality, with little if any regard for where and under what conditions certain developments should be discouraged. The political attractions of laissez faire and a policy of expediency are obvious. The consequences, in terms of both energy and environment, ought to be obvious as well.

States must begin to take action in several areas of urban development policy. They must modernize the housing industry, assure equal housing opportunity, provide environmental protection to areas of critical state concern, and ensure adequate mass transportation.

Each state must have an overall urbanization policy, but each state must also establish ground rules as to the extent to which local governments are permitted, encouraged, discouraged, or prohibited from taking their own steps to control growth. Localities across the country are already experimenting with alternatives such as placing an absolute ceiling on further population growth and enforcing it through building permits. Boca Raton, Florida, recently adopted a charter amendment limiting its future population to 40,000. This smacks of exclusionary zoning unless care is taken to make the impact nondiscriminatory among income classes. Ramapo, New York, and Livermore, California, among several other areas, are using the availability of public facilities as a means of slowing growth. Another alternative is refusing approval for large new residential subdivisions, as was done recently by Fairfax County, Virginia.

The decision to limit or stop growth would have a great effect on employment opportunity. Are the poor going to have to bear the brunt of a middle class environmental movement? Regardless of one's views on growth policy, it is clear that this problem is going to be one of the major contenders for attention through the 1970s.

How well state governments are able to confront these and other equally difficult and controversial issues will depend not only upon their own institutional strength and political resolve but upon the extent to which the federal government facilitates or frustrates a meaningful role for the states in the federal system.

Current Status of Federal-State Relations

The core of intergovernmental relations in the United States concerns federal-state interaction, and despite the repugnance with which many big city mayors view the term, the parallel sovereignty of national and state governments continues to be the hallmark of the American federal system. The ever-changing nature of the states' role was succinctly characterized by Woodrow Wilson half a century ago: "The question of the relations of the states to the federal government is the cardinal question of our constitutional system. At every turn of our national development we have been brought face to face with it, and no definition either of statesmen or of judges has ever quieted or decided it. It cannot, indeed, be settled by the opinion of any one generation, because it is a question of growth, and every successive stage of our political and economic development gives it a new aspect, makes it a new question."

Despite their legal parity in the federal system, the states' fiscal, administrative, and political status has been in a long decline since the 1930s. As indicated above, they have just begun to recoup. The growing fiscal dependence of the states on federal grants-in-aid, rising to a current average of 25-30 percent of total state revenues, has been one of the factors in this decline. A drastic shift beginning in 1937 from an exclusive federal-state relationship to one in which the federal-local axis competes in volume and vigor with its precursor has been another. A shift from "formula" grants, where a particular share was a matter of right, to "project" grants, in which state governments compete with one another as well as with local governments and universities for federal grants, could be added to the list. Decisions about who would receive the grants were made by program administrators and congressional subcommittees and staff, all of which were fond of playing God in intergovernmental relations. The increasing national tendency to look to the United States Senate rather than the state houses for national political leadership has been another factor. To be sure, Governor Nelson Rockefeller of New York kept the competition reasonably lively in recent years. The fact remains, however, that the last governor to serve as president was Franklin Roosevelt, and the last one nominated by either of the two major parties was Adlai Stevenson. The only governor to serve either as president or vice president since World War II resigned in disgrace in 1973.

Finally, perhaps the most pernicious factor of all has been the refusal of Congress and the executive branch to deal *selectively* rather than *generally* with state governments, insisting always in treating California, New York, and Michigan, for example, on exactly the same terms as Alabama, Nevada, and Rhode Island. For over a decade, the Advisory Commission on Intergovernmental Relations (ACIR) has been urging a selective approach to grants-in-aid. The ACIR has suggested that where a state meets two conditions—establishes adequate administrative machinery and, "buys in" to a federal-local program by putting up at least half the nonfederal share—the federal government should deal with the state rather than directly with local governments. ·

This selective approach has been resisted strongly from three quarters: senators who do not like to admit strong potential competitors such as governors into partnership; big city mayors who do not want to see a shift in the center of gravity from Chicago to Springfield, New York City to Albany, or San Francisco to Sacramento; and those states that have done little in the area of urban affairs, such as Tennessee, Missouri, Indiana, and others who contend that it is the "sovereign" right of the state to maintain exclusive jurisdiction over intergovernmental relations with Washington, the history of the last forty years notwithstanding.

In assessing the current struggle over centralization and decentralization in the American governmental system, it is apparent that a number of forces are operating strongly on opposing sides. Advocates of intergovernmental decentralization can count on a widely recognized failure to coordinate effectively from Washington an intricate network of over one thousand separate categorical programs, a majority of which have been of a "project" rather than a "formula" nature and have required a multiplicity of decisions by federal program administrators. Mayors and county officials, to say nothing of state legislators and governors, insist on the decentralization of decisions about program priorities. This insistence springs from differing sources and rests upon contrasting assumptions. Conservative officials would like to see some social programs killed and irritants such as community action, legal services, and day care left to wither on the vine. Liberal officials think they could make programs operate better and reach more people if operated under a bloc grant. Other officials would like flexibility to expand some programs and terminate others. Another illusion of conservatives is that decentralization will bring about a national condition of "limited government." President Nixon's administration is also committed to decentralization, but there is a question about the permanency of this commitment in the face of his greatly weakened political influence on Capitol Hill and in the nation.

The present constitutional climate requires strong proof of the need for federal action. Although Article X of the United States Constitution, which reserves all powers not vested in the federal government to the states, has lost much of its legal significance, there usually must be a reasonable showing of state and local inability or unwillingness to act before a new federal program can be passed through the Congress. If proponents cannot demonstrate that state and local governments have had a reasonable opportunity to act and have not done so, the opponents of federal action can usually obtain at least a delay until another Congress. The great flurry of legislative enactments following the Johnson landslide of 1964 dealt for the most part with proposals that had been discussed in the halls and corridors of Congress for quite a while. It had become clear long before that the states were unwilling or unable to act on these proposals.

Finally, a shift toward an income maintenance strategy lessens justification for federal service delivery programs. The federalization of three of the four welfare categories, increasing pressure for private pension reform and national health insurance, and the current call for housing allowances all underline the trend toward an income maintenance rather than a service strategy. Thus, service delivery problems are left to state and local government.

Forces Against Intergovernmental Decentralization

The opposition to decentralization is resilient as well as persistent. It rests on the assumption that the long-range trends of technological advance and increasing societal complexity and interdependence make inevitable and ever-expanding sphere of governmental activity, especially at the national level.

All major decisions to decentralize must be made at the center. The plaint of presidents that they often do not control their own house is uniquely justified when considering plans, decisions, laws, and regulations to carry out governmental decentralization. The bureaucracy may be resistant or slow to move on policies espoused by new administrations. In the case of decentralization, the bureaucracy is personally and emotionally involved. Empires of program review and princely states of regulation writing are threatened to the core by revenue sharing and grant consolidation. The committee and subcommittee fiefdoms of the Congress are most unfriendly. Even when decentralization legislation is passed on occasion through the combined persuasive efforts of governors, mayors, and political leadership of the executive branch, its implementation must depend on regulations drafted by the bureaucracy, and strings and conditions appear as if by magic. For a time it appeared that this factor might be mitigated to a considerable degree by the unusually responsive cabinet and subcabinet machinery constructed by President Nixon's White House staff before Watergate. However, changes in the central staff mean that the high-water mark of White House mastery of the bureaucracy has passed.

The vertical functional autocracy of program specialists that runs from Washington through state capitals to city neighborhoods, disregarding cabinet officers, governors, and mayors in the process, is difficult to curb. The growing insistence of state and local elected officials on effective policy control is currently a strong challenge to this force.

A combination of threatened categorical components that adds up to a theoretical majority is possible. Given the parliamentary situation, however, a two-thirds majority rather than a simple majority is needed. This would be somewhat difficult to achieve even if the threatened categorical programs had been universally successful in reaching their objectives.

The Crystal Ball

To depart from the discipline of objective analysis for the luxury of speculation is always tempting and will be indulged in briefly here. Over the short run, many decentralization objectives will be achieved. Over the intermediate term, there will be pendulum swings in both directions, but not approaching the pace of federal *programmatic service* activity in the middle and late 1960s.

There will be a continuing trend at the national level toward income maintenance in preference to a spoon feeding service approach. The judicial role will continue unabated, with state supreme courts assuming an increasingly aggressive role as more governmental decision making is devolved into the state-local sector.

Over the long term, societal complexity and technological advance will be determining characteristics of intergovernmental relations. Certainly eternal vigilance is required to assure that government does not expand extravagantly; but expand it will, because expand it must. States will continue to give a mixed but improving response to the demands of domestic government, but the Congress and the president will need to give them a prod from time to time, and the people will need to strengthen their insistence upon greater accountability from state government as the *quid pro quo* for public support of further institutional modernization at both state and local levels. Only state governments, for so long as this country chooses to maintain a *federal*, rather than a *unitary*, governmental system can provide the large and growing body of domestic law to cover the countless aspects of daily life that is necessary to maintain an ordered society.

The State and the Federal Government

DONALD H. HAIDER

The sweep of broad national social-economic forces over the past two decades caused New York State to confront new conditions beyond its immediate control. Rapid industrialization of agriculture and displacement of unskilled workers, particularly in the South, generated a steady stream of rural migration to New York City and other areas in the state. This resulted in the concentration of large numbers of low-income people, chiefly minority groups, in the cities. While migration increased the population, federal programs in highways and housing promoted the exodus of job-producing industry and higher-income residents to suburban areas. These national migration patterns of people and business produced a mismatch of social problems and fiscal resources. Fiscal disparities between cites and suburbs led the state to assume responsibility for supporting basic social services and redistributing larger amounts of its tax collections to local governments.

Federal efforts further compounded New York's problems. The national government had long been active in providing grants in aid to states, but the character of these grants changed significantly over the years. From the 1920s through the 1950s federal assistance to states progressed from flat grants for supporting minimum service levels to variable matching ratios in categorical grant programs to promote geographic distribution of wealth, transferring revenues from above-average-income to below-average-income states. These programs generally focused upon rural America and the poorer states, and as a consequence (with the exception of highways, agriculture, and rather marginal investments in health and education) were not very significant to a high-income state like New York.

During the 1960s the federal government shifted from assisting states in achieving their objectives to development and implementation of national programs. Congress asserted federal interest and authority in a wide range of functions that until then had been the exclusive or predominant province of states and local governments. The number of separate federal grant-in-aid programs grew in the decade from 120 to nearly 500, the greater proportion of which were experimental or project grants.

The New York Case

These federal programs and funds compelled New York, a progressive state with acknowledged leadership in service provision, to spend enormous amounts of new funds for narrow, detailed purposes. The threat of federal action forced the state to implement the programs in the manner prescribed by Washington. On numerous occasions Governor Rockefeller argued that as a consequence of federal aid formulas, New York had to pay more than other states in aggregate to acquire a share of these funds. Indeed, in program after program, federal grant requirements stipulated that funds could not be used as a substitute for existing state efforts in a particular area but had to involve "maintenance of effort" or be used for "enrichment" purposes.

New York's needs, however, were most often not for new, experimental programs and further stimulation of effort. Rather, New York needed funds to carry on existing programs and to enable local governments to provide basic services like police, sanitation, and education. The narrow confines of federal programs impeded the state from focusing its fiscal and manpower resources on basic local needs.

For its leadership and initiatives, New York was often shortchanged or penalized by federal authorities. The state failed to receive full federal reimbursement, for example, in its prefinancing of the nation's clean waters program or advanced work on the state's portion of the national highway system. It was also penalized by direct statutory ceilings placed upon programs governing the specific amounts that any one state could receive in a program. In public transportation, New York was limited to 12.5 percent of the meager funds provided, despite the fact that 35 percent of all commutation on public transportation occurs in the New York City area.

Similarly, in housing, federal limitations on costs per unit often restricted state and local participation. To take full advantage of the Medicaid program, the state would have had to expand significantly its existing program standards even though the state already had the most advanced program in the country. If it had raised its assistance levels to meet the original federal participation requirements, New York would have absorbed the total amount of federal funds appropriated for the entire nation for this program. Once Congress awoke to this possibility, it changed federal regulations and established cost levels so that New York was, in effect, penalized for its already high level of service standards. Federal grant programs thus created for New York massive confusion in planning, coordination, and management.[1]

Restoring the fiscal balance in the federal system became another Rockefeller goal. The federal government, with its fiscally superior base for collecting revenues through federal income taxes, had brought about a complete reversal of fiscal relations among government levels. State and local governments outtaxed and outspent the national government up to the 1930s. But by the 1960s the federal government collected in aggregate two-thirds of all taxes nationally and 90 percent of all income taxes. Federal tax receipts for the decade 1960-70 more than doubled from $77 billion to $146 billion, while state and local tax structures proved less responsive to economic growth. Nonetheless, state and local governments made three-fifths of all outlays for domestic programs. Further, only slightly less than one-half of federally collected dollars were being spent for domestic purposes. Rockefeller did not advocate more spending for domestic purposes at the expense of national defense. Rather, he consistently supported maintaining national security but criticized the lack of federal priorities and inefficiency in federal domestic allocations.

The federal government had the revenues. The states and localities were left with the problems. Like other states, New York had to raise taxes time and again merely to keep pace with rising expenditure needs. Meanwhile, the federal government indulged in five separate tax cuts during the decade, while expanding the national debt. New York State, heavily reliant on income and sales taxes, incurred large fluctuations in its tax receipts as a result of national cyclical movements and suffered a continuous shortfall in revenue estimates during the recessionary period of 1969-71.

Adding to the difficulties of state budgeting and planning was what

[1] U.S., Congress, House, Government Operations Committee, Subcommittee on Intergovernmental Relations, *Grant Consolidation and Intergovernmental Cooperation Hearings*, 91st Cong., 1st sess., 1969, pp. 85-108.

Rockefeller termed "rising expectations." Often the federal government made commitments to new programs in which the states were expected to participate but failed to commit fully the magnitude of resources initially promised once the programs were under way. In the case of Medicaid, for example, Congress's decision to curb eligibility levels meant that New York had to trim its Medicaid rolls by more than 1 million people who had been promised assistance. In total, the disparity between federal aid authorizations for major domestic programs and actual appropriations of moneys increased by more than $6 billion just between FY 1966 and FY 1970. This "dollar gap" created enormous hardships for New York State and the governor in planning budgets, setting priorities, and assessing long-term federal commitments. When federal funds were cut back in the Poverty Program and Water Pollution funding, New York State substituted its own funds for federal moneys. Thus New York had to contend with economic fluctuations and inflation, on the one hand, and steadily rising service demands and insufficient tax resources on the other.

As early as 1968, the governor issued a warning that public expectations would soon be "out-running our capacity to raise revenue on a sound basis."[2] Further major increases in taxes might seriously damage economic growth by discouraging new business and expansion of old, and by jeopardizing New York's competitive position in relation to other states. Nonetheless, the state faced a $620 million budget gap in 1969, a gap that the governor indicated might have exceeded $1 billion if reductions had not been made in various department requests. To balance the state's budget, the sales tax was increased and a 5 percent across-the-board cut in all spending instituted. These tax problems were further exacerbated by the fact that New York was surrounded by three industrialized, nonincome-tax states, New Jersey, Connecticut, and Pennsylvania. Once again the governor called upon the federal government for immediate action on revenue sharing, federal takeover of welfare, and increased aid lest the state become "an industrial wasteland if it was forced to raise taxes further."

In the mid-1960s New York received back from Washington only 6 cents on every dollar, or $1.4 billion in federal aid for the $22 billion in taxes sent to Washington. While federal aid increased gradually in subsequent years, the fact remained that New York recovered only 14 percent of its aggregate state and local revenue from the federal

[2] *The 1969-1970 Budget Message of Governor Nelson A. Rockefeller*, January 8, 1969.

government by the end of the 1960s and regularly ranked nearly last among the fifty states in percent of revenue derived from federal money.[3]

In sum, Governor Rockefeller argued that New York had upheld its share of the federal partnership and proved its responsiveness to public needs. It could not wait for other states to catch up. The state could raise taxes further and thereby drive industry and taxpayers out, cut back much needed services and local assistance, or seek massive federal aid—and the latter was the only real political choice. Resolution of New York's fiscal problems could not be accomplished, however, without the assistance and collaboration of leaders in other states.

Rockefeller in Washington

The modern governor discovers that relations with Washington are far too important either to ignore or delegate to his surrogates. The governor, if he is to be chief executive in more than name only, must be the chief proponent of his state's point of view in dealing with Washington. Contemporary federalism has turned states into clients of the federal government and governors into lobbyists.

Governors are rather belated entrants into the Washington lobbying scene, already inundated with competitors. They are often rivals of congressmen and senators, who view them as outsiders seeking to encroach upon their fiefdoms. Also, most governors' terms of office are so limited and their formal powers so restricted that sustained penetration into the intergovernmental communications system and the Washington lobbying complex is prevented.

Rockefeller's problem was thus formidable. He dealt with Washington through innumerable access points and pressure instrumentalities to present the New York case and promote the cause of reforming the federal system. Having served as governor during the Eisenhower, Kennedy, Johnson, and Nixon administrations, Rockefeller developed a warm working relationship with presidents of both parties. He courted their good will, advising them on domestic policies and informing them of programs established in New York that could serve as models for national legislation.

As governor of the state with the single largest delegation in Congress, Rockefeller exhorted delegation members to employ their size

---

[3] Data on New York State supplied by George von Frank, Chief Intergovernmental Relations Section, New York State Division of the Budget.

and strength on behalf of New York. He organized a bipartisan steering committee of the delegation, met with the delegation at least annually to present the state's agenda with the federal government, and attempted to mobilize it on bipartisan issues where the state's direct interests were at stake. The size of the New York delegation and the diverse political interests of its members, however, limited the success of the governor's efforts on many issues.

Rockefeller testified more times before congressional committees than any other incumbent governor and appeared at least once before every major committee of the House and Senate. He pressed New York's claims at the White House and with federal department heads. He used the state's Division of the Budget to analyze proposed programs and to develop alternative measures. He also invested considerable effort in attempting to mobilize fellow governors in a collective strategy for dealing with the national government.

On a broader scale Rockefeller hoped to persuade the National Governors' Conference and the Republican Governors' Association to form a united front in dealing with the federal government. Few of the governors were as well informed as he on proposed programs as to how they might affect their states. Governors of other states that profited from the grant system as it existed had no desire to change it. Still others feared partisan disputes, and divisions between North and South on race questions made united action practically impossible.

For five years, 1965-69, Rockefeller served as a member of the Advisory Commission on Intergovernmental Relations (ACIR), an agency established by Congress as a permanent bipartisan body representing all levels of government and the public. During this period, the governor viewed the commission as a forum for building a consensus among governors, mayors, and county officials on the need for overhauling the federal grant system and the sharing of more federal revenues with states and localities. The problem-oriented ACIR played a pivotal role in efforts to recommend federal action in areas such as grant reform, federal assumption of public assistance costs, and especially revenue sharing.[4]

Thus, on many fronts, with Congress and the state's delegation, with the White House and federal agencies, with lobbying groups and fellow governors, Rockefeller worked to build a broad coalition for change in Washington. No single case is more illuminating of the

---

[4] See Advisory Commission on Intergovernmental Relations, *Urban America and the Federal System* (Washington, D.C.; G.P.O., 1969).

Rockefeller style, persuasiveness, and effectiveness than the passage of the State and Local Fiscal Assistance Act of 1972, otherwise known as revenue sharing.

The Governor and Revenue Sharing

Federal revenue sharing was first considered and later dismissed by the Johnson administration when the expected fiscal dividend of the mid-1960s quickly vanished under rising defense expenditures and inflationary conditions. The concept was then embraced by the Republican presidential candidate, Richard Nixon, in his 1968 campaign. President Nixon introduced his revenue sharing proposal to Congress in August 1969, calling for the return of $500 million to states and localities in FY 1971 with incremental increases to $5 billion by FY 1976.

Initially, Governor Rockefeller's federal agenda called for grant-in-aid reform, federal takeover of welfare costs, and revenue sharing. For Rockefeller, full federal assumption of welfare costs would have been the most desirable alternative. It was unlikely, however, that Congress would approve full federal assumption of these costs in one move, particularly since one-half of AFDC recipients resided in only four states, the largest of which was New York.

Rockefeller had not been an early revenue sharing enthusiast, simply because he did not think the bill could pass Congress. However, confronting a possible $1 billion gap in the state's 1971-72 budget, the governor in November 1970 settled on revenue sharing as offering the most immediate prospect of providing large amounts of new federal funds to meet New York's needs. Accordingly, revenue sharing became the state's highest priority in its dealings with Washington.

Essentially the governor moved on three related fronts: (a) coalition building—bringing together citizen groups, the media, legislators, mayors, county officials, and city managers; (b) White House influence—sustaining the president's commitment to revenue sharing, which involved expanding its base from $500 million to $10 billion and making it the Nixon administration's highest domestic priority; and (c) congressional lobbying—focusing these efforts upon the Democratic majority in Congress and specifically on Wilbur Mills, chairman of the House Ways and Means Committee, under whose auspices any revenue sharing plan would fall.

Rockefeller gained endorsement for revenue sharing from the great majority of the state's forty-one member congressional delegation and its two senators and urged them to sustain a unified effort "to get more money back from Washington."[5] The governor stumped the state, conducting town meetings, holding press gatherings, and making special speaking appearances to highlight the state's problems with Washington and to build support for revenue sharing. He rallied the state's mayors and county officials, formed a New York State Citizens Committee in Support of Revenue Sharing, and, to cap the campaign, declared February 22, 1971, Revenue Sharing Day throughout the state. In dramatizing the importance of this legislation for each community, Rockefeller released figures showing how much each county and city in the state might receive under the program.

Having organized a revenue sharing constituency in New York, the governor then carried his advocacy to national gatherings of mayors, state legislators, county officials, and city managers. These officials became revenue sharing's principal support groups. In early 1971 he helped organize the National Citizens Committee for Revenue Sharing. This Washington based citizens lobby, composed of governors, mayors, and prominent citizens, was modeled along the lines of the New York committee and created outlets in more than thirty states and numerous congressional districts.

Maintaining the White House's interest in revenue sharing and raising the base amount for the program constituted an even greater challenge. The governor estimated that New York State needed a $500 million to $1 billion increase in federal aid "just to hold the line at present levels of activity."[6] His campaign for a $10 billion starting figure was at direct variance with the $500 million base contained in Nixon's original bill. In several meetings with the president and his White house advisers, Rockefeller presented the case for a larger revenue sharing program. Cognizant that the White House was reviewing the entire revenue sharing issue, Rockefeller proposed and received support for a strong resolution from his fellow GOP governors which recognized "an impending collapse of confidence in state and local government, particularly in urban areas," and concluded that "nothing less than a federal revenue sharing program of at least $10 billion annually . . . can save this situation."[7]

Armed with this public statement, Rockefeller again took the revenue sharing case to the president. He argued that an expanded revenue sharing plan, which was supported by the Republican administration

[5] *New York Times* (November 11, 1970).
[6] Ibid., (November 19, 1970).
[7] Press Release, Republican Governors' Association, Meeting at Sun Valley, Idaho, December 14, 1970.

and an alliance of state-local officials and was opposed by the Democratic Congress, could make the difference in the forthcoming 1972 elections. The president and his party needed an issue. What emerged from this debate was a $5 billion base figure, a compromise between Rockefeller's $10 billion plan and the president's budget advisers' figure of a more modest $2.5 billion.

President Nixon called for a $5 billion general revenue sharing plan in his State of the Union message in January 1971. The president's move took Congress by surprise and began the long, uphill struggle for gaining congressional adoption. Chairman Mills indicated his opposition. His announcement of hearings was interpreted as a move to kill the proposal by inaction. Partisan resistance was evident in the fact that only 12 of the more than 170 House-Senate cosponsors were Democrats.

Like Wilbur Mills, many congressmen viewed revenue sharing as fiscally irresponsible, because it separated revenue acquisition from control over expenditures. Congressional appropriations committees feared circumvention of their authority and a backdoor raid on the federal treasury. Democratic leaders were not enchanted with the idea of allowing a Republican president to gain credit for passage of a Democratic initiated proposal. Also, many congressmen and senators opposed relief of governors and mayors, many of whom were rivals and competitors, and apportioning large sums of federal funds without a clear sense of whose constituencies would be the principal beneficiaries. Opposition also arose from organized labor, professional associations, and others who deplored the venality of state and local governments.

Although Wilbur Mills had originally opposed revenue sharing, he gradually succumbed to pressure within his own party, the committee, and the newly developed pressure system. A massive Washington lobbying effort by state and local officials in the spring of 1971 had particular impact on his thinking. On November 30, 1971, Mills introduced his long awaited substitute for the president's bill. Unlike the Nixon plan, backed by Rockefeller, which split payments evenly between states and localities, Mills's bill apportioned funds one-third to states and two-thirds to local governments. The base figure would be slightly more than $5 billion, drawn by formula from tax receipts over which the appropriations committee would have no control, and the total allocation for five years would be $30 billion. Half the battle had now been won, yet Mills had made no promises concerning House deliberation on his bill. However, the situation had changed in one important regard—the Democrats who had a majority in both houses of Congress now had their own revenue sharing proposal. No longer were they faced with a plan initiated by a Republican president.

The original Nixon proposal tied revenue sharing payments to two factors, population and tax efforts, that were highly beneficial to high tax states and those with large urban communities like New York. The Mills bill, resulting from various compromises of political interests within the Ways and Means Committee, involved a complicated five-factor combination: state-local tax effort, state income tax effort, population, urbanized population, and population inversely weighted for per capita income (the so-called poverty index). Even though only one-third of the funds would be apportioned to the states, the Mills bill also provided a highly favorable allocation to New York. *

When the House took up the Mills bill in June 1972, the outcome was in doubt. Rockefeller personally sat in on major deliberations among House leaders, Mills, and others, and he called governors at the last minute to clinch undecided votes. By an 8-7 vote of the House Rules Committee, revenue sharing gained a closed rule that prevented the legislation from being substantively amended by the House. House Appropriations Committee Chairman George Mahon was defeated by a close vote in his efforts to bring revenue sharing under the congressional appropriations process and his committee. Once again, Rockefeller participated in final House deliberations and strategy sessions, aiding the leadership in convincing individual members who might otherwise have voted against them. The Mills bill passed by less than forty votes, a slim margin in House deliberations. In an eighteen-month campaign for revenue sharing, Rockefeller emerged nationally as its principal spokesman, advocate, consensus builder, and lobbyist.

Revenue sharing passed the House, but Rockefeller's personal victory for gaining a substantial share for New York State proved ephemeral. In the Senate, poorer and less populous states and their senators reacted strongly against the House's distribution formula. What emanated from the Senate Finance Committee, a counterpart to the House Ways and Means Committee, was an apportionment formula geared chiefly to the poorest rural states. The Senate also voted to impose an annual ceiling on the previously open-ended funding for social services programs that had been reimbursed on a 75-25 basis between the federal government and state-local governments. The federal costs for social services reimbursements, extensively drawn on by New York State, had increased sixfold since 1968 and was expected to exceed $2 billion in FY 1973. In spite of protests from high-tax-effort states, the

Senate Finance Committee version gained Senate approval and was sent to the conference committee.

In the final outcome, the House-Senate conference gained approval for an unusual compromise that left both formulas in the final bill, and each state's revenue sharing allotment was to be based on the formula that provided the most money so long as it did not exceed available authorizations. States, which got one-third of the money, could use these funds for almost any purpose, while local shares based on population, tax effort and poverty, had some limited restrictions as to use. Conferees also agreed to a $2.5 billion ceiling on social services. On October 20, 1972, Nixon signed the State and Local Fiscal Assistance Act of 1972 into law, authorizing payments of $30.2 billion to states and local governments from mid-1972 to mid-1977. By early December 1972, all fifty states and more than 38,000 local communities began receiving first installments of revenue sharing funds.

It is hard to judge Nelson Rockefeller's success or failure in influencing national policy. The results of the difficult projects that he undertook will take years to materialize. Revenue sharing is a case in point. The combination of revenue sharing and social services provisions holds the prospect of funneling more than $40 billion to states and localities over a five-year period, making it the largest domestic aid bill ever enacted. Obviously its passage involved many men, but probably no single individual outside the federal service played more of a key role in gaining its adoption than did Nelson Rockefeller.

State Aid to Local Government

DONNA E. SHALALA

Characterized in the past as the invisible branch of government—the fallen arch of the federal system—state government has finally arrived. Like a private foundation, the state has enormous funds to give away. New York State allocates over half its money to local governments, resulting in complex fiscal relationships with them. Opinions differ on whether states were pulled or pushed into taking more responsibility for their citizens, but clearly there is much greater involvement today than there was twenty years ago.

Indeed, before New York State became predominantly metropolitan, the level of interdependence was low; citizens demanded few services from their local governments and even fewer from the state. The one exception was New York City, whose vast population concentration made it a special case "which demanded special treatment."[1]

Both urbanization (the movement of people from rural areas to the cities) and metropolitanization (the redistribution of population and economic activities between city and suburb) led to increased interdependence between localities and state governments. The growth of the state's aid to localities program is but one reflection of this.

Direct payments to local governments in New York are made through the state's Local Assistance Fund. New York also assists its residents through the State Purposes Fund, which finances services performed by the state, such as the operating expenses of state-maintained institutions. This analysis, however, will focus on the seven

[1] Seymour Sacks, Robert Harris, and John J. Carroll, *The Role of State Aid*, New York State Department of Audit and Control, Comptroller's Studies in Local Finance, no. 3 (Albany, 1963).

categories of the Local Assistance Fund (LAF): General Purposes (formerly the Per Capita program); Education; Social Services; Health and Mental Health; Highways; Housing and Urban Renewal; and Miscellaneous (a variety of small programs).

A number of characteristics of the fund will be analyzed: growth patterns (for the total fund and by major category); changes in the content of the aid programs; and shifts in the pattern of distribution of state aid. The study will begin with fiscal year 1959.

The Growth of State Aid

Between 1959 and 1972, the Local Assistance Fund grew 357 percent. Direct aid grew from nearly a billion dollars in 1959 to over 4 billion dollars fourteen years later. Even when the consumer price index is used to deflate the aid to real dollars, there is still an increase of approximately 200 percent. Not surprisingly, the fastest growing sector has been Social Services, with an increase of 641 percent. No other major category has increased as rapidly, although all have shown gains, as table 1 demonstrates. The growth in social service activities accounted for the increase in its share of total state aid and for a decrease (or no increase in the shares) of other categories. Education continued to be the largest single recipient, but its proportion of total aid dropped from 60.4 percent in 1959 to 53.3 percent in 1972. Highways, Housing Subsidies, and Urban Renewal moneys also received less of the total state aid package in 1972 than they did in 1959.

TABLE 1

State Aid to Localities by Type of Assistance 1959–72
(in thousands of dollars)

	1959		1972		% of Aid Increase
	Amount	% of LAF	Amount	% of LAF	1959–72
Education	$560,668	60.4	$2,261,038	53.3	303
Social Services	151,251	16.3	1,121,159	26.5	641
General Purpose (per capita)	96,838	10.4	454,955	10.7	370
Highways	58,077	6.3	108,376	2.6	87
Health & Mental Health	41,803	4.5	199,455	4.7	377
Housing Subsidies and Urban Renewal	15,107	1.6	51,676	1.2	242
Miscellaneous	4,951	0.5	43,625	1.0	781
Total (Local Assistance Fund)	$928,695	100.0	$4,240,284	100.0	357

Source: *Annual Reports* of the Comptroller of the State of New York.

These proportional declines or lack of growth in the other categories do not necessarily mean that the state has become less active in any of these areas. In fact, the state has expanded its activities outside the Local Assistance Fund in each category that showed no proportional growth or a decline. For example, state aid to education does not include most of the aid supplied to the state's university system. Transportation bond moneys do not show up fully in the Highways category, nor are the Urban Development Corporation's expenditures part of the Housing and Urban Renewal figures. The expansion of state-owned mental health facilities is not included under Health and Mental Health. An analysis of the Local Assistance Fund, therefore, covers only part of the complex relations between the state and local governments.

Changes in the Aid Package

The state's priorities are, in part, revealed by the functions selected for aid. Education and social service programs have accounted for 80 percent of all aid increases between 1959 and 1972 (51 percent to education and 29 percent to social service programs).

State aid to education in New York is a billion dollar business. It is the state's biggest business. More than half of all aid to local governments is currently allocated to education; whether this will continue is not clear. The greatest proportion of total Assistance Fund aid to education was in 1964 (67.4 percent) and its lowest point in 1972 (53.3 percent). Despite this apparent decline, however, education has received substantial aid increases, surpassed only by assistance to social service programs.

About 90 percent of all education aid goes to public school systems. The large proportion that public schools take out of the total education aid package has continued, along with significant increases in aid to other programs such as the City University of New York and the community college system. Of the aid to public schools, 90 percent is general aid, for which there have been two different programs. The first was a foundation program developed in the 1920s and continued, with periodic modification, until 1962. In 1962, the recommendations of the Joint Legislative Committee on School Financing (Diefendorf committee) were accepted, and the state legislature adopted an equalization grant program which, with some minor revisions, is still in use. The basic goal continues to be to aid districts that are poor in property value per pupil. The modifications in the basic equalization formula have generally not altered the technical basis of the formula. There have been occasional special-category programs, but these have never made up more than 10 percent of total public school aid. Nor has the aid distribution pattern changed significantly over the years—the state's largest cities have usually found themselves getting on the average less aid per student than their surrounding suburbs.

No sector has grown as rapidly as state aid to localities for services for the poor, the old, the young, and the sick. In fiscal 1959, the state gave $151 million to local governments to help pay their welfare bill; this figure reached $1.1 billion in 1972, an increase of almost a billion dollars. In 1959, 16.3 percent of total state aid was earmarked for social service programs; in 1972, the proportion had risen to 26.5 percent.

The establishment of the Medicaid program, in fiscal 1967, was legislatively the single most striking change in public assistance programs during the fourteen year period under review. However, the social service program in its entirety has experienced vast growth and change. The growth seems to be the result of the basic character of most of social service aid: everyone who qualifies for assistance and applies for it, receives it. Sufficient funds are appropriated to meet the costs that the program has authorized. In this sense, appropriations are automatic.

In 1959, Home Relief made up 35.8 percent of total welfare aid, followed by Aid to Dependent Children, 20.5 percent, and Old Age Assistance, 19.1 percent. Since 1959, there has been a reshuffling among the programs. The introduction of the Medicaid program explains the shifts. Although the Medicaid program cannot be considered completely new, because it picked up existing medical costs in every needy category, the new legislation did increase the coverage of the program. Because of the difficulty of sorting out medical payments before the enactment of Medicaid—to Old Age Assistance, Aid to the Blind and Disabled, and Aid to Dependent Children—it is impossible, however, to explain the increases by category.

Alterations in the geographic distribution of aid have taken place. Three recent studies concluded that the urbanized areas (cities and suburbs) of New York State benefitted most from changes in state aid patterns over the last decade.[2] There is no question that aid to urban

[2] Jerry Wade, "Changes in the Distribution of State Aid Programs in New York State, 1959-1969," in Local Government Finances in New York State, 1959-1969, eds. Jesse Burkhead, Seymour Sacks, Donna E. Shalala, and Bernard Jump, Report to the New York State Temporary Commission on the Powers of Local Government,

areas increased at a faster rate than aid to the rest of the state, and this was particularly true for New York City. However, such a conclusion, based on an aggregate analysis, hides important and nagging discriminatory patterns.

The Case of New York City

In terms of total aid, New York City received a tremendous 462 percent increase between 1959 and 1972, compared with 290 percent for the rest of the state. Much of this increase (42 percent) is explained by the growth in social service aid, while educational aid represented 33.6 percent of the increase. The rest of New York State received 69.2 percent of their increased aid for education, and 16.5 percent for social services.

When individual years are examined, it becomes clear that the pattern for aid to the city has changed over this period. In 1959, almost half of the aid received went for education, but by 1972, education accounted for only 35.4 percent, while welfare represented 39.3 percent, compared to 27.0 percent in 1959. The rest of the state consistently received about 70 percent of its aid for education (see tables 2 and 3). When social service assistance is excluded from the aid totals, the trend toward the city looks very different. On a per capita basis (using 1970 population figures), New York City received an increase of $122.08 per capita, compared to $133.17 for the rest of the state. This disparity is explained by the current state education aid program. Despite the change in funding during the 1959-72 period to include the CUNY system, the large proportion going to public schools has continued, 96 percent in 1959 and 90 percent in 1972. In dollar terms, in 1972 New York City received $75.44 per capita to support public schools while the rest of the state received $171.60 per capita. For *total* education in 1972, it received $90.62 per capita while the rest of the state received $149.38 per capita.

The explanation for these differences lies in the character of the state's current school aid formula—a substantially modified version of the percentage equalizing grant. This provision misrepresents the financial ability of New York City to pay for its schools. Put simply, the city appears to be exceedingly wealthy based on the property value

October, 1971; Donna E. Shalala and Jerry Wade, *State Aid to New York City, 1961-1971*, Report to the New York City Commission on City-State Relations, June 1972; Richard Lehne, *Reapportionment of the New York Legislature: Impact and Issues*, National Municipal League (New York, 1972).

TABLE 2

State Aid to New York City by Type of Assistance 1959-72 (in thousands of dollars)

	1959		1972		Proportion of Increase in LAF 1959-72
	Amount	% of LAF	Amount	% of LAF	
Education	$157,197	43.7	$ 715,515	35.4	33.6
Social Services	97,167	27.0	793,858	39.3	42.0
General Purpose (per capita)	53,176	15.0	274,947	13.6	13.4
Highways	9,481	2.6	45,894	2.3	2.2
Health and Mental Health	27,360	7.6	134,720	6.7	6.5
Housing Subsidies and Urban Renewal	12,288	3.4	33,663	1.6	1.3
Miscellaneous	2,687	0.7	21,369	1.1	1.0
Total (Local Assistance Fund)	$359,356	100.0	$2,019,966	100.0	100.0

Source: *Annual Reports* of the Comptroller of the State of New York.

per pupil measure, which is the basis for school aid distribution. Since school aid is distributed on a per pupil basis, it is possible to argue that it is unfair to use per capita measures to reveal an aid disparity. However, New York City would gain under a flat per pupil distribution system as well. In 1972 the city had 32.5 percent of the public school students in the state but received only 25.2 percent of the aid.

TABLE 3

State Aid to New York (Excluding New York City) by Type of Assistance 1959-72 (in thousands of dollars)

	1959		1972		Proportion of Increase in LAF 1959-72
	Amount	% of LAF	Amount	% of LAF	
Education	$403,471	70.9	$1,545,523	69.7	69.2
Social Services	54,083	9.5	327,301	14.7	16.5
General Purpose (per capita)	43,662	7.7	180,008	8.1	8.3
Highways	48,596	8.5	62,482	2.8	1.0
Health and Mental Health	14,443	2.5	64,735	2.9	3.0
Housing Subsidies and Urban Renewal	2,819	0.5	18,013	0.8	1.0
Miscellaneous	2,264	0.4	22,256	1.0	1.0
Total (Local Assistance Fund)	$569,338	100.0	$2,220,318	100.0	100.0

Source: *Annual Reports* of the Comptroller of the State of New York.

It is clear that the current education aid program accounts for the disparity between the city and the rest of the state. And removing the welfare burden from the city would only heighten the present state pattern of providing more aid to the rest of the state than to New York City.

Conclusion

Three generalizations can be drawn from this analysis of state aid in New York from 1959 to 1972: priorities in the allocation of aid have remained fairly constant, the distribution of aid now favors urban rather than rural areas, and there has been a great increase in aid to New York City.

While the growth of aid has been significant, the state's priorities have not changed much. Considering the high levels of conflict in the state legislature during the budget season, one might have expected startling reforms. In fact, the only major new aid program, Medicaid, was stimulated by the governor and not the state legislature. What has occurred over the fourteen-year period is that more money has been added to existing programs. Thus, recent state politics and programs can be characterized, for the most part, as incremental ones.

This is hardly remarkable. In one sense, social service aid increases are outside the legislature's prerogative, because all those applying for the programs, who are eligible, receive assistance. Only by cutting the size of payments or eligibility standards can the legislature influence the various social service programs. In education, too, almost all the assistance is general formula aid. Without completely changing the formula, the legislature can only make minor adjustments that might slightly affect the direction of the aid flow, and the governor can do virtually nothing to affect the flow in the annual executive budget process.

If the largest and most heavily funded programs do not lend themselves easily to change, what then of the other categories that make up state aid? There have been some changes in the other programs; a major shift in the state's revenue-sharing program, for example, is the result of a 1970 statute tying the increase to personal income tax collections. However, this legislation did not change the proportion of the LAF which was allocated to the General Purpose category (10.4 percent in 1959; 10.7 percent in 1972). Thus, little change has occurred since 1959, relative to the priorities within the state aid program, or the distribution within each category. Nor has there been any significant initiatives, at least in fiscal terms, to change the character and substance of the aid programs.

The second major finding—that the distribution pattern of aid is shifting from rural to urban New York—is easily explained. Aid increases reflect the shift in population from rural to urban areas that occurred in the 1940s, 1950s, and 1960s. Most of the aid programs are distributed on a per capita, per pupil basis or, in the case of social services, where the needy recipients live.

The third finding concerns the remarkable increase in state aid to New York City. Almost half was the result of social service increases. The state's school aid formula provides the explanation for the disparity between what the city receives per capita, compared with the rest of the state. Thus, the character of the fund has been shaped by the political process which reflects the nature of the state's population and its representation in the state legislature.

New York City's loss of relative power—population and political— to the suburbs may well force an interval reevaluation of priorities resulting in a leveling off of expenditures. Change in the priorities, substance, or pattern of distribution of the Local Assistance Fund, in relation to the state's largest cities, will have to wait for new formulas based on some kind of need measure.

The State and the City

FRANK J. MACCHIAROLA

The relations between New York State and New York City are the product of a long and tumultuous history. Old political scandals, reform movements, party divisions, and power struggles of yesteryear all left their marks on the roles of the city and the state. The script is not a story of "good guys versus bad guys," but rather one of politics played against a background of economic realities. Relations today are tremendously complex chiefly because the state, especially under Governor Rockefeller's administration, at long last began to face urban problems. As pointed out elsewhere in this volume, after long periods of inactivity, the state moved rapidly and extensively into housing, health, mass transit, education, welfare, and planning.[1] Nowhere is this more evident than in the relations between New York City and the state. The interaction of these two governments can be seen first in a traditional legal context and then in their political and economic aspects.

The usual municipal experience has been one of restricted powers for cities and widespread rights of incursion into local affairs by the states. The almost universal operation of Dillon's Rule, which found cities without inherent rights and therefore "mere creatures of the state," acted to establish legally restrictive guidelines for municipal activity. Indeed, the view that cities were mere "municipal corporations," with only those powers granted in their charters, was endorsed

---

[1] See above, pp. 73-84.

The author wishes to thank Stephen Berger, Carol Brownell, Dall Forsythe, and Ronald Stack for their helpful comments and suggestions.

by the United States Supreme Court. It said that "a municipality is merely a department of the State, and the State may withhold, grant, or withdraw powers and privileges as it sees fit. However great or small its sphere of action, it remains the creature of the State, exercising and holding powers and privileges subject to the sovereign will."[2]

It was possible for the states to provide their own constitutional safeguards for municipalities in the absence of federal constitutional protections. Some states in their constitutions did so, by granting to municipalities powers that could not be taken away by state legislation and by restricting state governments from interfering in areas reserved for local government action. But for many years New York State gave no state constitutional protections to municipalities. In fact, the first legislative grant of general powers of local self-government for municipalities was not enacted until 1913; constitutional home rule protections did not come into effect until 1923. Without specific protections for municipalities, either in the laws or the constitution, New York courts were quite convinced that none existed. The New York Court of Appeals, the highest state court, declared that "in the absence of express restrictions placed by the Constitution upon the exercise of its legislative powers, the Legislature may create or destroy, enlarge or restrict, combine or divide municipal corporations."[3]

In essence, the legal traditions of city and state relations were quite clear. Local governments maintained a completely subservient status *vis-à-vis* the state. All local government powers had to be founded upon expressed state constitutional and legislative grants of power, and all limitations on the power of state government had to be expressly provided for in the state constitution.

These legal arrangements acted to restrict significantly local powers and to cause many local decisions to be made at the state level. Moreover, the wealth of New York City made it a particularly inviting subject for state intervention. As George Washington Plunkitt said in 1905, "This city is ruled entirely by hayseed legislators from Albany." The aggressive role of the state government in local affairs of the city gave rise to frequent political protests. The recent, well-known and semiserious 51st State movement followed by more than a century an attempt by Mayor Fernando Wood to have the city secede from the Union and the state at the outbreak of the Civil War.

[2] Trenton v. New Jersey, 262 U.S. 182, 187 (1923).
[3] La Guardia v. Smith, 288 N.Y. 1 (1942).

When local home rule was finally provided in New York State, it took two basic forms. Municipalities were given affirmative rights through the direct grant of powers of self-government. These rights varied from the authority to enact specific and detailed legislation to the right to enact local ordinances dealing with the "property, affairs, and government" of the municipality. Municipalities received further protection through constitutional limitations placed on the power of the state government to interfere in internal affairs of cities. This combination of affirmative grants of home rule powers and constitutional safeguards from external interference provided the legal underpinning for the development of local home rule.

Although the constitutional language could have provided a basis for a broad view of home rule, that did not occur. Legislation in support of home rule powers was framed narrowly to constrict local powers, and the courts have not always provided interpretations that would concede the fullest rights to municipalities. In fact, judicial interference in the orderly development of home rule has been a well-documented occurrence.

When local government relied on constitutional protections against interference in the internal affairs of the municipality, general state laws and harsh judicial interpretations were used to invalidate local laws. In New York State, the courts have acted in harmony with the legislature to approve incursions against fundamental home rule protections. The courts permitted the legislature to classify cities according to population and to pass ordinary or general laws applying only to cities in each class. Such general laws were passed to apply to cities with a population of more than 1 million residents—only New York City. Encouraged by the courts, the state legislature enacts many laws under the fiction of general legislation aimed at selected municipalities. Thus the state legislature has been able to avoid the constitutional requirements of a two-thirds vote for special legislation directed at a particular locality in the absence of a home rule message from the municipality. Therefore, legislation peculiar to New York City can be enacted despite opposition of the New York City legislative delegation, notwithstanding the concept of home rule. Thus the vacancy decontrol act, which repealed the rent control law in New York City, was a general law with statewide effect. Directed only to New York City, it was passed by the legislature despite opposition of city legislators and the Lindsay administration.

Political Aspects of Relations

The relationship between the city and the state must also be seen in the light of the very different nature of politics upstate and downstate. These differences are manifested in several arenas, most notably in the party system and in the legislature.

New York City's political electorate and leadership have been predominantly Democratic; leadership and party enrollment outside the city have been heavily Republican. Of course, there have been some exceptions. Parts of New York City like Bay Ridge, Brooklyn, sections of Queens and the Bronx, and Staten Island have Republican leanings, and there have been regions upstate, mostly the older cities like Buffalo, Albany, and Yonkers, which have been traditionally Democratic. There has also been an increasing number of independent voters not permanently committed to either of the major parties. Nevertheless, the Democratic party is the party of New York City, and the Republican strength has been found in the suburbs and upstate areas. To the extent that the Democratic party is identified as a New York City party, both the party and the city suffer.

In the legislature, New York City Democrats form the bulk of the minority and dominate the opposition leadership. Thus the Democratic party, the legislative minority, and the interests of New York City are perceived as one and the same. There are Republican legislators from New York City who have assumed leadership roles in the senate and assembly, and there are Democrats who have been considered as responsible and professional members of the opposition party by the Republican leadership, but the role identifications are clear. Democratic legislators are little more than observers in Albany.

Moreover, upstaters have had an advantage historically in the legislature because the New York State constitution mandated malapportionment. For years every county in the state was granted an assembly seat, and New York City was barred from equal representation in the senate, guaranteeing minority status without regard to population. Ironically, a major impact of the Supreme Court cases mandating one man, one vote was to reduce city representation, since the increase in the number of legislators occurred in the suburban counties of Westchester, Nassau, and Suffolk because of the major shifts in population that had occurred since World War II. Thus advocates of big city rights in New York State were instrumental in rapidly and dramatically increasing the number and power of suburban legislators. In many cases, suburbanites such as Joseph Carlino, Perry Duryea, John Kingston, and Joseph Margiotta played leadership roles in the legislature. Moreover, on account of the immediacy and intensity of many problems of New York City and the anti-New York City bias of suburban legislators, the city's political position in the legislature suffered. The changing demography of the city, its growing numbers of poor and minority population, and the changing demography of its suburbs with its disaffected city emigrants have ensured further conflict in the legislative arena. The "city" is New York City, and from the standpoint of many upstaters and suburbanites, the legislative agenda seems to be filled with problems that would not exist if New York City were not in the state. Thus the differences between the upstaters and the downstaters are reflected in the nature of the party and the legislative structure.

When the interests of the city were upheld in Albany, it was invariably because of the position taken by the executive branch and particularly by Governor Rockefeller. The governors, who must run for office statewide, historically paid more attention to New York City and its problems than did the leadership in the legislature. New York governors frequently had to fend off upstate opposition and build alliances with members of the Democratic minority in order to provide additional benefits to New York City. In many ways the governor had to walk an almost impossible political tightrope between the city advocates on the one hand and the upstate and suburban interests on the other. A recent example of the interest-balancing techniques of the governor was the Transportation Bond Issue of 1973, when conflict between New York City and upstate and suburban groups was intensified by problems over aid to subways or commuter lines and rapid transit or highway aid. On this issue, Governor Rockefeller effected a remarkable political accommodation supported by virtually every political leader in the state. Even this broadly supported compromise package, however, was rejected by the voters.

This attitude of aggressive and constant interest by the state legislature in the internal affairs of local government, particularly local government in New York City, is further compounded by a weak and ineffective city council. The New York City Council has almost invariably referred its most unpleasant tasks to the state legislature, claiming that it had no lawful power to act in the absence of enabling state legislation. Political convenience has determined the parameters of the council's legislative authority. Except for some popular causes, it has rarely assumed legislative power of a regulatory nature, which legally it could have. The New York City Council thus concedes the narrow view of local government power and permits the notion of limited home rule to work itself more firmly into legal precedents.

The New York City Council also acts from time to time in clear and knowing violation of state law when it wants popular support for an advocacy stance it chooses to take. Such actions included two unsuccessful attempts to fix a city minimum wage above that of the state in 1963 and 1964 and the restoration of the old form of rent control in the face of the state law that prevented a relaxation of the modified New York City rent control statute in 1973. The result is a city council that insists upon exercising too much or too little power as the political situation warrants.

This matter of style is further complicated by the fact that significant legislative activity is no longer conducted in the New York City Council. Councilmen have changed street names, and they have pioneered in enacting consumer legislation, but beyond that their legislative activity is unimpressive. The responsibilities of the city for providing basic services are grounded in general laws that apply uniformly throughout the state to education, welfare, health, transportation, police, fire, and sanitation activities. Even when special exceptions are warranted for New York City, they are provided for in state-enacted legislation that serves to place limitations upon the discretion of the city government. The most casual inspection of McKinney's *Consolidated Laws of New York State* reveals general legislation that applies state standards that frequently include exceptions for New York City and other selected municipalities throughout the state. Thus powers of local self-government within the context of the style and content of legislative politics remain significantly circumscribed. City councilmen, instead of being lawmakers, serve most effectively as brokers for their constituents and associates who face the maze of the city's bureaucracy. The traditional posture of government in Albany and New York City makes the effort to achieve significant municipal home rule power virtually impossible.

The relative weakness of local government and the strength of state government have not escaped the view of those whose continued prosperity depends upon the recognition and utilization of significant centers of political power. It is no accident that New York municipal unions have been most attentive to the decision makers in Albany. Increasing pension benefits for New York City employees began in Albany in the 1960s when several laws liberalizing these benefits were passed despite the objections of Mayor Wagner. Again Albany interfered in 1973 when the state legislature mandated decreases in pension benefits for new city employees. Union leadership understands fully the importance of Albany. Even the union of college professors of the City University of New York was named the Legislative Conference, attesting to the fact that its principal negotiating role was performed in Albany, with the legislature. The statewide consolidation of teachers unions was also encouraged by the perceived need for effective statewide power by the strong, but largely New York City based, United Federation of Teachers. The result is that from the standpoint of those who understand political power, Albany is the capital of New York City.

Further confusing the question of enlarged home rule powers for New York City has been the growing feeling that large cities are no longer responsive to citizen needs and hence are no longer desirable units of local government. This attack on the suitability of the current structure of city government has come from two directions. Urging improved administration of government to deal with major problem areas and issues—such as poverty, transportation, and the environment—some argue that city boundaries interfere with solutions to regional problems. City boundaries and home rule, they contend, limit regional focus and perspective. Thus they insist upon increasing the territorial bounds of government through a form of regional government with diminished powers to competing municipalities.

Others attack big city government for being too large and impersonal and urge increased political participation by the electorate. They want to foster decentralization and reduce the power of city government, particularly with regard to the delivery of services. In New York City this could mean the creation of more than sixty local governments if the community planning board districts were employed as basic local government units.

In either case, the forces urging structural change no longer look to the present, traditional structure of New York City government to solve problems. They advocate either bigger or smaller government. Sometimes, as with the state-created Scott commission, the seemingly contradictory demands have been merged. The commission advocated both regional government and decentralized local government as well as continuing the present structure of New York City government in a weakened form. In the midst of the uncertainty created by those demanding change, the prospects for reorganizing local government in New York City are quite limited. Indeed, there has been no real effort to define the roles of state and local authority, notwithstanding the fact that a state commission under Mayor Wagner was established to do precisely that.

Economic Aspects

The city's most critical difficulties with legislation that has come from Albany have usually centered on the allocations given to the municipalities under different formulas for state aid. New York State bases many state aid formulas upon need. When New York City brought in comparatively more revenue than other areas of the state and when it was considered "less needy," the formulas worked to the city's disadvantage. These formulas, however, now show New York City to be increasingly disadvantaged and therefore entitled to greater amounts of state aid. The city's revenue-raising capacities have diminished, its poor population has grown, and it demands more state funds. These factors have created some difficulties among upstate legislators who are keenly aware of the tremendous burdens currently placed on their more affluent, yet still hard pressed, constituents.

Another difficulty that New York City faces in the economic arena results from the city's limitations in raising revenue through taxation. These limitations stem from provisions in the constitution and the dispositions of the legislature, since all local governments in New York State are without any power of taxation except those powers that are directly conferred upon the municipality by the legislature. The authority for additional taxing power, moreover, has been invariably given only after last-minute appeals by the city.

Taxation policy for local governments, especially for New York City, has not been the result of policy study and policy planning. Since any new city taxes have been determined for the most part in the annual pilgrimages of the mayor to Albany, their content has frequently been set in a bargaining framework that is not tied to the most productive, efficient, or equitable use of the taxing power. Nuisance taxes have been necessary to balance the budget of a particular fiscal year, although the Lindsay administration resorted to such levies more sparingly than did that of Mayor Wagner. The result has not been a disastrous one, and the city's overall tax structure is somewhat more efficient and progressive than might be imagined, although there have been some notable inefficiencies (such as the procedures for collecting the city's personal income tax) and large inequities (as in the case of suburbanites paying a fraction of the rate charged city residents on income earned within the city).

In addition to the problem of dealing in tax matters with a hostile legislature, there has been one other important barrier to the freedom of the municipality to tax—the limit found in the state constitution on the power of the city to raise the rate of real estate tax. Any increases in yield have resulted from higher values of real estate and increases in the rates permitted for local debt service. Until recently these increases have been modest and have acted to set a property tax ceiling. As a result, in comparison with other large cities and with the surrounding suburban areas, New York City taxes real property (especially that of small homeowners) modestly. And the yield from real estate taxes is a continually diminishing proportion of the city revenue.

It should be noted that while the city government had complained in the past that the yield from realty taxes has been insufficient, and while the figures show that the city's use of the real estate tax has not been as productive as for other cities, there have been some positive results. The tax advantage has been an inducement for many members of the middle class to remain in the city, and neighborhood deterioration in many middle-class sections where most people own their homes has not been as severe as it might have been had the tax burden been greater on landlords and small homeowners.

Though the state limits the city's ability to tax independently, it does return a large proportion of the total state-raised revenue to local governments. Thus, although New York State currently taxes its citizens at the highest rate of any state in the union, it also returns revenue to local governments—municipalities and school districts—at the highest rate. Local services in health, education, welfare, and housing, for example, are performed by local governments, but with the state paying a large share of the cost. Concomitantly, on account of the state funding, state bureaucratic control operates to restrict home rule exercised by city government.

This approach—the state acting as a conduit for funds returned to the municipality—was developed in the days when New York City was regarded as a significant object of state taxes and when the state received far more from the city than it returned. In the past a favorite tactic of the upstate-dominated legislature was to tax New York City heavily and then to turn back money to local governments under formulas that gave New York City comparatively less. Upstate school districts were (and still are) subsidized; road construction favored larger, rural counties; many services were denied to the larger cities of the state. While this situation is changing as New York City becomes increasingly disadvantaged, home rule advocates have continually complained that the formulas for aid to local governments still discriminate against the city.

There are, of course, no clear and agreed upon ways in which questions of equity in the formulas for aid and in the distribution of state-collected revenues to localities can be resolved. For instance, should a Long Island resident, working in New York City and paying state income taxes be "credited" to the city as a city taxpayer or to Nassau County as a suburban taxpayer? Should his tax payment on behalf of his local government be credited to his place of employment or to his place of residence? It is almost impossible to sort out the equities. Some experts, including Governor Rockefeller, have claimed that the city is now receiving more from the state than its taxpayers contribute, and they used the argument successfully to counter the movement for a "51st State." One thing is clear—allocating state revenue on the basis of need, which for so long favored the out of city New Yorker, is now beginning to work to the advantage of the city.

Recognizing the strength of the upstate and suburban interests in the legislature, one should not be surprised to see a new formula developed to limit advantages for the city. Governor Rockefeller, in fact, reduced the percentage of personal income tax returned to the local governments, a move that affected the Big Six cities most adversely. Mayor Lindsay's efforts with the other Bix Six mayors were countered in fact and strength—if not in style and publicity—by coalitions of suburban legislators who also felt the pressures from rising local costs, especially education. The momentum of these activities is clearly against the city, notwithstanding well-publicized discussions between city officials and suburban county executives. What position the New York courts may take toward changing the formula for distributing aid is not clear. Some decisions in other jurisdictions and in some federal courts indicate that the judiciary may be sensitive to any efforts to abandon or severely circumscribe the formulas based upon need that have been used for the allocation of state revenues.

One further economic aspect of city-state relations poses difficult questions. If New York City were given freedom by the state to tax as it pleased, would its financial problems be solved? In other words, is home rule in taxing and spending really an answer to the city's recurring financial difficulties? In considering this matter one would assume that the city would remain part of New York State and that its taxing choices would be superimposed on already existing state taxes. In such circumstances it is clear that while more home rule in the tax area would be helpful, competition for tax sources would severely limit the city's options. Home rule alone in financial matters is too simplistic an answer. More equitable sharing of state resources as well as improved management techniques at both the city and the state level offers better prospects for financial stability.

Recent Trends in State-City Relations

Perhaps the most significant trend in state-city relations has been the inability of the city to meet the costs of government through its own means and the growing dependence of the city on external aid. In 1962-63, 26.5 percent of the city's expense budget was raised through state and federal aid; by 1972-73, that figure had risen to 46.4 percent. State aid to New York City climbed from $0.5 billion in 1962-63 to more than $2.5 billion, a fivefold increase in ten years.

New York City is more of a general-purpose local government than any other large municipal government in the nation. Most other urban areas have created numerous special districts to manage a wide variety of government functions. Independent school districts, as well as park, water, sewage, and library districts are common elsewhere in the nation. In New York all of these functions are handled by the municipal government. As a result, the per capita costs of New York City government have climbed tremendously in the last decade. The costs of every area of local government from welfare to schools has been reflected in the expense and capital budgets of New York City. In the period from fiscal years 1962-63 to 1972-73, the expense budget climbed from $2.7 billion to $9.4 billion, much of it due to mandated increases. In fact, state aid contribution of $2.5 billion in 1973 almost equalled the entire city expense budget of a decade before. By way of comparison, the city government of Chicago did not have its first billion dollar budget until 1974.

These increases in the costs of government for New York City and the inability of the city to meet its full share of the costs from its tax base have affected the independence of the city government. New York City can no longer raise money required to perform the staggering tasks of self-government through taxation. Further, city spending for new projects has not taken into consideration the full impact of the limitations upon the city's revenue generating capacity. In some cases, federal funds have provided incentives to spend, and when support by the federal government has been cut back, the city has had to assume added costs and responsibilities. While the leaders of city government have not adjusted their attitudes toward increased spending to account for the limitations on the capacity to expand, the state government has been attempting to put curbs on the spending habits of the city through increased oversight of municipal performance.

Albany has perceived the city as severely mismanaged, fiscally and governmentally. It has been charged that fiscal constraints were lacking, the capital budget was manipulated, cost rollovers were widespread, and productivity measures have seemed little more than gimmicks. Moreover, in areas where efficiency and economy can be measured, the city has been found at fault. Spending in education and welfare has been seen as wasteful. Administrative reforms through the establishment of municipal superagencies have been seen as a tactic for creating "no-show" jobs at extravagant salaries. The city's wage settlements with municipal employees have been costly, and the tendency to postpone the costs of collective bargaining to the next generation of taxpayers has resulted in widespread demands for reform of the municipal pension systems.

A poll taken by the Scott commission in 1973 seems to document the belief that the government of New York City has failed to perform the tasks of service delivery effectively. Further, differences between the state and the city over substantive issues have been heightened by personality clashes between their top executives.

Although Mayor Wagner and Governor Rockefeller had their differences, they were minor compared to the deep and bitter antagonism between the governor and the mayor that characterized the last term of the Lindsay administration. On one occasion in 1971 Governor Rockefeller charged that there was a growing loss of confidence in the city on the part of the public "deepened by accumulated evidence of declining city services due to inept and extravagant administration of city government and apparent inability to take effective corrective action." Mayor Lindsay replied that the remarks were "the latest in a series of ill-informed and destructive statements" and charged Albany with "attempted domination of City Hall and outside bossism." In a lengthy statement Lindsay pointed with pride to what he saw as municipal achievements in narcotics treatment, control of crime, and industrial development.

Unfortunately, the distrust and ill-will were not limited to these two executives; much of the hostility carried over into areas of policy implementation. Strong hostile feelings among city and state officials have been continually manifest in public assistance and social services and have not been far below the surface in other areas, such as housing, law enforcement, and mass transportation.

The problems of city and state relations, however, cannot be reduced to differences in personalities. It is certainly clear that many policy decisions of the city government have been directly responsible for the enmity that has developed between city legislators and officials and Albany. Albany has long felt that the increasing inability of the city to pay its own way has not been met by any genuine attempts to invoke self-discipline and to limit spending. The City University of New York (CUNY), unlike the State University of New York (SUNY), does not charge its students tuition. Yet CUNY was permitted to expand its educational mission and its student population in ways that have evoked charges of undisciplined growth. Estimates in the 1961 City University Master Plan called for 117,000 undergraduate students by 1975; the 1968 master plan called for 212,000 undergraduates by 1975; in 1972 a new master plan called for 228,000 undergraduates at CUNY by 1975. And the City University budget reached $.5 billion, half of which was paid by the state. Because of this rapid growth by the university and demands for an increased state subsidy for it, state officials showed dissatisfaction with the city's spending decisions in higher education. State legislators also appear to be severely critical of the need for further subsidies for the city's subways, because of mounting fares on the commuter lines and the city's failure to place tolls on the East River bridges.

The state's propensity for expanding its role also seems to have grown with its dollar contributions to the localities. State agencies have developed increased power to monitor and supervise some of the activities of local governments, particularly those of New York City. An inspector general for social services, an inspector general for education, a special prosecutor to deal with corruption in the Criminal Justice System, a Program Evaluation Unit in the State Budget Office, state-appointed members of the New York City Board of Higher Education, and the Scott commission are all recent manifestations of state government seeking to limit and control city policy and to obtain a more efficient and effective use of state revenues that are provided for the city. Further, the growing role of the ordinary units and agencies of state government in the day to day affairs of city agencies is also apparent. The Rockefeller administration undertook programs in many new areas, some of which formerly had been reserved to local governments, others of which were nongovernmental. These areas included mass transit, commuter railroads, middle income housing, industrial development, public college and university assistance, hospital and nursing home construction, and even planned residential and industrial communities. Thus the state began to participate more and more at the local levels and to concern itself with the details of policy implementation as well as with the general formulation of those policies.

The increasing activity of the state in the urban field and inflationary increases in other areas also have raised questions about its capacity to absorb these mounting costs. When Governor Rockefeller took office in 1959, the state budget was less than $2 billion. In 1973 it was $8.75 billion, and if federal and other funds are added, it exceeded $13.4 billion. In the closing days of the Harriman administration, the state government was still far from realizing its full capacity to raise revenue through broadly based taxes. The income tax was limited, and there was no state sales tax. The per capita tax raised by state government was less than $100 a year; in 1973 it was $460. In the last fifteen years the state and local taxes have grown at alarming rates. State tax increases were enacted in 1959, 1963, 1965, 1966, 1968, 1969, 1971, and 1972. Professor Alan Campbell of the Maxwell School of Syracuse University calculated that the growth of state and local taxes in New York City, at recent rates, will meet the total personal income produced by all the residents of the city by the second decade of the twenty-first century. New York State's sales tax and income tax are among the highest in the nation; the city also has a sales tax and the highest municipal income tax in the nation, as well as a real property tax.

Moreover, the state is being asked to assume an even greater role in the solution of urban problems by increasing grants to cities and by funding costs of certain functions previously financed locally. The Fleischmann commission, which was established by the state to study the cost of elementary and secondary education, recommended after an exhaustive study that the state assume full responsibility for the financing of elementary and secondary schools. In fact, the commission may have merely suggested what the federal courts were on the verge of ordering. Other official groups, most recently the Scott commission, recommended that the state assume administration of the welfare program. If these costs are passed on to the state government, it may well result in new expenditures for an already hard-pressed, and perhaps overextended, state government. The state debt, in full faith and credit bonds, which was $912 million in 1959, climbed to $3.4 billion in 1973. There is an additional $3 billion of borrowing power authorized by the voters for mass transit and water pollution bonds. A $6.7 billion debt—and $10 billion in authorization to incur debt—has been incurred through the borrowing of semiautonomous agencies, such as the Housing Finance Agency, the State Dormitory Authority, the Metropolitan Transportation Authority, the Urban Development Corporation, and the State University Construction Fund. The money for the repayment of these bonds is raised through user charges. While the state is not directly responsible for repayment of these obligations, repayment will be a matter of moral obligation for the state if users' charges should prove insufficient. Thus, although spiraling municipal costs seem to indicate the need for a new state-city agenda, this demand is taking place at a time of a critical shortage of state dollars.

As long-term solutions are awaited, one should watch two silent observers whose decisions in some of these areas will be most important. One observer is the judiciary. So far the courts have generally been silent concerning the responsibilities of states to allocate funds among local government units. Yet some cases concerning state responsibilities for providing social services and education may be foreshadowing a more aggressive policy by the courts in related areas of state government service. The second observer is the federal government. At best, the cities can hope for an increased availability of bloc grants and a modest growth in federal money through revenue sharing for the cities and the states. The growing resistance to impoundment and to presidential vetoes forms the basis for such an outlook.

New York State and New York City relations must be seen against the larger background of availability of state resources, the process of state politics, and the recognition of serious need on the part of the city. State resources appear to be getting scarce. New York City seems to have few political friends in Albany, and leaders of city government have yet to convince state decision makers that their problems are severe. And as long as the state leaders believe that the economy and well-being of New York City are secure, there seems to be little chance for a radical readjustment of the relationship between the state and the city.

Financing the State

SEYMOUR SACKS

As the public finances of state governments have grown since the end of World War II, and especially since 1957, they have become increasingly complex and increasingly interdependent with those of the federal government, as well as with those of their own local governments. This growth of state fiscal operations has been due not only to an expansion in traditional activities, but also to the states' entry into new and very costly responsibilities. While each state government remains unique, there are important elements common to all, since each state is an integral part of the federal system and subject to the major economic and social forces within the society. This is as true of New York, a leading state, as it is for its smaller and less innovative sisters.

The development of an analysis of the finances of New York State that is meaningful to the intelligent layman as well as to those professionally concerned with the complex system of finances is a major challenge. Extensive studies of state finances have been carried out by large commissions, by numerous public and private advisory bodies, and by individual scholars, yet there is still no definitive statement as to the nature of the issues involved either on a national or state level. Although there are studies on New York State, they have been limited in their approach, insofar as they failed to recognize the interdependence of the state with the federal government and with its own local governmental systems.

Even when one recognizes the complexity and interdependent nature of state government finances, questions must still be considered with respect to the particular domains of finance to be studied and the period under consideration. The tendency has been for basic and long-range studies to be neglected in favor of an understandable focus on immediate and pressing problems. Exceptions to this short-range focus appeared in the papers prepared for the abortive constitutional convention of 1957 and for the convention that was held in 1967. Both of these studies had a more general and fundamental flavor than the pervasive "budgetary" approach in which immediate issues must be resolved in order to maintain government in operation.

The "budgetary" approach involves partial and practical solutions to very immediate problems. The manner in which current fiscal activities are reported and perceived become very important in this context. In recent years, the broader fiscal-policy approach has involved a longer time span in which more fundamental changes are considered and questions associated with capital financing come to the fore. During the 1960s this approach was given a boost by the interest in the Planning, Program, Budget System (PPBS). Its problem, however, has been that it concentrated on individual program areas, rather than on the fiscal system as a whole.

A last approach involves a longer time span and a more comprehensive view in which the presence or absence of fundamental changes is the object of the analysis. Fundamental changes, however, now become operative within a few years rather than in the generational spans associated with World War I, the Great Depression, and World War II. The Korean war, the Eisenhower Era, the New Frontier, the Great Society, and the New Federalism all took place within a single quarter-century. Each had consequences for the system of state-local finances in which New York State is a major actor.

Experts in state and local government were strikingly unable to predict the explosive fiscal developments of the 1960s. In 1955 a distinguished group of political scientists and public figures gathered at Arden House on the Harriman Campus of Columbia University to consider "The Forty-Eight States: Their Tasks as Policy Makers and Administrators." While statements were made about the "effectiveness of our state governments [being] a matter of increasing importance in the affairs of the nation," there was no indication that, at the very moment when state government was about stabilized in the fiscal domain, the participants were prepared to face the changes in the fiscal role of states that were imminent. This was also true of the Kestenbaum commission, although by leaving the Advisory Commission on Intergovernmental Relations as a legacy, this commission did create a vehicle for analyzing the problems as they were to emerge. Finally, both the Bird commission and the Tax Foundation, studying New York State finances, were unaware of the forces that were about to transform the New York State government.

The analysis to follow will consider three interrelated sets of questions in the broader context of national developments. Following the tradition of public finance, the expenditure, revenue, and borrowing characteristics will be considered. An attempt will then be made to link these major elements together in a manner consistent with the long-term decision-making process within which they are enmeshed. The failure to recognize these linkages has been as great in the academic world as in the actual operating arena.

The first set of questions revolves around the "whats" of the system of expenditure-revenue and borrowing that characterizes New York State. In order to answer these it will be necessary to answer the question, What is the State of New York? This basic nonfiscal information is not only necessary for an understandng of the fiscal numbers, but it also indicates a greater range of operative factors than is traditionally envisaged. The second set of questions involes the "whys" of observed developments. The answers are presented in terms of the governmental forces rather than the presumed underlying forces that have so characterized the limited academic literature dealing with state government finances. Major governmental forces to be analyzed reflect the expansion of federal aid in highways (Eisenhower), in social welfare (Kennedy), and in education and ecology (Johnson). The impact of revenue sharing (Nixon) is too new to be considered in detail here. Similar attention will be given to forces operating on the local level. Finally, the forces operating within the state government for change and expansion of direct state activities will also be considered in detail.

The final set of questions involves the "hows" of accomplishment or lack of accomplishment in a fiscal sense. This analysis will focus on the enormous changes that characterized the period from 1957 to 1971. The year 1957 is chosen as the base not only because of the convenient availability of detailed data from the 1957 Census of Governments, but also because it was a truly meaningful year for national and state patterns. The final year, 1971, is chosen because data for it are the most recent currently available.

Answers to these questions are not only of interest to those specifically interested in New York State, but also accurately represent the problems of state finance from a general perspective, because of the historical leadership role of New York State and its governors, who are almost always candidates for the presidential nomination. In addition, since the *New York Times* has a national readership, New York State's fiscal problems are given wide publicity and are viewed as typical of those of states in general.

What is the State of New York?

The question as to what New York State is arises not only in the case of governmental obligations, but also in any attempt to make comparisons between New York and other states. The different sources give different figures which can be reconciled by recognizing that varying concepts of the state are being utilized. The Executive Budget, the Annual Report of the Controller, and the U.S. Census Bureau, the three principal published sources, report different totals. For the purpose of interstate comparisons only the census figures will be used. For other purposes the more restricted New York State data will be used.

The state government clearly covers far more than is reported in the general fund of the Executive Budget, and even inclusion of federal funds and other funds does not cover all the activities of the state. Some activities excluded from the budget are carried on directly by other states and would influence comparisons.

The New York budget document contains three main segments, of which only one—the general fund—is reported as subject to executive control. A complex set of federal funds forms the second segment. Finally, there are a number of other state funds that cover a wide range of activities but still do not directly cover major fiscal entities such as the Housing Finance Agency, the Thruway Authority, and the Power Authority of the State of New York.

The general fund, according to the Department of Audit and Control, contained 66.8 percent of all state expenditures in 1971. This contrasts with an estimated 81.1 percent in 1957 and 74.8 percent in 1965. The New York State accounts are almost unique in that there is separate information on federal funds. Although there is information on the federal funds *received* by states, there is no comparable information on the amounts of such aid *spent* by states for their own functions as distinguished from the combined state-federal totals reported by the census as intergovernmental aids. The problem of such fund accounting is that in any single budgetary period a change may be made (such as a transfer of the federal funds to the general fund) that seriously distorts the accuracy of comparisons with other years.

Thus fund accounting tends to violate the rule that all fiscal elements must be combined to achieve meaningful planning for the future, as well as meaningful interpretation of past developments.

The Scale of Fiscal Activity

New York and California stand apart from all other states in their scales of fiscal aggregates. Depending on the particular aggregate, either one or the other is the more important. In each of the major elements of state finance, on a census basis, New York showed a more rapid growth rate than the average of all other states for the period 1957-71 even though New York's population and income grew at a slower rate than the remainder of the nation. The average annual rate of growth in expenditures in New York for the entire fifteen year period was 12.7 percent, with a more rapid rate of growth at the end of the period than at the beginning. This growth rate, it should be noted, is the compound interest growth rate and not the simple interest growth rate.[1] For states other than New York, the increase averaged 10.6 percent for the same period.

Federal aid, most of which New York passed on to its local governments, grew by an average of 17.6 percent during this same fifteen year period. The figure for other states was 14.0 percent. The more rapid increase in federal aid to New York was in part due to state policy, as will be shown later. The magnitude of the changes in federal aid can be seen by noting the fact that in 1957 federal aid was equal to 12.6 percent of state general revenues, and in 1971 it had grown to 23.2 percent. The growth of federal aid did not slow down the growth of revenue from the state's own sources; indeed, it probably is responsible in part for the fact that such revenues grew on the average by an 11.5 percent rate in New York as compared to 8.8 percent in all other states. At the same time that expenditures and revenues were showing such extraordinary growth, it is not surprising that the debt of the state and its subordinate agencies grew by 11.1 percent annually, while for all other states the comparable figure was 9.0 percent. The overall picture is thus one of enormous growth in New York when compared to the national totals exclusive of New York. Before looking at the "why" and "how" questions, the components of these observed

---

[1] The compound interest growth rate represents the average rate of growth for each pair of years during 1957-71. The simple interest growth rate compares the 1971 level only with that of 1957. As a result the compound interest rate is much lower than the simple interest rate, 12.7 percent as compared to 26.6 percent.

changes should be analyzed, since not all components participated to the same extent.

The Pattern of Expenditure Growth

The principal area of expenditure growth relative to other states and within New York State occurred in intergovernmental expenditures. Although the census does not distinguish between state-financed increases in aid and those financed from federal funds, New York State does make that distinction in its own accounts. The most rapid rate of growth occurred in the public welfare area at a rate of 17.5 percent, or $1,784 million, followed by general local assistance, which grew by 14.1 percent, or $504 million. Educational aid, which showed the largest aggregate assistance, grew by 13.1 percent, or $2,252 million. The slowest rate of growth was recorded by highways, which grew at an 8.2 percent rate, or by $96 million. The more rapid growth of intergovernmental expenditures altered the overall pattern of state finances during the period. In 1957, 52.4 percent of all state expenditures were for direct state functions; by 1971 this percentage was reduced to 43.9 percent. The major shift was associated with the intergovernmental aid for public welfare, which grew from 22.4 percent of all intergovernmental aid in 1957 to 33.8 percent in 1971.

The growth of intergovernmental aid in New York far outstripped that of other states, 14.1 percent as compared to 10.6 percent. The higher rate in New York reflected the much greater extent to which it was tied into the federally aided Medicaid program than were other states. As a result, public welfare expenditures made to local governments increased by 17.5 percent in New York, whereas the comparable figure for all other states was 10.5 percent. This probably led to greater increases in state and local taxes than would have been the case had the program not been introduced.

Federal aid for public welfare in New York dominates the overall pattern of such aid to a greater extent than in any other state. The per capita amount is also at a very high level compared to all other states.

State aid to education is still the most important single component of the intergovernmental system in New York, as it is in most other states. During the period 1957 to 1971 such aid in New York grew at a more rapid rate than the national average exclusive of New York— 13.1 percent as compared to 11.2 percent. The very high growth rate for New York is only partly explicable by the enactment in 1965 of the Elementary and Secondary Education Act, which was operative in all states. The high growth rate is partly explained by the wide scope of educational functions included in the total. In addition to aid for public schools, aid for the City University of New York and for the community college system that emerged in New York during the period under consideration are also included in the census totals.

General assistance also showed a major set of increases, partly as a result of timing since per capita aid responds primarily to the decennial census. In addition, there were the increasing demands of general purpose governments evidenced during the late 1960s. Aid for highways generally grew at much lower rates not only than aggregate state aid, but also at a lower rate than any of the major components of state aid in New York, both in and out of New York. Nevertheless, even here the rate for New York was 8.2 percent, while for other states exclusive of New York it was only 6.4 percent. The overall pattern is thus dominated by the enormous dollar increase in aid to education financed mainly out of state taxes and the greater proportional increase by the public welfare payments which were jointly financed by federal and state funds.

The question of intergovernmental payments in New York is indissolubly linked to the special problems of New York City. With a large percentage of the state's population and with an unparalleled concentration of property in middle and lower Manhattan, the city has had difficulty in playing the role of the supplicant to the state.

The operative New York City population through 1960 was the 1950 census figure of 53.0 percent of the state's total population. By 1970 the proportion had fallen to 43.1 percent and was continuing to fall at a time when the Supreme Court's one man, one vote principle was beginning to take hold. The decline was due to the migration to the suburbs, and the fiscal impact was especially great in the education area, since the number of children attending suburban public schools was large relative to the total population. In spite of a number of specific state programs designed to help the city and other urban centers, the result was a reduction in state aid to the city's public schools from 29.3 percent in 1957 to 26.8 percent in 1971. However, during the same period, because of the enrollment changes, per pupil aid in New York City rose from 66.5 percent to 75.9 percent of the level received by the rest of the state.

The major changes in the treatment of the city in the aggregate were associated directly and indirectly with changes in federal policy, although this was due in part to state action in the case of the medical assistance program. The state aid figures are also partly influenced by the federal programs to which they are tied. In 1957, 65.5 percent of all state aid (exclusive of federal aid) for social services went to New York City. By 1971 this aid rose to 70.8 percent. Simultaneously, federal aid to New York City for the same group of services rose slightly from 65.3 percent in 1957 to 69.1 percent in 1971.

As a result of the relatively more rapid growth of social service aids than the overall total and because federal aid rose more rapidly than state aid, the city share of total assistance to all local governments increased from 43.8 percent in 1957 to 49.4 percent in 1971, or from $423 million to $3,825 million.

These changes obscure the intense set of problems faced by the aid system as it tried to provide increased sums associated with the growth of the city's problems during the period. That such aid was partly successful has been indicated by a number of New York City studies which show that, relative to income, the share raised from New York City residents had not increased during the decade. However, the intensity of the problems far exceeded the pressures indicated by these statistics. The failure of New York City to achieve a truly dramatic increase in its share of total state aid distributions resulted from the maintenance of pressures in behalf of public schools in other parts of the state, as well as the persistence of the "hold harmless" philosophy in both theory and practice. This meant that despite the increase in total distributions, the overall share to New York City tended to show great stability.

Direct State Expenditures

The growth of direct expenditures was lower than that of intergovernmental expenditures, 11.3 percent as compared to 14.1 percent. The pattern was primarily that of catching up in the domain of higher education, as well as strong increases in other areas. The major emphasis of the state was in the building up of its own institutions of higher education, providing Scholar Incentive payments for in-state pupils and some money distributed to private institutions of higher education on the basis of degrees earned, i.e., the so-called Bundy money. Without considering the appropriate growth rates, this emphasis can be seen by the change in New York's ranking in direct state expenditures for state institutions of higher education. New York outlays rose from 29.1 percent of the median state in 1957 to 59.5 percent of the median state in 1971. This change was accomplished by 20.4 percent per annum increases as compared to a 12.3 percent rate for all other states.

The state of New York had changed from an essentially two-function government in 1957, excluding general functions, to one that was more varied in its behavior. The two major functions, highways and mental health, made up over half the total of state direct expenditures in 1957, but only 34.3 percent of the total in 1971. While both showed slow growth rates relative to higher education, they were of the same order of magnitude as the national growth rates during the same period.

The changes that took place over the period were not, however, continuous. In the case of both intergovernmental and direct expenditures of the state government, external forces were operative, although it was the attempt to catch up in higher education that led to the increase of direct state expenditures.

The Reasons for the Changes

The reasons for the changes or their absence have been alluded to in the explanation of their magnitude, but now they may be assembled systematically. First and perhaps foremost was the very rapid change characteristic of the entire era and of all state governments. During this period, increases in personal income were not associated with any reduction in the demands on state governments. If anything, the relatively lower salary levels at the outset of the period led to a degree of general catching up that was characteristic of the entire state and local sectors. In some states such as New York the forces for catching up with the federal government and with the private sector were probably more pronounced than elsewhere. The period also witnessed the introduction of collective bargaining on a massive scale, which also enhanced the pressure on the state government as it did on local governments in New York.

The second set of forces were external in part to the state, but it was the state's acceptance of these forces that was critical. The immense expansion of the federal sector that occurred during this period was reflected not only in the federal totals, but in the state totals which were also increased during this period. This was true, for example, in the cases of medical assistance and of the very substantial increases in other programs.

The enormous responsibility given to the localities in New York, which still ranked first in per capita local taxes in 1971 in spite of the fact that intergovernmental payments were 261 percent of the national average, provided an extraordinary set of pressures on the state government. The massive aid was not reflected in lower local taxes but in higher expenditure levels and was most evident in aid for education, which was widely dispersed, as well as in the more concentrated types of welfare assistance.

The desire of Governor Rockefeller and various localities and interests for special aid in the construction of new facilities was consummated through obligations of public authorities and municipalities as well as through the use of earmarked revenues. The range of capital construction included State University facilities, those of the Department of Mental Hygiene, and the South Mall project in Albany. Other office buildings have been financed under lease-purchase agreements with the New York State Retirement System.

The extent to which this differentiated New York from other states can be seen by the fact that the long-term full faith and credit debt of the state went up by only 5.5 percent a year during the period 1957 to 1971 while the long-term nonguaranteed debt went up by 12.5 percent during the same period. In the former case the increase was less than the average, excluding New York, while in the latter case it was almost a 50 percent increase over the average of 8.2 percent.

The net long-term debt of New York grew at a rate that was only slightly more than other states taken as a whole. The major differences were not in the size of the increase in debt and presumably in state capital construction, but in the form in which capital construction was financed.

Several elements contributed to the growth of state expenditures: increased federal aid, a more extensive use of the state tax system, and the expansion of the state debt by the use of a variety of instruments. The more rapid growth of New York than all the other states combined indicates that in the aggregate the changes must have been sharper than elsewhere.

The New York State Tax System

Compared to other states, New York's tax system emerges as almost unique. In most states a high proportionate tax effort by the state government is associated with a low per capita local amount and a high local proportionate tax effort is associated with a low per capita state figure. California, which ranked second in local effort, ranked fifteenth in state tax effort. New Jersey, which ranked third locally, ranked thirty-seventh statewide, and Massachusetts had respective ranks of fourth and nineteenth. In contrast, New York State in 1973 ranked first in per capita local tax effort and third in per capita state effort. Thus, unlike most states, New York did not have low taxes at one level of government to offset high effort elsewhere in the system, and perhaps most important, it had a much higher level than its neighbors, New Jersey and Connecticut, in both state and local taxes.

New York's 10.9 percent rate of growth was slightly higher than the 9.3 percent average for other states during 1957-71. Comparisons on an individual tax basis are difficult, especially when they involve the introduction of taxes that were formerly not utilized. Nevertheless, such comparisons are meaningful when the underlying changes are specified. There is no way of indicating the growth of the general sales tax in New York, because it simply was not operative at the outset of the period. The 10.9 percent growth rate outside of New York reflects the fact that eleven other states also introduced this tax during the period, and numerous others increased their rates.

The selected sales taxes and the taxes on licenses increased at much lower rates inside New York and in other states. The corporation income tax showed only a modest growth relative to the rest of the nation because of the recession and the fact that other states introduced this tax during the time period.

The largest single increase in state tax revenues occurred in the case of the personal income tax, which was even larger than the increase due to the introduction of the general sales tax. The increase averaged 12.7 percent a year, reflecting changes in the levels of state personal income and increases in rates and coverage. The increase outside of New York was an enormous 14.9 percent. It represented not only higher incomes and rates, but also the entrance of some relatively large states into this domain.

The important consideration here is the overall change in the tax system that grew at a 10.9 percent rate as compared to a 9.3 percent rate outside of New York. Changes on a per capita basis were larger in New York than in other states. The general picture is one of basic national trends in which New York participated. The major shift involved the introduction of a statewide general sales tax; the most important increase in existing taxes occurred in the case of the personal income tax.

The growth of fees and charges on the state level was associated with the financing of capital facilities in State University and in mental hygiene. The manner of financing in a more general context has already been considered. In a specific context it involved the activities of the Housing Finance Agency, Municipality Debt, and most recently the Urban Development Corporation.

Conclusion

New York has played a more complex role than most states in the overall system of state and local finance. At the same time it has been among the leading states in providing state aid and has moved from a below average state in direct expenditures to slightly above average. As a result, New York is ranked very high with respect to state and local taxes.

The growth of state finances in New York exceeded those of other states, because of a number of major decisions on the state level. These decisions included the rapid expansion of the higher education sector, both in direct state activity as well as aid to local government, and the assumption of Medicaid as a major state responsibility, while maintaining other responsibilities at increasing levels.

To facilitate these changes, a number of alterations of the system were undertaken. The one major tax, the general sales tax, not previously used by New York was introduced. At the same time the system of financing capital outlays became far more complex as a variety of arrangements were introduced. These arrangements have created special problems mentioned above.

Some results of these developments seem quite evident. New York fiscal technicians fashioned a system for managing a flow that exceeded more than $100 billion with full checkbook control, while no long-range overall policy determination was ever articulated. Such conceptualizations must be developed before the political structure can operate the necessary democratic acceptance and the technical-fiscal bureaucracy can engineer the necessary apparatus.

With all of these it should be noted that New York State essentially followed national patterns. It went beyond these national patterns, partly because of historical reasons and special problems. The historical reasons included an area in which the state was behind, higher education, as well as two in which it was ahead, educational and public welfare aid. The special problem was associated with the New York City and the urban malaise generally. Here, too, New York State made a major effort.

Higher Education

DONALD AXELROD

The New York State system of higher education has been shaped by a combination of factors, pressures, and strong personalities, bearing the imprint of two activist governors, Thomas E. Dewey and Nelson A. Rockefeller, a sympathetic legislative leadership in both parties, and several outstanding committees and commissions that have helped develop new policies. In 1948 the New York State Legislature and Governor Thomas E. Dewey established the State University of New York (SUNY), with twenty-nine existing teachers colleges, institutes, and special colleges providing a nucleus for the new institution. The state also voted funds for the first time to provide minimal support for the New York City municipal colleges, which later became the City University of New York (CUNY). By 1973 the state and city university systems had become the first and third largest systems of higher education in the country. Although in 1948 public higher education in New York was conceived simply as a supplement to the state's 138 private colleges, by 1973 the percentage of students in private colleges had dropped from 70 to 40 percent. Moreover, the precarious financial shape of the private institutions raised serious doubts as to whether they could continue to be a viable alternative to public higher education. Private colleges were relying more and more on federal and state aid, and thus there was a growing tendency to look at both systems as related resources of the state.

The major issues affecting higher education can be considered in four periods. From 1948 to 1949, SUNY was established, community colleges gained a foothold, and the state recognized the need for financial support of New York City's municipal colleges. The second period,

1950-58, encompassing the last five years of Governor Dewey's tenure in office and the four years of the Harriman administration, was a time of modest, incremental growth. SUNY and CUNY enjoyed no special priorities during those years. The 1960s, the third period, were the golden years for public higher education in the country and, largely because of the efforts of Governor Rockefeller, in the state. After ten years of rapid expansion, the fourth period, the early 1970s, has been a time of leveling enrollments and financial crisis. By the middle of 1973 is became clear that public colleges were in trouble and private colleges in danger.

The Beginnings

With the end of World War II the Board of Regents, as head of the State Education Department, prepared to cope with the flood of veterans who would clearly swamp existing higher education facilities. To meet these needs the regents sought the expansion of private colleges augmented by a vast increase in state scholarships, the establishment of emergency two-year colleges subsidized by the state and administered by a consortium of private colleges, the development of a new teachers college in addition to the eleven that were already under the regents' control, and the founding of twenty-two state-supported institutes of applied arts and sciences that would offer two-year post-secondary-school programs. This last recommendation represented a major innovation and foreshadowed the community college movement.

The Dewey administration and the legislative leadership embraced wholeheartedly the emergency program for veterans, but otherwise agreed only to a limited increase in the number of scholarships and to the establishment of five institutes of arts and sciences on an experimental basis. At the same time they were disquieted by mounting pressure for expanded higher education facilities, charges of racial, ethnic, and religious discrimination in college admissions, claims that low-income groups lacked opportunities, and unflattering comparisons between New York and other states with regard to public support of higher education. To resolve these issues the governor and the legislature in 1946 established the Temporary Commission on the Need for a State University, headed by Owen D. Young.

The commission's report in 1948 laid the basis for a long overdue commitment to public higher education. It proposed the creation of the State University of New York to be headed by a board of trustees appointed by the governor but under the general jurisdiction of the

Board of Regents. At the outset SUNY was to be composed of the twenty-nine state-operated institutions that then existed, including the teachers colleges and technical institutes previously under the direct control of the regents, the specialized colleges, and the several contract colleges at Cornell University. The system, it was planned, would expand in accordance with need and would also include one or two medical centers. In a pioneering move the commission also proposed the establishment of a network of locally sponsored community colleges as an integral part of the SUNY system with the state paying one-third of the cost. As a matter of equity it also recommended that the state fund teacher education in the New York City municipal colleges since it was already supporting upstate teachers colleges.

The regents, joined by many of the private colleges, fought against the establishment of SUNY and, as a fallback position, agreed to its creation only if it were under their direct control. In a now legendary battle the governor and legislative leadership not only supported the Young commission recommendations, but actually strengthened them. In 1948 the legislature approved the creation of SUNY, effective April 1, 1949, under a board of trustees appointed by the governor.

In the following decade SUNY underwent only limited expansion, as is evident from the size of the budget and enrollment figures. SUNY's budget grew from $28.9 million in 1949-50, the first full year of operation, to $44.1 million in 1958-59, and full-time enrollment rose from 25,525 to 38,642 during the same period. The new SUNY administration slowly took hold of the twenty-nine campuses. The first community colleges were established. Two private medical colleges were purchased and became the Downstate Medical Center in Brooklyn and the Upstate Medical Center in Syracuse.

The Rockefeller Years

It remained for Nelson Rockefeller, who became governor in 1959, to take steps during the 1960s that brought about a rate of growth in higher education unmatched by any other state. Spurred by the sharp increase in the college-age population, the unprecedented demand for admission to college, and the limited capacity of private institutions, the governor and the Board of Regents toward the end of 1959 asked a committee headed by Henry T. Heald to undertake a review of higher education needs and facilities in New York State. It is no exaggeration to suggest that the committee's report served as a blueprint for the further development of higher education in the state and was largely instrumental in transforming SUNY from an ill-coordinated collection of small colleges to one of the major systems of higher education in the country.

Going beyond the timid estimates of the past, the Heald committee proposed doubling combined full- and part-time enrollments from 401,000 in public and private institutions in 1959 to 804,000 in 1970 and 1,102,000 in 1980.[1] In view of the limited capacity of private institutions it foresaw a drop in their enrollments from 60 to 40 percent of the total by 1985. This of course implied a heavier burden for public institutions. The committee consequently stressed the urgency of expanding and strengthening SUNY by establishing two comprehensive university centers, converting the teachers colleges to liberal arts colleges, sharply expanding community college enrollments while increasing state support to one-half of operating costs, and converting agricultural and technical colleges to community colleges. The committee was appalled by the administrative and fiscal constraints to which SUNY was subjected and urged greater flexibility in budgeting, hiring personnel, purchasing, and constructing facilities.

The Heald committee regarded increased state aid for the New York City public colleges as essential and urged state representation on the New York City Board of Higher Education. In order to strengthen private colleges and universities, the committee recommended that state aid be given for each degree granted, with larger grants for graduate degrees. Total amounts would not exceed 10 percent of the cost of instruction. The committee also suggested contracting with private colleges for certain programs, thus avoiding outright grants that might raise the church-state constitutional issue. To expand medical education, it proposed grants to private medical schools, the establishment of two or three additional state medical schools, and the drafting of a master plan by a new study group.

As a basis for future development of the entire university, the committee proposed a comprehensive planning process whereby SUNY would prepare triennial master plans for review and approval by the Board of Regents. These would also take into account the activities of private institutions. Although the committee was not explicit, it presumably intended that the New York City municipal colleges be included. To strengthen master planning, the committee urged that the governor and Board of Regents appoint a state council of higher educa-

[1] In total the committee's 1970 projection was relatively accurate since 765,000 students actually enrolled. However, the committee overestimated part-time enrollments and underestimated full-time enrollments.

tion advisers to evaluate programs, goals, and objectives, and to recommend appropriate action. It also saw the need for yet another state
agency to act as a consultant in improving the management of higher
education institutions.

With regard to students, the committee recommended doubling the
number of regents scholarships to reach 10 percent of each year's high
school graduating class, year-round attendance, shortening the four-
year period for a degree, and the use of statewide proficiency examina-
tions to obtain credit toward degrees regardless of formal class attendance.

The Heald report, which was submitted in November 1960, has
been cited at length because it shaped the expansion of higher education during the 1960s. Although it was not followed in every detail,
it led to a wide consensus on the part of the governor, the regents, and
the legislature, whose reservations, if any, were resolved in large part
by a study made in 1963 by its own consultants headed by Herman B.
Wells, chancellor of Indiana University. The Wells committee not
only endorsed the proposals of the Heald committee, but went beyond
them, especially with regard to graduate and research programs.

Aid to Private Colleges

One other major study was influential in fixing higher education policies in the 1960s. The Heald committee had anticipated the need for
state aid to private colleges and universities. By 1967 Governor Rockefeller and the regents were convinced that private institutions were
facing a serious financial crisis and appointed the Select Committee on
the Future of Private and Independent Higher Education in New York
State, chaired by McGeorge Bundy, to investigate the problem. Later
that year the Bundy committee reported that the needs of the private
colleges were "real and important but in most cases not desperate."
Acknowledging a lack of precise data, it nevertheless estimated a loom-
ing combined annual deficit of $20 million to $25 million and a backlog of deferred maintenance costs ranging from $45 million to $55 million for these institutions.

The Bundy committee set the course for the present program of aid
to private colleges. It recommended direct support to private institutions for each degree awarded: bachelor's, $400; master's, $400; doctorate, $2,400. Its goal was to get the state to provide approximately
5 percent of the operating income of private institutions. Cautioning
against automatic grants, the committee urged that state aid should

be available only to institutions that met high quality standards and should "not be used to sustain at a subsistence level institutions which would better be dissolved or merged." It saw no contradiction between continued expansion of public universities, which it strongly urged, and "prudent attention" to the strengthening of the private sector. To provide aid to institutions with religious affiliations, it proposed an amendment to the state constitution. Other major recommendations were designed to strengthen the planning and management of private institutions, provide comprehensive data on programs and costs, improve the planning and evaluation capability of the State Education Department, and increase contractual arrangements for graduate education.

The 1968 legislature quickly followed Governor Rockefeller's enthusiastic lead and provided for grants in accordance with the Bundy formula, requiring the recipient institutions to submit comprehensive reports and long-range plans to the State Education Department. During the 1969-70 academic year, $24.8 million was distributed to fifty-seven eligible institutions to start a program that has continued to expand.

To meet the critical need for more physicians and dentists, the governor supplemented the Bundy program by providing a formula for aid to medical and dental schools that expanded their enrollments as well as their facilities. This formula had the effect over several years of increasing medical enrollments by the equivalent of a new medical school.

Three other major steps rounded out Governor Rockefeller's higher education program in the 1960s. In 1961 he approved legislation setting up under one governing board the City University of New York, eventually to comprise ten senior colleges, eight community colleges (legally part of SUNY), one graduate center, and one affiliated medical center. However, New York City's chronic financial problems prevented the needed expansion until 1966, when the Democrats in control of the assembly persuaded the governor to have the state support half of the costs of CUNY's senior colleges. Under another statewide formula, the state was already paying 50 percent of the capital cost and up to 40 percent of the operating costs of community colleges. The effect of these changes was to accelerate sharply the growth of CUNY. In 1972-73 the state's share of CUNY's operating costs came to $197 million, fifteen times the level of support in 1959 when the governor assumed office.

To equalize higher education opportunities for all students regardless of background and economic status, New York State developed an unprecedented program of student aid in the form of scholarships, grants, and loans. While exceedingly helpful, especially to bright, middle-class students, this aid did not meet the needs of average or poor students and members of minority groups. Black and Puerto Rican students still ranked low in college attendance in proportion to their numbers. To correct this imbalance, two programs were pioneered by CUNY with the support of the governor and the legislature: SEEK (Search for Education and Elevation Through Knowledge) in 1967 and the Open Admissions Program in 1969. SEEK provided special testing, counseling and remedial services, and subsistence and financial assistance to selected students who would not ordinarily qualify for college admission. Beginning with 1,416 students in 1967, the program expanded to include 9,800 students in 1973. The Open Admissions Program guaranteed every high school graduate admission to a New York City institution of post-secondary public education. More than any other program it brought about a surge in CUNY enrollments during 1970-73 that strained resources and significantly increased operating costs.

With the momentum generated by these programs, the governor and the legislature concluded that they could do no less in upstate areas. The Full Opportunity Program (FOP) in community colleges, the Educational Opportunity Program (EOP) in the State University, and the Higher Education Opportunity Program (HEOP) in private colleges and universities were developed to provide tutorial aid, counseling services, and financial assistance to eligible students. For 1971-72, $32 million was appropriated for over 18,000 students enrolled in HEOP and EOP programs. This amount supplemented funds for six urban centers that emphasize vocational training and job upgrading and five cooperative college centers designed to prepare disadvantaged students for admission to community and senior colleges. The latter two were also programs initiated by Rockefeller.

The effect of these programs, combined with the expansion of SUNY, CUNY, and the community colleges, was to put the state well on the road to providing universal access to some form of post-secondary education. Still unsettled, however, were critical issues such as whether low-income students could afford low-cost or even free education and the nature of appropriate programs for educationally and culturally deprived students.

Another hallmark of the Rockefeller era was the administrative and fiscal flexibility accorded SUNY, a departure from the model of other state systems of higher education. This flexibility was largely the work of two strong chancellors, Samuel B. Gould and his successor, Ernest L. Boyer, and Rockefeller's budget directors, T. Norman Hurd and Richard L. Dunham. Out of their efforts evolved a strong central SUNY administration, a freedom from state controls not enjoyed by any other program, and a budgeting system which is program-oriented and based on the joint development of standards, criteria, unit costs, guidelines and formulas, and a continuing series of cost-effectiveness studies. At the same time the governor's budget office worked closely with SUNY, CUNY, and the State Education Department in an attempt to strengthen long-range planning capability.

In 1962 Governor Rockefeller initiated the establishment of the State University Construction Fund, a public benefit corporation responsible for designing and constructing academic facilities. Bonds are sold for this purpose by the New York State Housing Finance Agency (HFA) using tuition, fees, and other unrestricted income to pay the debt service. Without this mechanism the state could not have developed in time the facilities necessary to accommodate the enrollment expansion of the 1960s. To assist private colleges, the governor had enlarged the mission of the New York State Dormitory Authority in 1959 to permit it to sell bonds and design and construct facilities in private institutions just as it had built dormitories and dining halls for SUNY since 1955. Beset with construction slowdowns and impressed by SUNY's example, City University obtained legislative and gubernatorial approval in 1966 to establish a City University Construction Fund and to resort to comparable methods of financing capital construction. CUNY uses the State Dormitory Authority for financing just as SUNY uses the HFA.

Cutback and Consolidation Phase

In a dramatic reversal of trends of the previous decade, the higher education bubble appeared to burst in the early 1970s. For a variety of reasons, enrollment began to reach a plateau. As New York experienced its worst financial crisis in years, budgets for higher education were stabilized and, wherever possible, cut back. Inflation effected further reductions. No longer could public higher education systems count on annual budgetary increases of 10 to 20 percent. Other programs began to compete with public higher education for scarce resources. Federal aid for many programs dried up, with a particularly painful effect on those private institutions accustomed to "soft" money. In several disciplines, job prospects for graduate students looked particularly bleak. Significant numbers of vacant student places developed at private colleges and universities. Tuition rates continued to go up inexorably, making less expensive public institutions more attractive to students and intensifying competition.

In this climate Governor Rockefeller and the legislative leaders announced on November 7, 1971, in uncharacteristically gloomy tones that "the problems of financing and operating higher education, including medical and other professional training have continued to intensify. The fiscal plight of private institutions worsens while funding for public higher education is jeopardized by the general fiscal crisis."

The political leaders created a task force to focus on fiscal problems, student aid, tuition, and the feasibility of intensified public-private cooperation. The burden of the study fell essentially on Dr. T. N. Hurd, secretary to the governor and a member of the task force. Failing to reach agreement on recommendations, the task force came to the conclusion that it could serve best by identifying explicitly the fundamental problems of higher education and developing available options to facilitate debate and public policy choices. In February 1972 it proposed the creation of a special commission on higher education finance to formulate an action program.

The governor agreed and in October 1972 appointed a new task force headed by Francis Keppel to "develop a program to strengthen both public and private higher education in the State by proposing better methods of financing and helping to improve the quality of the State's system of higher education."

In March 1973 the task force laid out a far-reaching program: a "student bill of rights" guaranteeing New York high school graduates the right of access to at least two years of post-secondary education; financial aid if needed to complete the bachelor's degree; outright grants and loans to low-income students to attend public or private institutions; discontinuance of "Bundy" grants to private institutions for baccalaureate degrees in view of the proposed availability of student aid as a basis for supporting institutions; imposition of uniform tuition charges in all public institutions including the City University of New York, which was tuition-free for undergraduate day students; somewhat higher tuition rates at public colleges to narrow the gap between public and private institutions; increasing state support of CUNY from 50 to 60 percent and for community colleges from 40 percent (or less) to 60 percent; authorizing the governor, in view of expanded state aid, to appoint more than half the members of the governing boards of CUNY and the community colleges; requiring the governor rather than the legislature to nominate members of the Board of Regents; and the establishment by the governor, with the concurrence of the regents and the senate, of a state planning council to plan and coordinate post-secondary education and to develop mechanisms for interinstitutional and regional cooperation.

The task force estimated that its recommendations would save local governments about $88 million but increase state costs by $156 million. At the same time it pointed out that if the higher education provisions of the Federal Education Amendments of 1972 were fully funded, New York State institutions could receive as much as $350 million in 1973-74.

The Keppel Task Force recommendations could constitute the agenda for debate and action during the 1974 session of the legislature. It remains to be seen how seriously they will be regarded by Governor Wilson and the legislative leadership.

Problems Searching for a Solution

Any future planning must be tempered by the fact that the period of dramatic growth in enrollment is over. From 1961 to 1971 undergraduate enrollment in New York State increased 123 percent with the public system experiencing an overall rise of 245 percent, community colleges 438 percent, and private colleges 42 percent. In 1972 came the rude awakening when full-time enrollments declined at private institutions and at some public colleges as well. The outlook is for moderate growth until 1980 with possible decreases thereafter to the levels prevailing in 1972 or, in the view of some, to even lower levels. Table 1 indicates estimates of college enrollment by 1980 and 1990, which the New York State Education Department claimed to be conservative.

These estimates take into account declining birthrates and a continuing rate of about 70 percent of high school graduates going on to post-secondary institutions. They also give some weight to less

TABLE 1

Estimates of College Enrollment in New York State, 1980 and 1990

	Actual 1972	Estimated 1980	Estimated 1990
High school graduates	240,050	270,000	242,000
Full-time, first-term freshmen	142,650	161,900	146,000
Full-time undergraduates	473,894	526,000	483,200

Source: New York State Education Department.

tangible factors such as changing social attitudes toward the value of a college education and the removal of the spectre of the military draft. At the same time it is clear that at least some of the anticipated decreases will be offset by the growth of nontraditional and experimental forms of post-secondary education in which the State University has pioneered. Among these are the Empire State College (the University Without Walls), external degrees based on a combination of courses taken at various institutions and personal experience, lifelong education on a come-and-go basis, and extensions of college education beyond the customary four years.

Considering all these factors, it may be that State University, City University, and the private colleges and universities have projected overly ambitious 1980 enrollment targets in their 1972 master plans. If this is so, some agonizing program reevaluation and decision making will be in order particularly for the private institutions that are experiencing persistent financial problems compounded by increasing numbers of vacancies—56,000 claimed in 1971.

Without the Bundy formula aid, the financial situation of private colleges would now be even more critical. In 1971, if not for $23.7 million in Bundy aid, combined deficits totaling $16.8 million would have exceeded $40 million. Deficits declined in 1972 to $700,000, an improvement that reflected not only Bundy aid but also austerity measures undertaken by the private colleges. Chief deficit-producing factors have been student aid and auxiliary enterprises, such as dormitories and food service; in 1972 losses in these areas were $45.3 million, an amount that actually exceeded the entire state subsidy. Notwithstanding some apparent success in trimming costs, the governor and the legislature were persuaded that inflation had eroded the value of the original aid formula. In 1973, therefore, they agreed to a formula change to provide 60 percent more to eligible institutions: $800 for each bachelor's degree, $600 for a master's, and $3,000 for a doctorate. In addition, for the first time they provided $300 for each associate degree earned in private junior colleges.

Of $31 million distributed in 1972-73, one-half went to six major institutions: Columbia, Cornell, Fordham, New York University, Syracuse, and Rochester. Five smaller institutions in the New York City-Long Island area received 16 percent of the funds. No strings were attached. All chartered institutions that met existing standards and constitutional requirements were eligible, the money going equally to rich and poor, outstanding and mediocre, efficient and inefficient, socially responsible and indifferent. Bundy's admonition that aid should not be channeled to marginal and low-quality institutions seems to have been overlooked.

Overall data obscure the serious problems of individual institutions that may worsen as enrollments decline and the gap widens between public and private tuition. In 1972 the average annual differential between tuition in state-operated colleges and in private institutions was $1,802 despite a sharp increase in SUNY tuition. Whether some private colleges will be permitted to fail remains one of the critical educational and political issues in the state. To narrow the gap, New York will have to consider such options as increasing public tuition for students who can afford it, undertaking a vast program of direct aid to students so that they can choose freely between public and private colleges, mandating tuition at CUNY, consolidating institutions and programs, eliminating low enrollment and unnecessary programs, improving management and productivity, differentiating sharply among the missions and optimum size of public and private institutions, and significantly revising downward enrollment targets and construction plans.

The community colleges and City University, which accounted for more than 60 percent of public, full-time enrollment in 1972, have special problems of their own. The phenomenal growth of community colleges masks serious difficulties of governance, finance, and program effectiveness. Legally they are part of State University, which approves courses, budgets, tuition charges, and capital facilities. In the upstate areas, they are controlled for all practical purposes by the counties that sponsor them and in New York City by the Board of Higher Education. Under present laws a sponsoring county may pay less than 5 percent of its community college's budget and yet control it. Despite state support, which ranges up to 40 percent in accordance with administrative and cost control formulas (the student pays one-third, except in New York City, and the sponsor the rest), state oversight and coordination through the State University are minimal. The result is a patchwork quilt of two-year colleges with marked disparities in access, equality of opportunity, costs, program comprehensiveness, quality, governance, and tuition.

Although the system served reasonably well during the last two decades, the evidence suggests that the time has come to develop a network of colleges that would be correlated more rationally with population, student demand, and manpower needs. One suggestion made in recent studies is to develop community college service areas that would serve several counties. Upstate, the colleges might come under the direct control of State University through regional boards. In New York City, the Board of Higher Education might assume legal as well as actual control of the two-year colleges. In both cases the state might pay 50 percent of the costs with the remainder divided between the students and the counties.

The development of CUNY is hampered by the uncertainty of financial support from the city and the university's ambiguous relationship with both state and city, neither of which appears to have clear oversight of its affairs. The state controls CUNY's expenditures indirectly by approving programs and facilities in the master plan. Once the plan is approved the state pays half of net operating costs without further budgetary review. At the same time New York City exercises only limited review because of the de facto autonomy of the Board of Higher Education and its legal status as a creature of the state. The Keppel Task Force proposal to increase state support and give the state majority control of the board appears to be a way out of the dilemma.

There is no question that the state, through the governor, the legislature, and the regents, is committed to placing in appropriate postsecondary-education programs every high school graduate with the necessary motivation and aptitude regardless of economic status, race, ethnic origin, religion, or sex. Can New York afford this unprecedented commitment for the near and long term? Estimates by the State Education Department and the Keppel Task Force suggest that by 1980 state support for public and private higher education may range from $1.25 billion to $1.556 billion in contrast to the $846.6 million spent in 1972-73. The figure may go even higher if student aid programs expand sharply and expected federal aid is not forthcoming. Assuming that the state continues to allocate nearly 11 percent of its budget to higher education and growth of the economy produces necessary revenues, it will probably be in a position to pay these sums for the richer educational mixture. However, there are three imponderables that may affect future decisions. Will higher education continue to enjoy the priority of the Rockefeller years? Will the New York State taxpayer, who pays the highest per capita state-local taxes in the country, revolt and force a cutback in expenditures? Will the public and private higher education establishments demonstrate that they can manage their resources wisely and effectively enough to hold public confidence?

The latter issue is very much to the fore at this moment. One needs no particular clairvoyance to anticipate the following developments:

emphasis on realistic, quantified, and price-tagged master plans; resource allocations that follow enrollments, not hypothetical lists; further cutbacks in capital construction programs; priority shifts to favor some graduate and professional programs (for example, medical manpower) and to eliminate, reduce, or consolidate others; higher tuition in public universities for those who can afford to pay; insistence on greater productivity as measured by higher student-faculty ratios and increased teaching hours; tenure limitations so as to avoid unnecessary long-term commitments; controlled growth of faculty salaries and fringe benefits, collective bargaining notwithstanding; and joint use of public and private facilities. The big question is who will take the lead in implementing these difficult policies—the higher education establishment, the legislature, the governor, or the Board of Regents?

Increasingly the governor and the legislature are looking to the Board of Regents and the public and private higher education systems to plan, coordinate, and manage their programs more effectively and to account for the use of resources made available to them. In theory New York State has the mechanisms to achieve these ends. It has one of the most advanced master planning processes in the country through which the regents every four years prepare for the governor's approval an updated statewide plan for the development of post-secondary education and every two years evaluate and report on the results of programs. The plans that the public and private higher education systems are required by law to submit constitute the basic data in the process. To promote regional and interinstitutional cooperation among public and private institutions, the regents have established eight regions for developmental purposes and fostered the appointment of college cooperative service boards in these regions. SUNY has created four regions that are compatible with the regents' field structure. Regional boards and advisory councils are working jointly on a coordinated approach to admissions, data collection, use of facilities, cross-registration (so that a student can take courses in several institutions), and program development.

There has been some progress. Master plans have become more useful guides to action in contrast to the noble and visionary statements that characterized planning in the 1960s. Regional groups show modest accomplishments, although there is little disposition to alter the power and authority of individual institutions.

Despite all the work done in master planning at the state and regional levels, plans fall short, in the view of some observers, of measuring adequately the quality and results of state-funded higher education. Should SUNY aim to develop "peaks of excellence" comparable with the best at the Massachusetts Institute of Technology, Berkeley, or Michigan, or continue a highly regarded overall program combined with universal access to post-secondary education? What impact has open admissions at CUNY had on program quality? While private institutions play a predominant role in graduate and professional education, their ratings in evaluations of graduate education sponsored by the American Council on Education are not especially high, although they are superior to assessments of graduate programs in public institutions. What can be done to improve the quality of graduate programs and to eliminate underfunded and marginal programs? What steps should be taken to reduce the high attrition rates in community colleges and open admissions programs? These are merely illustrative of the issues with which an appropriate accountability system would deal.

To use higher education resources more effectively and to balance public and private interests equitably may require a more tough-minded approach. The Keppel Task Force proposed that a state planning council rather than the regents serve as the planning, evaluative, and coordinating body in higher education. This approach would be more in line with the pattern in other states. A single-purpose agency would not be diverted by the multiplicity of programs now within the ken of the Board of Regents. The state planning council would look to regional councils to develop unified plans that avoid duplication and maximize use of existing facilities and programs. The Keppel Task Force did not go so far as to propose the preparation of regional budgets that take all funds, public and private, into account, but this may well be an essential next step. The New York State mental health program is moving in this direction and might serve as a prototype.

Public and private higher education institutions can also anticipate intensified external reviews in addition to those by the Board of Regents or the state planning council. The Legislative Commission on Expenditure Review, the Joint Legislative Committee on Higher Education, the Department of Audit and Control, the Budget Division, the governor's office, and the staffs of the legislative leadership and fiscal committees are all involved in major program and management audits. Higher education may suffer from lack of funds, but clearly not from lack of attention! It is enough to make one yearn for the simple problems of the late 1940s.

The State and Social Welfare

BLANCHE BERNSTEIN

If a social welfare recipient who lives in a city in New York State were asked who provides the benefits he receives or determines the conditions under which he receives them, he would probably say "the city." The reason for this answer is that he deals with a city agency and city personnel, and his bimonthly cheques are drawn on the local government treasury. If he complains, the city gets the blame; if he is satisfied, an unlikely situation, the city gets the credit. He is only dimly aware of the tripartite—federal, state, and local—system of financing, of the complicated formulas that determine federal and state reimbursement to the city for different categories of recipients, or of which level of government has the initial or final responsibility for establishing overall policies and detailed regulations.

In fact, both the federal and state governments carry larger shares of the financial costs, as well as the responsibility for overall policies governing the public assistance and Medicaid programs. But while some social programs are administered directly by state authorities, in New York, as in many other states, welfare and Medicaid as well as other programs such as food stamps, day care, and homemaker services are operated under a system briefly described as "state supervised—locally administered." This essay considers the role of the state government in determining welfare and Medicaid policy and administration. What has "state supervised—locally administered" meant in New York over the last decade? What have been the results of this welfare system? What have been the recent changes in the roles of the federal, state, and local governments, and what changes can be anticipated?[1] Further, the discussion will illustrate how administration, though presumably something distinct from policy, is actually intertwined with policy.

The state's role in social welfare must be defined both in relation to the federal government and to its own subdivisions. Since the passage of the Social Security Act of 1936, large amounts of federal funds have become available for specified programs, and New York, along with other states, has taken the necessary steps to utilize these funds and to meet the administrative requirements laid down by the federal government.

The introduction of federal funding into what had previously been a state and local function meant, of course, a sharing of policy making between the federal government on the one hand and the state and local governments on the other. The most frequent pattern is represented by the public assistance program, under which New York State establishes its own benefit standards and eligibility requirements subject to federal regulations with respect to the federally aided categories of recipients. A similar pattern was originally established for Medicaid, but in 1967, in reaction to the unanticipated size of expenditures under the program, the federal government issued its own definitions of the medically indigent. This action limited the state's role in establishing eligibility standards. It should be noted, however, that state-city financed programs of both welfare and medical assistance cover persons not included in the federally aided categories.

The major tool for federal control of public assistance and Medicaid programs is the requirement that the state develop a plan, which must be approved by the federal government. The state is held responsible for ensuring that the program is carried out in accordance with the approved plan. The federal government permits the state to choose whether it will do so by direct state administration of the program through a single state agency or through cities and other local subdivisions supervised by a single state agency.

New York chose state supervision rather than state administration,

[1] The major reference sources include *Social Services in New York City*, Task Force on Social Services, State Study Commission for New York City; Blanche Bernstein with Anne Shkuda and Eveline M. Burns, *Income-Tested Social Benefits in New York: Adequacy, Incentives and Equity*, Subcommittee on Fiscal Policy, Joint Economic Committee, Congress of the United States, July 8, 1973; *Annual Reports* of the New York State Department of Social Services, especially 1969 through 1972 and various news releases issued in 1972 and 1973 by the New York State Department of Social Services and the New York City Human Resources Administration.

a choice permitted under Article XVII of the state constitution. In accordance with this article, the Social Services Law spells out in some detail the role of the state in relation to local administration. The commissioner of social services and the State Department of Social Services are responsible for determining the policies and principles upon which public assistance and services shall be provided within the state; establishing regulations for administration of public assistance and service by local governments; supervising all public welfare work, as this may be administered by any local unit of government; and establishing minimum qualifications for local staff in consultation with the Civil Service Commission.

The law also contains other authorizations. The commissioner may approve or disapprove rules, regulations, and procedures established by local social service officials. The state department is authorized to withhold or deny reimbursement to any city in the event of failure to comply with the laws, rules, or regulations of the department. The department may also on its own motion review the decision of any local public welfare official with regard to applications or grants of assistance and make decisions binding upon local officials. The state commissioner may initiate charges against local commissioners who have failed to perform their duties, according to law, rules, or regulations, and if these charges are substantiated by the local appointing authorities, the state commissioners may remove such local officials.

It appears from this description that the federal government maintained only a loose rein on New York State, but that the state held a tight rein on the localities administering the programs. This may have been the case in the past. It would, however, be an inaccurate description of the situation in the 1960s, a period marked by increasing federal intervention in policy making and administration of social welfare programs and by a loosening of supervision by New York State over the localities, especially in New York City. The causes of these developments varied.

The federal government's contribution to social welfare programs shifted from a relatively small proportion to the leading share; concomitantly, its desire for control expanded. The federal government began to intervene directly in the administration of welfare programs. In the expansive mood of the 1960s, it instituted self-declaration by welfare applicants in place of a field investigation to determine eligibility. In the more restrictive atmosphere of the late 1960s and early 1970s, the federal government established various work requirements for welfare clients. Whether or not one approved of particular federal requirements, one must recognize them as an encroachment on the authority of New York and other states to administer the programs as they saw fit under general federal guidelines.

Despite the heightened federal role, New York State retained substantial power with respect to the administration of social welfare programs, and it was quite active in the exercise of this power. Area offices were established in New York City and in other areas to provide supervision and consultation, but the degree of receptivity to such supervision varied. In New York City, which was responsible for about 70 percent of the total state caseload, the desire for home rule was strong, and there was little enchantment with state supervision. For a number of years some considered the state area office for New York City as more of an advocate for the city than an instrument of supervision.

Another important factor was that the New York State Board of Social Welfare, composed of knowledgeable citizens appointed by the governor, determined public assistance policy and set the welfare standards. In addition, the board had the authority to appoint the commissioner of social services with the approval of the governor. The board was, of course, sympathetic to the needs of the disadvantaged, as one would expect and indeed require. However, in recent years it tended toward a rather uncritical acceptance of the recommendations of the state commissioner whom it had itself appointed. It appeared reluctant to engage in the unpleasant combat with welfare officials throughout the state necessary to achieve strict administration of the state's welfare policies.

Thus by 1970, the state had on the books vast authority to determine policy and to oversee and control the administration of welfare programs; however, it had ceded considerable authority over policy matters to the Board of Social Welfare and was only loosely exercising its supervisory powers, especially in New York City. The picture began to change in 1971, as Governor Rockefeller and the state legislature moved to reassert their authority over crucial policy issues and to deal with the twin problems of eligibility and employability of welfare recipients. The impetus for this change derived from the fact that during the 1960s, despite increasing prosperity and decreasing unemployment, the public assistance caseload in the state tripled and expenditures quadrupled. While the rise in caseload was evident statewide, it was particularly heavy in New York City. Medicaid, a program instituted in 1966 to cover both welfare recipients and the medically indigent, expanded rapidly and quickly exceeded by wide margins estimates of anticipated costs. By the end of the 1960s, the view was widely, though not universally, held that the number of ineligible persons on welfare greatly exceeded the tolerable limit of 3 percent established as the guideline by the federal government.

Governor Rockefeller's Welfare Reform

In March 1971 Governor Rockefeller sent a special message to the legislature on welfare. He first stated that the federal government ought to take complete responsibility for welfare by establishing national standards and paying the full costs but that it was unlikely to do so in the near future. He therefore proposed a welfare reform package designed to control the growth of the welfare caseloads, reduce the rate of ineligibility, and encourage employment of welfare recipients. His six-part program, as well as developments that stemmed from it, are described below.

The New York State Board of Social Welfare was separated from the Department of Social Services on July 1, 1971, and became a division of the Executive Department. The board's policy functions with respect to welfare were transferred to the commissioner of social services and to the department. The legislature exercised the authority it had assumed the year before to fix the public welfare standard. Additional legislative changes provided for the appointment of the commissioner of social services by the governor with the advice and consent of the senate in place of the previous arrangement. Thus the governor acquired direct control over the top officials in the department. Further, the Department of Social Services was reorganized to strengthen its control over the administration of public welfare. The Division of Operations was established and made responsible for the development and implementation of administrative procedures, the supervision of local welfare districts, and the direct services of the department. In addition, the Division of Program Development and Evaluation was set up to prepare new programs designed to reduce welfare dependency and to evaluate existing programs.

As a means of dealing with questions of eligibility, the legislature, on the governor's recommendation, established the Office of the Welfare Inspector General to receive and investigate complaints of alleged welfare abuses, suspected frauds, and other violations of the welfare system. After his appointment by the governor as inspector general, George F. Berlinger moved vigorously to investigate the thousands of complaints of abuse that his office quickly received and to conduct spot audits of samples of cases at various welfare centers. His analyses indicated a rate of ineligibility in New York City as high as 30 percent. His findings, however, were vigorously challenged by city authorities who generally regarded his operation as nothing short of a disaster. His estimate of the rate of ineligibility, while not altogether substantiated in subsequent studies, was a significant factor in the decision to transfer the responsibility for the quarterly audits of a sample of the caseload, required under federal law, from the local departments of social services to the newly created office of Audit and Quality Control established July 1, 1972, in the New York State Department of Social Services. The latest state audit covering the last half of 1972 indicated a statewide rate of ineligibility of 17.6 percent among Aid to Families with Dependent Children (AFDC) cases, which constituted the bulk of the caseload, a far higher rate than ever uncovered in audits conducted by New York City or other localities.

Accumulating evidence of high ineligibility rates also led to changes, initiated in 1972, in the application procedure. In place of the short-form self-declaration of need, the State Department of Social Services instituted a new eleven-page form that required considerable documentation before a final determination of eligibility was made; emergency relief, however, may be granted for a few days. The result was a significant drop in the percentage of applications approved.

The eligibility problem has been attacked from another angle as well, the recertification of persons already on welfare for continued eligibility, a procedure which from the late 1960s until mid-1973 had been based, like the original application for aid, on a self-declaration mailed by the recipient. Prior to state action in this area, Jule M. Sugarman, administrator of New York City's Human Resources Administration, had announced in April 1972 that a face to face recertification procedure was to be instituted in the city. In the summer of 1972 he advised New York State Commissioner Abe Lavine that pilot tests had been successfully completed and that citywide operations would begin in September. Subsequently, however, citywide use of the procedure was postponed until April 1973, a delay that the Scott Commission's Task Force on Social Services estimated, on the basis of a potential ineligibility rate of 10 percent, cost over $50 million. In fact, the face to face recertification procedure was not started even in April, except on a very minor scale.

Meantime, the State Department of Social Services announced in February 1973 that face to face recertification procedures would become mandatory throughout the state as of July 1, 1973. Under the new policy, all AFDC and Home Relief cases are subject to face to face recertification interviews within the first ninety days after they have entered the rolls and thereafter at intervals of six to twelve months depending on the nature of the case. The plan was to complete the recertification of the total caseload within nine months after the policy was implemented.

Commissioner Lavine stated his belief that the procedure would prove to be "the single most effective reform yet introduced into the eligibility determination and redetermination process."[2] Indeed, preliminary figures issued in October 1973 indicated that close to 20 percent of cases examined for recertification were closed before the interview, for failure to report, or for ineligibility found during the interview. However, some of these cases will probably be reopened because of a continuing need for assistance by clients who misunderstood the new procedures.

Controversy over the issue between New York State and New York City authorities continued. The city is conducting the face to face recertification only after a case has been on welfare for a year. It claims that the state approved this procedure as an interim measure until additional city personnel become available in 1974. Moreover, the city will take considerably more than nine months to complete the recertification process. The issue of whether the recertification takes place before the client has been on welfare for ninety days or after one year is apparently crucial to the success of the procedure since it appears that with the new application form initial eligibility is high, but within a few months the client frequently finds other income sources that remain undiscovered if the recertification is postponed. The state commissioner of social services has followed a hard line in New York City and has announced the imposition of a penalty of $750,000 against the city for the last two weeks of August and another one of the same amount for the first two weeks of September, because of the city's failure to apply the recertification procedure to an adequate number of cases.

The New York State Department of Social Services is also planning to institute administrative reforms in the Medicaid program similar to those described for public assistance, including a variation of the eleven-page application form, face to face recertification for families receiving Medicaid only, and a new way of reviewing the utilization of inpatient services paid for under the Medicaid program.

[2] Abe Lavine, commissioner of the New York State Department of Social Services (Speech presented to the Rotary Club, Ithaca, New York, September 19, 1973), p. 9.

Another important aspect of the welfare problem, which involves questions of both policy and administration, relates to the employability of welfare recipients, job training and referral, and, of course, the availability of jobs. Throughout the 1960s, New York State policy permitted mothers in AFDC families to choose whether they wished job training or employment, or whether they wished to remain at home caring for their children. It was generally assumed that the AFDC mother was not employable. The 1970 report of the State Department of Social Services indicated that "of the 1.8 million persons who received some type of assistance only about 6 percent were considered employable." Excluded from the employable category in the main were the AFDC mothers on the grounds that they were needed at home to care for the children. While a variety of work training, job referral, and work incentive programs were in operation throughout the 1960s, these affected only a small portion of the caseload.

The 1971 state welfare reform sought to change this situation. Indeed, the 1972 report of the State Department of Social Services declared: "The heart of the 1971 welfare reform program in New York State was the emphasis on the value of work." The major element of the effort was a new requirement that all employable welfare recipients report twice a month to the New York State Employment Service offices to receive employment services, including referrals to job openings, employment counseling, and training, and at the same time to pick up their welfare checks. Further, it redefined employability and limited the discretion of local social service districts to declare an individual unable to work. Included among those defined as employable were AFDC mothers whose children were six years of age or older, who were not otherwise incapacitated by illness or injury, or who were unable to work because they needed to take care of their children full-time despite diligent efforts to find other means of care for the children. Exemptions for illness or injury were to be reviewed every ninety days.

The legislation also contained several other important provisions. Localities were required to arrange for a public works program to which the Employment Service would assign welfare recipients. The Employment Service was directed to locate and develop employment opportunities for unskilled public assistance recipients and to provide job preparation and follow-up service. Finally, it denied welfare to an employable recipient who quit a job without good cause or refused a job that he or she was able to perform.

Full implementation of the 1971 program with respect to employment of welfare recipients was interrupted by a suit against the application of the law to AFDC mothers. The federal court deciding this case held that the state program conflicted with the federal Social Security Act since the area of work and training for AFDC recipients had been preempted by the Federal Work Incentive Program. An appeal to the United States Supreme Court resulted in a reversal of the lower court decision in mid-1973, but as a consequence of the litigation the program became fully operational only in September 1973. It should be noted that while the judicial process was under way, the 1972 Talmadge amendment to the Social Security Act brought the federal government into this area of policy. It defined as employable the AFDC mothers whose children were six years of age or older and who were not otherwise incapacitated and required that they accept available employment.

In all candor, it must be said that the program has not succeeded in placing huge numbers of welfare clients in jobs in the private sector of the economy. In the first twelve months of operation, from July 1, 1971, to June 30, 1972, slightly more than 29,000 obtained jobs. In the first half of 1973, about 6,200 were placed in jobs. In addition, a monthly average of 13,400 recipients of home relief were employed on public works projects in 1972. But while it has achieved only a limited success so far in placing welfare recipients in jobs, the program has been effective in uncovering a significant number of persons ineligible for welfare because they refused employment, failed to follow through on referrals, or, if offered jobs, failed to report to work. During the first year of the program's operation, 53,000 persons, or about 3 percent of the total caseload, were dropped from the welfare rolls as a result of the work reporting requirement.

Several other aspects of Governor Rockefeller's welfare reform of 1971 were less successful. Residency requirements as a condition for eligibility for public assistance had been declared unconstitutional by the United States Supreme Court some years before. The governor attempted, nevertheless, to institute a one-year residency requirement for a period of five years on the grounds of an emergency situation in New York State with respect to housing, an epidemic of narcotics addiction, and overburdened social services and health resources. It was declared unconstitutional by a federal court, and the decision was upheld by the United States Supreme Court.

The governor also proposed an incentive scheme on a demonstration basis to encourage members of welfare families to work, attend school or take part in training programs, or participate in supplementary education programs or community improvement projects. Essentially, the Incentives for Independence program provided a basic welfare payment of $2,400 for a family of four other than the aged, blind, disabled, or mothers unable to work. It also allowed supplementary benefits up to the current state level of about $3,900 as the family earned points for the various activities enumerated. The proposal irreverently, but with some justification, quickly came to be characterized as the brownie point plan. Overwhelming opposition from social and civic groups, as well as the enormous administrative difficulties involved in implementing the system led to a redesigned program so that the family received the full welfare benefits, but subtractions could be made from them if the family did not engage in the required activities. Court challenges of the demonstration program resulting in a temporary restraining order issued by a federal court prevented immediate implementation. In 1973, however, the Circuit Court of Appeals upheld the state's position, and the United States Supreme Court refused to review the decision. Whether the Department of Social Services will reinstate the demonstration program remains to be seen.

A separate Public Service Opportunities Project directed particularly toward AFDC mothers was also designed on a demonstration basis covering about 25 percent of the AFDC caseload. As in the case of Home Relief families, its main feature required employable AFDC mothers for whom private employment could not be found to accept public service jobs and to work the number of hours needed to equal the assistance grant at the rate of pay for the job. Like the Incentives for Independence proposal, it was temporarily restrained by a federal court order, but the state's position was upheld in the Circuit Court of Appeals in 1973. Plans are now underway to start the demonstration program.

Trends Toward a State Administered Welfare System

Clearly, Governor Rockefeller's 1971 welfare reform program, which was adopted almost in toto by the legislature, indicated dissatisfaction not only with the way the "state supervised—locally administered" system was working, but also with the system itself. It is a system with built-in irritants with respect to state-local relations. In a situation where one locality, New York City, is responsible for 70 percent of the caseload, the suspicion arises that administration is being used to circumvent rather than implement policies. Further, the federal government is involved more heavily than before in both policy and administrative matters. The situation easily leads to the notion of a federal or state administered system. In fact, the federal government took over the administration of public assistance to the aged, blind, and disabled in January 1974. What will happen to the rest of the welfare program, by far the largest part, remains to be seen.

The notion of establishing a state administered system in New York is not new. It was recommended by the Moreland Commission in 1963, by the New York State Citizens Committee on Welfare Costs in 1965, and by two management consulting firms in the late 1960s. As an interim measure, looking toward federal assumption of the responsibility for all welfare costs, a state administered system was also recommended in principle by the New York State Board of Social Welfare in 1969 and reiterated more explicitly in 1970. Despite this background, the 1971 State Welfare Reform Program did not mention the possibility of setting up a state administered system. It was solely related to improving state supervision and local administration. Nevertheless, support for a state takeover of the administration of public assistance and Medicaid has been gathering momentum. In 1972 the Temporary Commission to Revise the Social Service Law recommended such action, though with a proviso that the localities continue to determine eligibility, a proviso with which few agree. New York City officials have for several years urged state takeover although they may have done so only in the hope that the city would be relieved of all of its share of welfare costs, an expectation unlikely to be realized. Whatever the motivation, New York City proposed a plan in February 1973 for state administration of public assistance and Medicaid; Jule M. Sugarman was quoted as stating that it could end "this eternal haggling" between the state and the city.[3] The State Study Commission for New York City—Task Force on Social Services in its report issued in March 1973 stated: "For a variety of reasons the State may now be in a better position than the City [i.e., New York City] to operate a tight, efficient, objective operation that will protect recipient rights while assuring the security of the program."

In April 1973 the time had apparently come. The governor submitted a proposal to the legislature for a gradual takeover of the administration of public assistance and Medicaid including determination of eligibility, payments to recipients, and, particularly in the case of Medicaid, payments to the providers of the service. The localities

[3] *New York Times*, February 1, 1973.

would retain responsibility for the administration of social services. They would continue to pay their current share of welfare and medicaid costs. The legislature postponed action on the proposal for at least a year, but during the 1973 session it adopted legislation establishing the Division of Local Income Maintenance and Medical Administration with an administrative board as a first step toward a state administered system.

Further legislation is likely to be enacted during the 1974 session of the legislature. In the meantime, a number of steps have been taken in anticipation of state administration. Several computer companies were asked to develop a state system for administering welfare, a decision that led to a heated controversy between state and New York City officials over the fate of the system already developed for the city. In November 1973, however, agreement was reached for the joint development of a computer system. Further, the five-man administrative board of the Division of Local Income Maintenance and Medical Administration was established. The governor was authorized to name three members of the board, and he appointed the director of the Division of the Budget, the commissioner of the Department of Social Services, and the welfare inspector general as well as the remaining two members on the recommendation of the senate majority leader and assembly speaker. The principal responsibility of the board is to develop a plan for state assumption of administrative responsibility for income maintenance and medical assistance programs, prepare a proposal for the establishment of a public benefit corporation to implement and administer such a program, and develop and implement, under authority provided in the enacting legislation, a data processing system for income maintenance and medical assistance in New York City.

While the form of state administration cannot be predicted—it may either be by an expansion of the responsibilities of the state's Department of Social Services or by creating a public benefit corporation—it seems probable that the state will take over the welfare function during the next year or two.

Issues in Welfare

In summary, beginning with 1971 welfare reform, the state took a series of actions directed toward reducing the rate of ineligibility among welfare and Medicaid recipients and toward a new emphasis on work, especially by redefining employability for AFDC mothers and by increasing efforts to find private or public employment for welfare recipients. Other issues, however, need attention.

Although New York's welfare standards are among the highest in the country, it has, nevertheless, been generally assumed that only a dismally low standard of living was provided, an assumption based on the frequently quoted figure of about $3,900, the public assistance standard for a family of four. This is indeed the current average *net* standard for cash assistance, including an allowance for rent. What was not generally taken account of, however, was that the family on welfare is also entitled to purchase food stamps that provide a bonus of about $360 per year, to free school lunches worth about $95 for one child, and to medical care costing approximately $1,200 annually. The sum of these benefits is over $5,500 and is equivalent to a gross income of almost $7,000 per year when income and social security taxes and work expenses are considered. The sum of $7,000 is 89 percent of the Bureau of Labor Statistics' lower-level living budget (in 1972 prices), which provides for "the maintenance of physical health and social well-being, the nurture of children, and participation in community activities" though, obviously, at a lower level than the BLS moderate or higher level budgets. It is equal to what a wage earner working a thirty-five-hour week at $3.80 an hour would earn and therefore can be considered a fairly generous standard of welfare. If the family is living in a publicly subsidized housing program, as about 20 percent of New York City welfare families do, the gross income equivalent of its benefits from social programs will be even higher.

When the value of the package of social programs including medical assistance is considered in conjunction with the regulations that reduce benefits as income from earnings or other sources increase, it becomes apparent that there is no practical advantage to the ordinary four-person family to increase its income from zero up to $7,000. Indeed, at various points on the income scale the family can be actually penalized. The loss in benefits exceeds the gain in disposable income (gross income minus taxes and work expenses). As earnings rise above $8,000 the family begins to be better off and the greater the rise in income, the more substantial the difference in the level of living achieved compared to the welfare standard. But for those who, because of limited education or skills, or discrimination, or other reasons, are unable to earn more than $6,000 to $7,000 per year, the present set of eligibility criteria does not provide any incentive to increase income. In fact, the result is quite the opposite.

A family headed by a woman, especially one that qualifies for the work incentive which allows it to disregard $30 of monthly earnings plus one-third of the remainder, is somewhat better off and always gains something from working. But even for the female head of a family, marginal tax rates are high, almost 70 percent of each $1,000 increase in income. Further, when her earnings reach about $9,400 she loses the remaining cash assistance benefits as well as food stamps, school lunches, Medicaid, and some day-care benefits.

While the incentive offered to a family headed by a female on welfare increases the incentive to work, it creates serious inequity between this type of family and the intact family or the female headed family that does not qualify for the $30 and a third disregard. The effect is such that for families with earnings of $5,000, the difference in disposable income plus benefits may be as much as $1,900, a large sum at this income level.

Other inequities derive from the granting of some types of benefits such as food stamps or Medicaid on the basis of public assistance status rather than income. As a result, a female headed family of four in which the mother is earning $7,000 obtains a disposable income plus benefits from food stamps, school lunches, and Medicaid of about $7,900 per year. The nonpublic-assistance family with earnings of $7,000, eligible at this income level for only a small amount of medical assistance, would be left with a disposable income plus benefits of only about $5,800. Further, the variety of eligibility criteria, definitions of income, income disregards, and procedures for verifying income in public assistance, Medicaid, and other social programs is so bewildering that one is not assured that those who are eligible for benefits will receive them or that those not eligible for benefits will be denied them. In addition, the variety of policy making bodies involved has led to serious inconsistencies in policies which establish who should benefit and to what degree from various programs.

While stricter administration and work requirements can be effective in counteracting the lack of incentive to work created by a basic welfare package equivalent to a gross income of almost $7,000 per year, it does not eliminate all problems. Under present regulations a family may be worse off if it increases its earnings by a few hundred dollars than if it does not. There is inequity in varying benefits available to different types of families on welfare or to those who are and those who are not on public assistance.

Finally, public assistance and Medicaid must be considered in relation to other social programs such as food stamps, day care, and subsidized housing. The current irrational pattern of definitions of income, of income disregards, of fee scales, and of different eligibility criteria for various social programs needs to be changed and made more rational and equitable. Like other states, New York is, of course, under a variety of federal constraints, but there is nonetheless considerable room for changes in state policies that would enhance equity of treatment among the residents of the state.

Public Employee Labor Relations Under the Taylor Law

RAYMOND D. HORTON

Enactment in 1967 of the Public Employees' Fair Employment Act, or the Taylor Law, created a formal labor relations system
in New York State built around the principles of employee organization and representation, collective bargaining, and neutral administration. The purpose of this study is to describe and evaluate New
York's experience with this law over the past six years. What important changes in the relations between public employees and state and
local government have occurred as a result of the Taylor Law? What
are the major strengths and weaknesses of the state's program? Finally,
how well has the Taylor Law served public employees, governmental
units, and the New York public?

No formal labor relations program existed for state and local employees prior to 1967 except in New York City. In earlier years, however, an informal and intensely political system did exist. Public employees, like other political interest groups, were forced to seek their
goals by employing political tactics, including lobbying, lawsuits, and
political alliances with elected politicians.

The parameters of public employee labor relations before the passage of the Taylor Law were defined largely by the politics of the
state's civil service system and, to a lesser extent, by the common law
(later statutory) ban on public employee strikes. The civil service or
merit system was introduced by state legislation in 1883. In 1894
the merit principle was incorporated in the state constitution. Vesting
the civil service system with a cloak of state statutory and constitutional authority proved important, because it helped direct the attention of civil servants and civil service reformers toward Albany, the

governor, and the legislature. This focus, in turn, helped mold the political strategies of civil service reformers into very traditional forms. Public employee "associations," as they were commonly known for more than a half century, were primarily lobbying organizations.

This combination of organizational form and political strategy was not particularly successful. For example, it was not until 1937, more than five decades after the first civil service law was passed, that reformers managed to extend civil service protections beyond such matters as hiring, promotion, and job security to include an employee classification and compensation scheme. It was not until 1950, when state employees were expressly granted the right to organize by executive order of Governor Dewey and a rudimentary grievance procedure was instituted, that even small steps were taken toward a modern labor relations system. Since organizations of employees had existed de facto if not de jure for over fifty years, Dewey's initiative, which was continued by Governors Harriman and Rockefeller, was no large concession.

When a few civil service groups finally began to employ a new political tactic—the strike—the state legislature reacted very quickly to suppress this activity. In 1947, after public employee strikes in Rochester and Buffalo and the threat of a strike by transit workers in New York City, the Condon-Wadlin Law was passed. This measure codified the common law proscription against public employee strikes and added stiff penalties for use against striking employees. Weak organizationally, possessing no special forum in which to press their claims, and constrained by tradition or law against acting militantly, public employees throughout the state historically were dominated by their governmental employers.

Early in the 1960s, the first serious discussion of a more positive labor relations program began at the state level, spurred in part by the introduction of such a program in New York City in 1958. The Condon-Wadlin Law was amended in 1963 to soften somewhat the mandatory penalties against striking government employees. Governor Rockefeller, in a memorandum approving the 1963 revision of Condon-Wadlin, noted "the need to consider possible improvements in the overall relationship between state and local employees and their employers." This was the first suggestion from an important official that something affirmative finally might be done about public employee labor relations.

Two serious strikes in New York City—the welfare strike in 1965 and the transit strike in 1966—provided much of the immediate impetus for the Taylor Law. The two strikes shocked political leaders and the public, who were unaccustomed to such behavior by civil servants. A consensus rapidly emerged that penalties alone could not prevent public employee strikes and that some collective bargaining machinery was necessary to ensure labor peace. Shortly after the transit strike was settled in January 1966, Governor Rockefeller appointed a prestigious five-man committee of labor relations experts, headed by Professor George Taylor of the University of Pennsylvania, to assay the situation. The Taylor committee ratified the emerging policy consensus by recommending, after a two-month study, that the Condon-Wadlin Law be repealed and that a new law be passed creating a modern labor relations system for all state and local employees in New York.

The Public Employees' Fair Employment Act was passed the following year in essentially the form recommended by the Taylor committee. Employees were guaranteed the dual rights of organization and representation, public employers were required to negotiate with employee organizations, and an administrative board was created to help resolve anticipated labor-management disputes. However, the strike ban was continued. The carrot did not completely replace the stick in the state's labor relations program. The major deviation from the Taylor committee report was a clause inserted at the behest of New York City Democrats that permitted local governments to create their own labor relations schemes if they were "substantially equivalent" to the state's program. The local option clause permitted New York City to implement its own newly devised labor relations program.

Major Facets of the Taylor Law

The transition from an informal to a formal labor relations system in New York required some important structural and substantive innovations, including a new agency to administer the system, rules governing access to and the conduct of collective bargaining, and an impasse procedure to assist in resolving bargaining disputes. The particular route charted by the Taylor committee and ratified by the state legislature was both creative and comprehensive, at least for 1967. When compared to approaches that have been tried in other states since 1967, New York's program remains distinctive in several important respects.

The New York State Public Employment Relations Board (PERB) administers the Taylor Law. PERB represents the so-called independent agency that most new public employee relations programs include in some form or another. While PERB is a three-man umpire, it is not a tripartite organization in which representatives of employees, management, and the public share control according to some arithmetic mix. Rather, PERB's three officers, each of whom serves a six-year term, are appointed by the governor with the consent of the state senate. That PERB has managed to acquire a reputation for neutrality despite its formal membership selection process is testimony to the quality and fair-mindedness of its leadership, a fact generally though not unanimously recognized by civil service union leaders. The willingness of the state's political leaders, primarily Governor Rockefeller, to refrain from extensive involvement in the affairs of PERB has also enhanced the board's reputation of neutrality.

PERB's major functions include the resolution of disputes concerning union representation, determination of appropriate bargaining units, provision of conciliation services (mediation and fact-finding) in the event of a bargaining impasse, and, as a result of 1969 amendments to the Taylor Law, adjudication of "improper practice" charges, which can be brought by either negotiating party. In addition, PERB is empowered by the Taylor Law to suspend the dues checkoff privileges of unions involved in strikes, including New York City unions, and to perform other essentially housekeeping functions.

In six years PERB has imposed considerable order on state and local labor relations, except in New York City, which uses its tripartite Office of Collective Bargaining, an organization similar to PERB. While PERB is not a judicial body, its decisions and dicta represent something akin to a body of common law that labor and management refer to for advice, if not direction, in the conduct of their separate and joint business. In this limited sense, the Taylor Law has centralized the labor relations process in New York State.

The most important change introduced by the Taylor Law was, of course, collective bargaining. The most obvious effect of collective bargaining was to provide public employees a privileged forum for the pursuit of their goals, one from which all other political interest groups were directly excluded. The Taylor Law has not depoliticized the state's labor relations process; rather, it has added another political forum. Two other important by-products of collective bargaining under the Taylor Law are important. First, collective bargaining has contributed to a marked decentralization of the labor relations process. Second, it has infused new life into public employee organizations in New York State. These conditions are important in determining how well and for whom collective bargaining works.

If the state house and executive mansion were once the most important place for public employees to be represented, that is less the case today because of the Taylor Law. While some very important issues, such as the attempt at public employee pension reform in 1973, still involve state officials heavily in the labor relations process, collective bargaining has become increasingly important in such places as New York City, Syracuse, North Castle, and Oyster Bay. In the Taylor Law's first six years over 15,000 collective bargaining agreements have been reached. Some 1,100 public employers, 750 of which are school districts, negotiate contracts covering approximately 2,500 separate bargaining units. The Taylor Law imposed substantial new responsibilities on the state's smaller governments that had no background in formal collective bargaining, but opened up new opportunities for the employees of those governments.

That the Taylor Law has contributed to the vitality of public employee organizations in New York State is indicated by the fact that 900,000 of the 1,000,000 state and local employees are represented by unions. In comparison, only about one-third of the state's private, nonagricultural employees are unionized. Although the unionization of many public employees, those in New York City, occurred for reasons having little to do with the Taylor Law, the impact of the law on employee organizational life elsewhere in the state cannot be disputed. Through 1972, PERB received over 900 representation petitions from public employee groups and conducted 234 elections involving over 350,000 state and local employees. It should be noted that union organization, spurred by the introduction of collective bargaining under the Taylor Law, produces important spillover effects away from the bargaining table. Newly organized or refurbished unions are convenient and effective vehicles for the expression of traditional public employee political strategies, such as lobbying and electoral support, which are aimed at influencing the behavior of local or statewide officials.

Unlike many other public employee labor relations statutes, the Taylor Law contains no "scope of bargaining" or "management rights" clause; it provides simply that the terms and conditions of employment will be determined bilaterally. This means that in addition to economic benefits, public employee organizations may bargain with management representatives over civil service and managerial rules. These three subjects, then, must be examined in order to measure the nature and extent of change actually occasioned by the Taylor

Law. However, since the law created a new decision making process, opened up a broad range of issues for resolution in that forum, and assisted the organizational development of public employees, it would appear that collective bargaining under it does not simply represent a cosmetic change involving new structures only.

Impasse Procedures

Under the Taylor Law, parties to negotiation are free to develop their own impasse procedures. If this option is not utilized, as it most frequently is not, or if the procedures are not successful, PERB may enter the impasse situation either at the motion of the parties or on its own initiative. PERB's initial response is mediation; if mediation does not bring about a settlement, PERB is empowered to appoint a fact finder who may make nonbinding recommendations for a settlement.

About 70 percent of the contracts negotiated in the state are now achieved without PERB's assistance. Nevertheless, the volume of cases reaching the impasse stage is increasing; and, increasingly, fact-finding is displacing mediation. In 1970, a total of 696 cases were closed during the impasse stage, 60 percent by mediation; in 1972, 839 cases reached the impasse stage, but by then close to 60 percent went through the fact-finding procedure.

If neither mediation nor fact-finding produces a settlement, the Taylor Law provides for finality by vesting the appropriate local legislative body with the power to impose unilaterally a final solution. As a practical matter, the legislative hearing has not been used frequently as a final step. Normally, the parties reach a settlement on their initiative when one or both are hesitant about permitting a legislative body to impose a settlement. Less than 10 percent of all impasse proceedings reach the legislative hearing stage, and less than 1 percent of all impasse decisions represent binding, unilateral decisions imposed by the appropriate legislative body.

Strikes

The impasse procedures of the Taylor Law are touted as a substitute for strikes. The argument is that the availability of impartial, expert conciliatory services renders public employee strikes unnecessary. Nevertheless, the Taylor Law attempts to provide double protection against strikes by declaring them illegal and by making possible the invocation of a series of penalties in case of strikes. Contempt convictions against union leaders growing out of failure to obey injunctions against strikes are available, public employers are permitted to dock striking employees two days' pay for each day they strike, and PERB is empowered to impose the penalty of loss of dues checkoff privileges if it finds the union responsible for the strike.

In theory these are reasonably stiff penalties, but in fact they are only as stiff as the backs of those public officials, including jurists, who must enforce or implement them. The enforcement record, dating back to the period when the Condon-Wadlin Law was on the books, has been weak. However, the inclination of public officials to enforce strike penalties appears to be increasing. In 1972, PERB invoked forfeiture of dues checkoff for periods ranging from three months to a year against twenty-three employee organizations. New York City officials, who long were remiss in this regard, have also recently begun to enforce the punitive provisions of the Taylor Law more energetically.

Whether penalties in the Taylor Law play any substantial role in easing the strike problem is not clear. Aggregate strike data disclose very little information. Fifteen strikes in 1967 resulted in almost 800,000 lost man-days of work; thirty-four strikes in 1970 cost only 29,000 man-days of work. While more strikes occur now than before the Taylor Law was enacted, this may result more from factors like improved union organization and the sharpness with which issues are focused at the bargaining table than from any changes in the penalties against strikes.

Strengths and Weaknesses of the Taylor Law

Not surprisingly, consensus concerning the strong and weak points of the Taylor Law is lacking. Deep-seated divisions among various groups about what should be included in public labor relations programs make agreement difficult. The absence of a management rights clause, for example, is viewed by civil service union leaders as a positive feature and by many management officials as a negative one. But consensus is in part made difficult because so little research has been conducted that might demonstrate empirically the consequences that follow from specific features of the Taylor Law.

One positive feature of the Taylor Law is the composition of its administrative overseer, PERB. A broad spectrum of potential organizational forms exists for agencies that perform functions similar to

PERB's, from a tripartite, politically independent structure to one dominated politically by an elected chief executive. No structure is free from theoretical or potential operational weaknesses. Administrative units dominated by mayors or governors may serve but one interest in their deliberations; tripartite units, in theory dominated by no specific interest, may easily become biased toward unions. PERB's members, who are appointed by the governor and thus are theoretically subject to his political control, have been permitted considerable discretion in their decision making functions. This discretion has helped PERB develop a significant reputation for fairness. If one, two, or all three of PERB's members begin to show signs of favoritism or ineptitude, a political process exists that permits removal from office, albeit not immediately. This form of political control is less easily exercised in tripartite administrative organizations where government representatives are usually in the minority.

A second positive feature of the Taylor Law, closely related to the first, concerns the system's impasse procedures. The objection that PERB's members are appointed by "management" are largely mooted by PERB's lack of authority to impose binding settlements. So long as an administrative agency such as PERB and its mediators and factfinders perform only advisory functions, composition and the process of membership selection are relatively unimportant. But when politically independent administrative agencies are accorded the power of binding arbitration, as in the case of New York City's Office of Collective Bargaining, important issues of democratic control and public policy are raised.

In the event of an impasse under the Taylor Law, the ultimate authority to reallocate expense budgets and to determine particular management policies of government rests with legislative bodies that may range from a school board to the state legislature itself. Such a body is a more fitting forum than an independent administrative agency for the resolution of decisions so central to political life. Also, as the Taylor Law experience suggests, locating final authority with a legislative rather than administrative body tends to increase the likelihood that final settlements will eventually be negotiated by the parties rather than imposed on them. While New York City's Office of Collective Bargaining has possessed the power of imposing binding arbitration for a relatively short period, recent evidence suggests that compulsory arbitration will increasingly become a substitute for collective bargaining in New York City.

It should be noted, however, that one effect of the legislative finality provision in the Taylor Law is to force organized public school teachers into a very difficult and seemingly unfair impasse procedure. The appropriate legislative body in such a situation is the school board itself, a body unlikely to reach a binding decision much different from its own final negotiating offer. In the absence of a right to strike, teacher unions in the state's independent school districts would seem to be disadvantaged by the finality provision of the Taylor Law.

A third positive feature of the state's program concerns the determination of bargaining units. State employees are divided into a small number of bargaining units, only eight. At the local level, except in New York City, PERB has attempted to minimize the number of bargaining relationships so that governments are not forced to negotiate with many separate unions in a large number of units. New York City inherited an extremely fragmented bargaining process from the Wagner years, one which the Office of Collective Bargaining has attempted to restructure. From 1968 through 1973, the number of bargaining units in New York City was decreased 36 percent, but almost 250 separate units still remain. Such a large number of bargaining units places considerable strain on management negotiators and encourages leapfrogging of union demands. An excessive number of units disrupts sound labor relations, at least from management's viewpoint.

While there is considerable opinion to the contrary, one failing of the Taylor Law seems to be the absence of a clause limiting the scope of bargaining. The rationale for a limited scope rests primarily on the assumption that efficiencies in the delivery of public services are sacrificed when trained, experienced management personnel are deprived of the authority to decide policies having to do with matters like deployment of manpower, introduction of technology and other labor-saving devices, and the setting of standards for work performance. This is not an easy assumption, for certainly the history of public sector management in New York and elsewhere discloses more than a few examples of managerial apathy or ineptitude.

If one assumes, however, that managers *generally* know more about management than employees and their bargaining agents and are *generally* more interested than employees in devising means of increasing productivity and lowering unit costs, the absence of a limiting clause in the Taylor Law becomes a problem. While PERB has attempted to limit the scope of bargaining on management issues through its decisions in "improper practices" cases, it has not been successful, partly because the Taylor Law contains no clause covering the scope of bargaining or the rights of management. In the *Hunting-*

ton case, a recent decision involving this issue, the New York State
Court of Appeals stated:"Under the Taylor Law the obligation to bargain as to all terms and conditions of employment is a broad and un-
qualified one, and there is no reason why the mandatory provision
of that act should be limited, in any way, except in cases where some
other applicable statutory provision explicitly and definitively pro-
hibits the public employer from making an agreement as to a particular term or condition of employment."

Given this sweeping dictum and the experience in New York City,
where decisions once reserved to management officials are now regularly negotiated and even determined in binding arbitration decisions
by the Office of Collective Bargaining, it is more than likely that
significant changes will occur in the nature of public service management in New York. Civil servants and managers have quite different
ideas about what the rules, techniques, and technology of service
delivery should be. Indeed, the most significant changes brought about
in state and local government by the Taylor Law may occur in this
area rather than in the economic benefits of civil servants. Clarifying
legislation that defines the scope of bargaining and management rights
would seem desirable, though this step probably would not definitively limit the scope of bargaining.

Whether the Taylor Law's ban on public employee strikes is a strong
or weak point is a much-debated issue. The conventional wisdom is
that legalizing public employee strikes would place government in
an untenable position at the bargaining table and would promote in-
terruptions in the flow of services to the public. In maintaining the
state's long-standing ban on public employee strikes, New York has
followed what is clearly the dominant position nationally on this
issue. The classical argument in favor of legalizing public employee
strikes is based on the quite different assumption that public employees, rather than management, need help at the bargaining table and
that the right to strike would help equalize bargaining power and
thus permit meaningful bargaining.

The other side of the argument favoring legalization of strikes raises
interesting questions, which are now beginning to be considered.
While legalization of strikes would indeed provide public employees
the right to strike, it would also provide management the right to
accept strikes. It would seem, a priori, that management's ability to
accept certain strikes as a rational bargaining strategy is just as essential for meaningful collective bargaining as a union's freedom
to employ the strike as a rational bargaining strategy. What is good

for the goose would seem, logically at least, good for the gander.

An interesting and perhaps fundamental realignment of positions on the strike question may be occurring, one which may make modification of the Taylor Law ban on strikes possible. While virtually all union leaders publicly argue for the right to strike, some union leaders are beginning to appreciate the many pitfalls they would face if public employee strikes were legalized. In most strike situations management probably enjoys the stronger hand since most civil service groups perform services that the public and management could do without for considerable periods if the need arose. Because membership expectations concerning the fruits of success in strike situations would not often be realized, gaining the right to strike would probably put most union leaders in a difficult situation not conducive to extended tenure in office. The growing support of union leaders for compulsory arbitration schemes represents, at least in part, their appreciation that bargaining-arbitration scenarios are likely to be more profitable for them than bargaining-strike scenarios.

Conversely, some public officials are beginning to recognize the problems associated with labor relations programs that impose arbitration or other finality procedures as a substitute for the strike. When third-party organizations like PERB or the Office of Collective Bargaining intervene on their own initiative to institute conciliatory or binding procedures, managers lose an important political resource—the ability to accept a strike when faced by what they consider unreasonable union demands. This problem is compounded from management's point of view when outside parties impose settlements that management finds unacceptable but cannot reject.

The day may not be far off when proposals to legalize strikes elicit no solid phalanxes of union support or managerial opposition. The strongest argument for the prevailing view that strikes should be illegal involves widespread recognition that certain strikes, such as those by firemen and possibly policemen, simply cannot be tolerated because of the threat they post to public safety and property. This very real problem, however, in no way justifies the blanket ban on strikes found in the Taylor Law. It may justify a limited ban, as now exists in Pennsylvania and Hawaii, that permits certain employee groups to strike and provides a system of compulsory arbitration for others.

No issue is as widely misunderstood as the strike, in large part because so little empirical research on the causes and effects of public strikes has been conducted. The chances seem good that serious research would dispel many myths about the impact of public employee strikes and the efficacy of laws banning strikes. One such myth is that laws prohibiting strikes help management at the bargaining table.

An Evaluation of the Taylor Law

It is not difficult to recount the major rule and institutional changes occasioned by the Taylor Law; it is far more difficult to evaluate the law, because to do this, one must know something about its consequences. On the surface, the transition from an informal to a formal labor relations process in New York State involved some seemingly important changes. But formal changes in the way decisions are made sometimes do not produce changes in decisions themselves. A second way of evaluating change, then, is to see if the content of decisions reached under the new system has changed.

This way is not common for evaluating public sector labor relations programs that utilize collective bargaining. Students of the subject spend far more time discussing the process by which collective bargaining decisions should be reached than analyzing the decisions themselves. The reasons for this are not difficult to understand. Bargaining is valued highly in this society because it is thought to ensure two important results: group participation in decision making and acceptable decisions (if bargained decisions are not perfect for all, they are assumed to be at least acceptable to all). Because collective bargaining is perhaps the purest example of the participation principle, strong incentives exist to impute greater merit to bargained decisions than to those unilaterally imposed. Also, collective bargaining began in the private sector where it was assumed that the unseen hand of the market would minimize the incidence of bad decisions and protect consumer or public interests.

The desire by some to extend collective bargaining to the public sector collided with the almost unanimous impression that the private sector and governmental operations were inherently different. These alleged differences led opponents of public sector bargaining to conclude that it represented a dangerous experiment that should not be attempted; proponents of public sector bargaining were less skeptical, of course, but they nevertheless focused most of their attention on how to structure governmental bargaining in the most advantageous way. As a consequence, the literature of public sector labor relations is heavily biased toward normative, legalistic, and formalistic concerns. Little attention has been paid to developing conceptual and methodological schemas that would permit measurement of the tangible effects of public sector bargaining.

One such conceptual schema centers around the political economist's assumption that the purpose and consequence of political change involves the redistribution of political benefits and costs. Few examples of political change escape this iron law. Since the substance of collective bargaining under the Taylor Law includes some very important and very tangible public resources, such as money and control over policy making, it would seem appropriate to evaluate the law by examining the consequences of collective bargaining decisions. If a redistribution of benefits and costs is occurring because of the Taylor Law, decision analysis permits stronger inference about the extent and nature of change that has resulted than a simple comparison of old and new programs permits. Further, this approach helps make it possible to say something about who benefits and who loses as a result of the law.

If the Taylor Law has changed public employee labor relations in New York State, the best evidence of change should be found in specific transactions made at the bargaining table. Have salaries and fringe benefits of public employees increased as a result of the Taylor Law reforms? Have specific public and managerial policies of government changed as a result of their inclusion within the scope of collective bargaining? Has the introduction of collective bargaining affected the cost of government in New York State or the quality and quantity of public services?

Unfortunately, little research on these questions has been conducted. Until more is known about the consequences of collective bargaining decisions in New York, a definitive evaluation of the Taylor Law will be impossible. The formal changes that have been described in this study and the limited, empirical research that has been attempted suggest that the following working hypotheses about the impact of the Taylor Law warrant consideration.

First, organized public employees benefit from the Taylor Law; as a result of improved union organization and the availability of the collective bargaining forum, organized public employees are better compensated. For essentially the same reasons, plus the absence of a scope of bargaining clause in the Taylor Law, they enjoy more influence over the management process. Unorganized public employees, including many managerial employees, do not benefit from the Taylor Law, or benefit less than organized employees. Not only are there relatively fewer financial resources available for distribution, but they possess less control over the formulation and implementation of management policies.

Second, the impact of the Taylor Law on government operations in New York State varies widely; the impact of a formal labor relations system on New York State government is less than that of a similar system on the government of New York City. Local governmental units are more affected by the Taylor Law than the government of New York State. Government policies having to do with the management and delivery of services are, and increasingly will be, affected by the Taylor Law.

Third, the Taylor Law contributes to a redistribution of personal income in New York State. A small but growing segment of the public—organized state and local employees and their families—benefits from the redistribution of personal income. A large but shrinking segment of the public does not benefit from this redistribution. Finally, the quantity and quality of public services in New York State will not increase as a result of the Taylor Law.

Health Care

ARTHUR L. LEVIN

Sandwiched between the federal and local governments, many of which had strong departments of health as far back as the early 1800s, the state governments have played a significant, though often ambiguous, role in national health affairs. They have frequently found themselves in the unenviable position of having health policy making preempted by Washington, while being criticized by local governments laboring under the day to day management of their health problems.

Nevertheless, the states have remained an essential part of the tripartite governmental health structure. Indeed, they are more important now than ever before. Federal health spending increased some 170 percent in the 1960s, and in 1974 federal outlays for health will total more than $23 billion, over $5 billion more than two years ago. Most of these increases have been to plan, finance, or otherwise support the delivery of health services. And of these moneys, with the important exception of the Medicare program, most are funneled through the states.

With the passage of the Medicare and Medicaid acts in 1965, federal spending to finance health services took a quantum leap. The increment of several billion additional dollars for health placed a serious strain on intergovernmental relations. The federal government looked to the states to control health prices while localities, hard-pressed for funds, resented state efforts to police their operation of health programs or to limit their use of federal-state money.

Medicaid was the most significant source of intergovernmental conflict. This law, enacted in July 1965, required that as a condition for receiving federal funds states plan to deliver by July 1, 1975, "comprehensive" health services for all citizens unable to meet their health care obligations. This commitment, however, was short-lived. Faced with the burgeoning costs of a program that quickly became the biggest item in their budgets, many states petitioned the federal government for relief. A series of amendments passed between 1965 and 1970 drastically curtailed both the scope of services and the number of people eligible for them.

The basic problem with both Medicare and Medicaid was that vast amounts of new dollars were being forced into the health system without adequate controls over costs or third-party reimbursement rates. The result was grave inflation. Health prices became the fastest rising component of the consumer price index, with physicians' fees and daily hospital rates rising at some 7 and 15 percent per annum respectively. Much of the latter rise reflected the pent-up demands of hospital workers for higher wages to bring their incomes up to the level of comparable workers in other industries. Hospitals, in turn, passed on these higher labor costs to third-party payors, particularly Blue Cross and the government, who were eventually forced to pass them on to the public in the form of higher premiums or taxes.

To make matters worse, at the time Medicare and Medicaid were passed, there was little governmental planning of health services. Hospitals were often built where they were not needed or where there was no manpower to staff them. There was a serious imbalance in the nation's supply of acute and long-term care beds, with not enough of the latter. There were shortages in many geographic areas of "primary care" physicians or of other types of manpower.

The Comprehensive Health Planning Act, passed in 1966, was the federal government's reaction to this chaotic and potentially dangerous situation. This act provided funds to states and local governments to establish agencies that would, it was hoped, foster the more efficient and effective delivery of care. These agencies were envisaged as encompassing all aspects of health planning, including facilities, manpower, and even financing.

By 1974 all fifty states, and more than 150 local areas, had established comprehensive health planning agencies. But the total planning envisaged by the 1966 law has proven difficult to implement. The federal comprehensive health planning (CHP) agency was established far down in the depths of the bureaucracy, a position that gave it no predominance over other programs, such as Hill-Burton. At the state and local level, similar mistakes were made. At the local level, there is still the sense of confusion over the role of the CHP agency. In New York City, for instance, an areawide facilities planning body is still separate from the city's CHP entity.

Thus, well into the 1970s, vast amounts of money—more than 7 percent of the nation's GNP—are being spent for health. But the basic dilemma of how to find ways to increase health services while maintaining quality and holding the line on prices persists. The problem remains, for all levels of government, of the best way to exert some kind of rational control over a system that, in its pluralism and complexity, is most difficult to encompass.

New York State's Health Progress

New York has always undeniably been a leader among states in the attention paid to health. Nelson Rockefeller in his fifteen years as governor had not only a continuing interest about the availability of health services but a growing concern with rising costs. Year after year his annual messages to the legislature emphasized the necessity for increased funds for research as well as the more systematic planning of medical care facilities and health services. As early as 1961 he noted that health care costs were increasing at the annual rate of 10 percent. In a long special message in February 1967 he outlined an expanded health program covering research, manpower training, health education, and planning. He stated that he had five basic objectives, which were to ensure enough skilled hands to meet health needs, communicate disease-fighting knowledge, intensify research in areas where little was known, improve health planning, and establish a network of hostels for the mentally retarded.

The success of the governor's efforts can be seen in the fact that New York spends more money per capita on health care than any other state —approaching $100 a person in 1974. In the last decade, spending for New York's own health programs increased 132 percent, and state aid for local programs more than doubled. The state's share of its Medicaid program is some $500 million. Within the state, local governments also spend large amounts; New York City's health budget is more than $1 billion annually, second in magnitude only to federal outlays.

In several areas New York can, with some justification, claim significant health accomplishments and innovative leadership. The state has an impressive record in the construction of new facilities. In the last fifteen years, New York has built 23 new state mental health facilities and has constructed or expanded 109 voluntary and municipal hospitals and nursing homes. Since 1966 the state has provided $5.8 billion in long-term, low-interest mortgage loans for public or non-profit health facility construction through the sale of bonds by the State Housing Finance Agency.

This aggressive building program has resulted in a stock of more than 85,000 hospital beds, or 4.6 beds per 1,000 population—one of the nation's highest ratios. Moreover, the building of facilities with long-term beds has allowed the state to close many nursing homes and other institutions that did not conform to present standards. The state has succeeded in maintaining a fairly appropriate ratio of long-term to acute-care beds, both through construction and through a well organized planning effort.

With more physicians for its population than any other state, New York has the nation's richest supply of health manpower. These manpower resources have been fostered by several state programs. The State University has achieved, as part of its overall spectacular growth during the last decade, an increased capability to train health professionals. In addition, the state provides funds to private schools of medicine, nursing, and dentistry—more than $20 million in 1973-74. These moneys are granted for the purpose of enabling these schools to increase their enrollments. This incentive has been adopted by the federal government in its own manpower training grant programs.

Equally important, the state has made efforts to remedy the maldistribution of health manpower. The health commissioner identifies physician-shortage areas throughout the state for the purpose of awarding scholarships to medical students. This effort operates in conjunction with a federal loan-forgiveness program for physicians who work in such physician-deprived areas.

Finally, the state has recognized the need to introduce new types of health manpower. In 1971 the legislature enacted one of the nation's first laws legalizing two new categories of health paraprofessionals, physicians' associates and physicians' assistants. Graduates of approved training programs are now able to work in these roles. In addition, the Nurse Practice Act was amended in 1972 to allow expanded roles for nurses. Both of these laws should encourage new types of manpower that can improve the productivity of physicians.

The history of health planning in New York dates back some thirty-five years. The Health and Hospital Planning Council of Southern New York, a private nonprofit body, was incorporated in 1938 to foster hospital planning in the New York City metropolitan area. With passage by the legislature of the Metcalf-McCloskey Act in 1964 and the Folsom Act in 1965, the state health commissioner was charged with approving all new health facilities construction. A state planning council and seven regional councils, some of which, like the metropolitan New York one, had existed for many years as nonofficial bodies, were given official authority to make recommendations to the commissioner. New York was thus the first state to mandate statewide planning for health facilities. Through this mandate, the state has in large measure succeeded in halting the construction of unneeded facilities and in fostering such efficiencies as combined hospital operation and hospital mergers. In addition, planning has improved the mix of facilities and encouraged the building of long-term-care beds and other nonacute types of facilities.

With passage of the federal comprehensive health planning law, the state acted to institute comprehensive planning. The Health Planning Commission was established in 1967 as the state CHP agency, and regional CHP agencies have also been established. The problem of duplication of planning efforts now exists; the old hospital planning bodies and the newer CHP agencies are operating side by side. This problem has been recognized by state officials, and the immediate future should see a merger or other organizational changes designed to achieve a single planning system throughout the state.

New York was one of the first states to give its officials broad powers to control costs. The Folsom Act, in addition to its planning provisions, gave the health commissioner power to audit the costs of hospitals and other facilities. Equally crucial, it also authorized the commissioner to certify that reimbursement rates paid hospitals by the state (under Medicaid, for example) or by other third-party payors, such as Blue Cross, were "reasonably related to costs."

At the time of its enactment, the Folsom Act was probably the nation's strongest cost control law. In 1968 and 1969 the act was further strengthened, giving the commissioner power to certify that third-party payments for hospital and "health-related services" were reasonably related to "the costs of efficient production of such services."

In addition to the cost control law, the state passed several laws regulating the private insurance industry. These laws were aimed at eliminating certain abuses such as "dread disease insurance" and at requiring that insurers offer consumers individual protection when they leave a group plan. In 1972 the state passed a landmark "Truth in Health Insurance" law. This law required that insurers present a clear, concise statement of coverage and exceptions on the face of every health policy sold within the state. The law also required that the policy state information on the percentage of premium income used for benefits versus operating costs and profits. Legislation was also passed in 1972 requiring that insurance agencies make home care coverage available, on request, in policies providing reimbursement for hospital care.

New York has also taken wide-ranging actions to control the quality of care. In 1963 the Department of Health was given authority to audit the quality of medical care practiced throughout the state. In 1965 the Folsom Act gave the commissioner power to license medical facilities and to audit both the quality of their care and their utilization. The Department of Health has also been given the function of approving laboratories that perform chemical, bacteriological, and other types of health tests. Finally, in addition to its role in licensing physicians, nurses, and a wide range of other health manpower, the department now certifies the newer categories of physicians' associates and assistants.

New York has one of the nation's most ambitious programs to finance health services for low-income individuals and families. Despite recent cutbacks, eligibility criteria and the scope of benefits are more liberal than in any other state with the possible exception of California. At present, the program costs some $1.8 billion annually and an estimated 2 million to 2.5 million persons are served. In addition to its role in paying for care, the program has also instituted certain cost- and quality-control innovations, such as the use of a drug formulary to promote the most efficient provision of pharmaceuticals and audits of medical and dental practices for those providers serving large numbers of Medicaid patients.

Of all specific state health programs, mental health deserves particular mention. Until fairly recently, mental health programs were almost entirely state supported. New York has good reason to be proud of the results of that support. In addition to a vigorous building program, the state has emphasized efforts to move the treatment of mental illness from an institutional to an outpatient or community basis. Indeed, it was in a New York State mental hospital in the early 1950s that the initial research was started in the use of psychotropic drugs. This research has been the single most important factor in allowing patients to be discharged from mental institutions and treated while functioning in the community. Over the last fifteen years, the number of hospitalized mental patients in the state has declined from 90,000 to less than 50,000, a dramatic reversal of a previous trend. New York can justifiably claim to have provided national leadership in this revolution in the treatment of mental illness.

Health Problems of the 1970s

New York's high health expenditures plus the state's high per capita income might lead one to infer that its citizens enjoy health levels that are as good as those in any state. Paradoxically, the most recent objective evidence obtainable suggests that health status in the state may not be as good as its level of health spending would warrant.

Although New York had the highest per capita health expenditures of any state in 1970, there were thirty-seven other states that could boast lower overall death rates than New York's. Moreover, this situation was substantially unchanged from a decade ago, when forty-three states had lower death rates. In New York City, death rates and life expectancy have not altered appreciably in the last ten years.

Overall death rates in 1970 were 10.3 per 1,000 persons in New York, but only 9.4 for the entire nation. In 1968, the most recent year for which data are available, New York's rate was higher than the nation's for three of the five leading causes of death. For heart disease and cancer, the two leading causes of death, New York's rates were more than 120 percent above the national averages. For the ten leading causes of death, New York's rates exceeded the national rates in five, including the categories of pneumonia and diabetes, in which medical care is generally quite effective.

These comparative data pose more questions than they answer. Could the state's poorer performance be due to the fact that many people come to New York seeking medical care that is unavailable elsewhere? Could it simply be due to more accurate reporting of the causes of death within the state? Or could the data, indeed, say something about the quality or distribution of health care services in New York, the nation's richest state in health resources?

By themselves, of course, the above comparisons do not necessarily mean that New York's citizens receive substandard health care, or even care that could be more effective. These data do, however, provide a dramatic illustration of how a state can spend large amounts of money while still lagging behind in measurable indexes of health status.

This inability to purchase good health with the state's health dollar will continue to be the central problem in the coming years. No one would deny that many aspects of a state's status are not amenable to influence by alterations in the health delivery system. On the other hand, improvements in many areas might well affect health levels. Some of the more important of these problem areas are discussed below.

Assuring the quality of care has always been a paramount public health concern. Licensing of health professionals and institutions are long-standing methods designed to promote quality. More recently, emphasis has been placed on postgraduate education for health workers and on peer review of the workers' actions and decisions.

There is, unfortunately, a dearth of systematic data concerning the quality of care in New York State. In the early 1960s, however, two extensive studies of the quality of hospital care agreed remarkably in their results. As many as one-fifth of hospitalized patients received medically inferior care. The same proportion of hospital admissions was not medically justified. A significant proportion of surgical operations—one-third of all hysterectomies, for example—was found to be medically unindicated.

In another study of the quality of care within the state, the authors concluded that 42 percent of all prenatal deaths were preventable, and in three-quarters of the preventable deaths, errors in medical judgment were a factor. Several other more recent studies, though not all done in New York, have pointed up notable variations in the quality of medical care in diverse specialties such as radiology, pediatrics, and mental health. Finally, during the past two years, articles in the popular press have highlighted what appear to be grave examples of poor quality care, such as the questionable practice by physicians of administering intravenous medications to office patients.

Taken together, these studies and anecdotal evidence suggest that the problem of ensuring high-caliber health care continues to be a crucial one for state and local health officials. This problem is compounded by the difficulty and costliness of monitoring the quality of services and by the dilemma of how to discipline offenders. These difficulties notwithstanding, as government pays for a greater proportion of health services, it seems inevitable that more attention must be given the quality of those services, if only to eliminate practices that are unindicated or of questionable efficacy. This effort on the part of government at all levels can be expected to increase in the next few years.

There is also much evidence that health resources are not being used as appropriately as they might be. This misuse of resources is, in large measure, responsible for New York's high cost of health care. Misuse of hospitals, the most costly form of health care, has been well documented. Studies in three metropolitan areas have shown hospital overuse of some 25 percent and nursing home "patient misplacement" at 20 percent. A recent study of New York City's municipal hospitals found one-fifth of all beds empty and 40 percent of patients hospitalized beyond twenty-one days not in need of acute hospital care.

There are several reasons for this misuse of costly hospital care. Doctors responsible for admitting and discharging patients have little or no financial stake in using beds as efficiently as possible. Also, many health insurance plans encourage hospital use by not paying for alternative forms of care, such as ambulatory or long-term care. The New York metropolitan Blue Cross plan, for example, does not reimburse for most forms of ambulatory care or long-term care. Finally, there is a positive incentive on the part of hospital administrators to ignore unindicated bed use, since higher occupancy rates mean higher revenues.

All these misplaced incentives make it extremely hard to control the problem of hospital misuse. Various forms of utilization review have been attempted, and the results speak for themselves. There is little doubt that hospital misuse will continue to vex health officials in the years to come. One suspects that a combination of peer review plus monetary penalties for hospitals (and possibly for third-party payors such as Blue Cross) will be required. In addition, a closer look will have to be taken at certain scarce services within hospitals—intensive care is an example—to assure that these services are utilized by those patients who most need and can benefit from them.

Health manpower, another scarce resource, could also be used more appropriately and efficiently. The productivity of health workers in hospitals, for example, has actually fallen during the last decade, as measured by the number of employee hours per patient-day. As a result, New York State now has the highest cost per hospital case of any state, nearly twice the national average.

While health care probably will and possibly ought to remain a labor-intensive industry, there are already proven methods of using that labor more efficiently. It has been known for some time, for example, that many tasks performed by physicians can be delegated to less highly trained personnel. In experimental programs, nonphysician manpower has been able to save 60 percent of a physician's time while improving the caliber of care delivered.

The change of labor patterns has, however, been slow in coming, particularly in hospitals where the delivery of care is highly stratified and organized. Vested interests and fears of professional groups—

nurses, for example—have operated to discourage the use of physicians' assistants. Overly rigid educational requirements imposed by the government have been another slowing influence.

A related problem, and one of much more concern to government, is physician misallocation. In New York State, it is well recognized that areas of severe physician shortages exist next to areas of excess. As a result, the burden of caring for low-income patients falls on a very few doctors. In New York City only about one-third of practicing physicians participate in the Medicaid program. These related problems, the misuse and misallocation of health manpower, can be expected to remain pressing challenges for state and local governments during this decade.

In the area of financing there continues to be a need for a system that does not deter any citizen from seeking care for illness and that offers positive incentives for preventive care. Such a system would save lives and money as well. Prepayment plans, such as New York City's Health Insurance Plan (HIP), which cover ambulatory care and thus preventive services, show less hospitalization and improved health levels in enrollees. Moreover, HIP has demonstrated that low-income persons, commonly thought to be overusers of care, acquire the use patterns of middle-income groups when they are enrolled in the prepayment system.

Unfortunately, many private insurance plans offer coverage that is far less comprehensive than HIP or the Kaiser plan, both of which actually deliver services as opposed to merely financing them. "The private insurance industry generally, and Blue Cross as well," noted Governor Rockefeller's Steering Committee on Social Problems, "have not been sufficiently aggressive in marketing coverage to meet patient needs more adequately."

The committee went on to estimate that comprehensive care could be provided at a yearly cost of $227 a person. Even if this estimate were doubled to provide for New York's excessively high costs, the resultant figure would still be far below what it now costs to deliver fragmented care that is less than comprehensive under the fee-for-service model.

Thus far, states have put aside consideration of health insurance for their citizens in hopes that the federal government would initiate such legislation. It would seem, however, eminently feasible and economically wise for a state like New York to undertake such a universal insurance plan. As a less optimal solution, the state could enact legislation mandating more comprehensive coverage by private carriers. One thing seems sure: without an increase in the number of citizens covered for comprehensive health services, many other efforts to improve the delivery of care will be difficult, if not impossible, to implement.

Two related and persistent problems are how to achieve regionalized health delivery and how to eliminate the dichotomy between public financed and private care. Two New York studies, the Piel commission and the health report of the Governor's Steering Committee, have labelled these goals as desirable ones. Yet, thus far, progress toward either has been limited.

Rationalization implies a health system that holds health providers accountable to a given population and that expeditiously refers patients to the proper kind and intensity of care. New York is, at present, far from such a regionalized system. New York City, for instance, is subdivided into some thirty health districts, but within each district there may be outpatient clinics, as well as numerous physicians who are unaffiliated with any hospital. Smaller, less elaborate hospitals may lack linkages with larger, more comprehensive ones.

The split between public and private care, exemplified by the municipal hospital system, has produced dual delivery systems which, aside from whatever inequities they foster, are obviously inimical to regionalized, efficient delivery. That inequities do exist has been documented by numerous studies. As recently as last year, the Scott commission found serious deficiencies in New York City's municipal hospitals. The commission heard testimony on the lack of adequate staff, as well as insufficient capital expenditures. In addition, municipal hospitals in general are acknowledged to receive lower reimbursement rates from Blue Cross and other third-party payors than do nonmunicipal institutions, a fact which, in light of their needs, is clearly inappropriate.

It is well within the power of state government to promote regionalization and the unification of public and private care. The establishment of regional health officers with the authority to institute measures to rationalize the allocation of operating funds as well as health manpower would go far toward eliminating many of the inequities and disparities that now exist.

The Future Role of the State

The rest of this decade should see continued changes in the state's role in health affairs. More aggressive state governments are already deeply involved in ensuring that their citizens enjoy access to high-caliber health services at a reasonable cost. They are exploring new ways to improve the use of health resources and to render insurers and providers more accountable to the public. The federal government has encouraged these efforts by providing funds not only for planning, but also for research and development in the delivery of health services.

The next few years should see a continuation of the trend away from a concern with categorical health programs (e.g., cancer, venereal disease, and tuberculosis) and movement toward programs that foster comprehensive services, such as community health and mental health centers. There should also be a trend away from efforts designed solely to augment the supply of health resources, whether bricks and mortar or manpower. State governments will find themselves forced to concentrate more on how existing funds and resources can be used most effectively. In so doing, they will find themselves compelled to exercise even greater control than at present over the operation and management of health care institutions and over the practices and procedures of health professionals.

In financing care, both state and federal governments, by virtue of their large financial participation, will undertake stronger efforts to control costs. The performance of hospitals with regard to utilization review will come under closer scrutiny. The role of Blue Cross and other third-party payors in influencing efficiency and in discouraging unneeded or ineffective services will also face reexamination.

On the other side of the cost-effectiveness coin, states will undoubtedly play a greater role in monitoring and ensuring the quality of care. It is dubious whether professional societies and groups, by their very nature unaccountable to the public, will be allowed free rein or autonomy as guarantors of quality in hospitals and nursing homes or in doctors' offices and clinics. Efforts such as that initiated in New York City to monitor the quality of physicians' office care under Medicaid can be expected to be expanded to encompass care delivered to all consumers, regardless of their income status.

Finally, states will have to address themselves to perhaps the most basic question, Who really runs the health care system? Health is a particularly perplexing industry because of the myriad of agencies, public and private, profit and nonprofit, which exert an influence in the field. In addition, dozens of professional groups and labor organizations seek a voice in the way services are regulated.

This extreme pluralism carries with it both strengths and weaknesses. One weakness is the distinct lack of authority of any single entity for overseeing the entire delivery system. If regionalization is to be promoted and the dualism of public-private care abolished, state government will have to accept greater responsibility for this governance.

In the near future, perhaps more than any other level of government, states will have to come to grips with this question of who exerts control over the health system. They will have to do so, if only because resource constraints will make it economically impossible to afford anything but a unified, coordinated system that discourages use of hospitals and other high-cost components. Health, like every other endeavor, is entering the era of scarcity. And in this era there will be a great and grave role for the states to play in assuring that the public interest is best served.

Housing

FRANK S. KRISTOF

Except for New York, the direct participation of states in meeting the housing needs of their citizens has been minimal until recently. This sector of public action has been assumed primarily by the federal government, with resources channeled directly to private beneficiaries or municipal public agencies. Housing became the subject of national public policy during the historic transitional years of the 1930s. By persistently reelecting President Franklin D. Roosevelt, the American public demonstrated its acceptance of a new political premise that the state of the economy was a legitimate area of public action. Housing became a leading contender for government attention for several mutually reinforcing reasons. First, shelter is a fundamental human need. Second, areas of housing blight are highly visible and disturbing symbols of individual or community poverty. Third, the nation's economic health is linked to the level of residential construction, which accounts, directly or indirectly, for about a tenth of the gross national product.

Thus, directing public resources toward new or improved housing for families who would not normally be in the market serves the dual objectives of meeting social needs while stimulating the nation's economy. Until recently, this duality of objectives had a powerful political constituency that, in the past decade, comanded an unprecedented flow of federal resources into publicly assisted housing.

The Movement of States into Housing Development

In less than a decade, there has been a complete reversal of state non-participation in housing activities. Between 1966 and 1973, the number of states with housing finance or development agencies has increased from three to thirty. Most of these agencies have been created within the past three years.

Three events influenced the states to move into housing finance and development. Probably the most important was an amendment to the National Housing Act of 1968, introduced by Senator Javits of New York, that opened direct participation in the housing subsidy benefits of the FHA Section 236 program to state and municipal housing finance and development agencies. The program gave the federal government the power to subsidize the market interest rate (approximately 7 to 8.5 percent) down to 1 percent for newly constructed or rehabilitated housing built by developers for families of moderate incomes ranging from $5,000 to $12,000, depending upon family size and community income levels. This subsidy, contracted for the life of a forty-year mortgage, effectively cut the market rent of new housing by 35 to 45 percent—the latter in communities that additionally authorized real estate tax exemptions for moderate-rent housing. The initiative for Javits's amendment came from New York City's Housing and Development Administration officials, who perceptively foresaw the possibilities for effective use of the 236 program in redeveloping the city's urban renewal areas.

As it turned out, the Javits amendment became the foundation stone for revolutionizing state-federal housing relationships. This amendment provided the state housing agencies with an unprecedented opportunity to develop an avenue for housing subsidy funds directly to such agencies from the Department of Housing and Urban Development (HUD) in Washington. This avenue was exploited swiftly and vigorously with the sympathetic cooperation of Secretary George Romney and his executive staff.

A concomitant of this opportunity for the allocation of federal subsidy funds to developers through state housing agencies was the rapid development within the states of an awareness of the new possibility to provide leadership, as well as federal assistance, to deal with the varying problems of those in need of housing across the state.

A second influence that enhanced the political outlook for state housing legislation was the 1961 one man, one vote Supreme Court decision that broke the back of rural domination of state legislatures. Since housing is seen as an essentially urban problem, the increased proclivity of redistricted state legislatures to pass urban-oriented legislation has had a positive influence on the rapid proliferation of new state housing finance agencies.

The third event that helped accelerate the movement of states into the housing field was the creation in 1968 of the New York State Urban Development Corporation (UDC). In UDC, observers from other states saw a working example of an organization that had succeeded in undertaking an extraordinary volume of new construction in a very brief time. Although the legislative concepts that underlie UDC may appear unique to non-New Yorkers, this agency's creation was the logical result of a long history of innovative housing legislation in New York State.

New York State's Housing Program: 1920-68

The first known use of state policy to stimulate housing production occurred in New York State over a half century ago. In 1920, the state legislature authorized New York City to grant exemption from local taxation until 1932 to all new residential construction, except for local improvements, started by April 1922. It is not surprising that the origins of legislation for assisted housing should be found in the city. Because New York City was the principal port of entry for European immigration, a chronic housing problem was created by this large inflow of newcomers. Furthermore, World War I disrupted residential construction, and the slowness of its resumption during the postwar inflation created a serious housing crisis in the city.

The 1920 tax exemption legislation touched off what subsequently became the greatest housing boom ever experienced by any city in America. Between 1923 and 1928, 564,000 housing units were completed at an average of 94,000 annually, a number sufficient to house the present 1.5 million population of Detroit, the nation's fifth largest city. The Upper West Side of Manhattan, much of the Bronx, and large sections of Queens were developed during this brief period. Initiated by the tax exemption program, this boom was sustained by the completion of rapid transit lines to some of the newly developed areas.

In 1926 the first state-authorized, limited-dividend statute in the nation was enacted. It provided for tax exemption to encourage construction of modest-cost multifamily housing on vacant land. The power of eminent domain was made available for site assembly purposes. The New York State Division of Housing, the first state agency to administer a publicly assisted housing program, was created the same year to administer this program. Twelve years later, in 1938, another major advance was made. In article 18 of the new state constitution, the use of public funds to provide multifamily housing "for families of low income" was authorized, and the state's municipalities were permitted to utilize federal funds to build low-rent public housing. Soon after, the State Division of Housing was made responsible for administration of the state-financed, low-rent public housing program.

The landmark New York State Limited Profit Housing Companies (Mitchell-Lama) Act of 1955 was one of the most sophisticated pieces of legislation ever devised to produce below-market priced housing. Its terms included use of tax-exempt, long-term (up to fifty years) public financing, local real estate tax exemption, use of eminent domain for site acquisition, a limit of 6 percent return on equity, and limits on incomes of occupants in order to provide moderate-rent housing for middle income families.

Not only did this statute break new conceptual ground in providing housing production subsidies for families that are not poor, but its basic principles subsequently were embodied in the Section 221(d)(3) below-market interest rate (BMIR) program of the National Housing Act of 1961. A further extension of this conceptual approach was realized by the 1 percent interest rate program in Section 236 of the 1968 National Housing Act. In 1960 the State Housing Finance Agency was created to provide a continued source of revenue bond financing for the Mitchell-Lama program administered by the State Division of Housing and Community Renewal.

Aside from the federal government's urban renewal program, designed to clear slums and to provide vacant land for urban reconstruction, and its Model Cities program, a more sophisticated program for community redevelopment assistance, there is little in the armory of federal housing assistance for low- and moderate-income families that has not been either forecast or replicated by New York State.

New York's Urban Development Problems of the Late 1960s

Despite New York State's long history of assistance to housing production, events of the years 1966-68 threatened to bring urban renewal and housing production programs to a halt. The inflation of these years, which caused both rapidly rising interest rates and unprecedented increases in union construction contract settlements, had severely adverse effects upon municipal redevelopment activities. Sharply increasing costs of constructing and financing state limited profit projects drove rents of these developments from $30 per room a month in 1964 to $40 in 1966 and $60 in 1968. The usefulness of this program in urban renewal areas was rapidly disappearing as this housing, despite tax-exempt bond financing and real estate tax exemption, priced itself out of these markets. Urban renewal developments across the state stagnated for lack of developers and usable public programs.

Even without these impediments, a growing disenchantment was developing among private entrepreneurs with the extraordinary amount of time (from three to six years) that was required to work through the labyrinth of state, local, and federal requirements to process a housing development, whether on urban renewal or privately owned land, with the city or state housing agencies. This unhappiness was matched by disaffection of public development agencies with private developers because of their unwillingness to undertake any serious expenditures (in itself a source of delay) prior to obtaining a guarantee that a proposed project would be processed to a satisfactory conclusion. The public agency could not give this guarantee, because of the seriatim nature of statutorily required approvals by other public bodies involved in the development process.

More specifically, a developer of an urban renewal site in New York City had to obtain official approvals from ten separate departments or agencies of the city, state, and federal governments, seven of which had to be obtained serially. Failure at any one of the seven serial stages could terminate the proposed project, while negative reactions obtained in the other six halted processing until objections were overcome. Adversary relationships between developer and public agencies engendered in this process was the source of many costly delays.

The difficulty in using existing programs in the face of the inflationary conditions of the late 1960s, the increased reluctance of private developers to undertake added risks engendered by these conditions, and the corresponding reluctance of public agencies to confront the public with skyrocketing costs of subsidized housing programs led senior state housing officials to seek new mechanisms that could cope with these problems.

Both the state and the New York City housing agencies had serious deficiencies. They were heavily dependent on the skill, knowledge, initiative, and integrity of the private developers chosen as sponsors of developments. This dependence gave the agencies little control over the location (except for renewal sites), the rate, or the timing of new developments. Public agencies could only react to proposals brought to them by developers, and even after they approved proposals, the agencies were often at the mercy of inept developers. This was a major cause of antagonism between developers and the public agency.

Another deficiency of the public agencies was their lack of statutory authority either to initiate development or to expend funds to investigate the feasibility of proposed developments. Statutory changes were needed to enable public development agencies to simplify and expedite the process of meeting legal requirements administered by other public agencies involved in housing development. There was also a need to broaden the definition of a public agency's powers to permit a wider range of development activities consistent with urban development requirements of the state's communities. Prominent among these activities was the authority to undertake industrial, commercial, and civic development. A mechanism to finance the expanded development objectives was required.

The Powers of the New York State Urban Development Corporation

After an extensive study by senior state officers of the deficiencies in the housing program, Governor Rockefeller proposed to the legislature that the New York State Urban Development Corporation (UDC) be created. This agency was unique in the breadth and depth of its power to initiate, finance, construct, and supervise the management of residential, commercial, industrial, and civic facilities. The legislature was extremely reluctant to act until the governor threatened to withhold patronage and keep the houses in continuous session. This hesitation stemmed largely from the proposed grant of power to the new UDC to overrule local building and zoning ordinances that legislators feared would lead to low cost housing for minority groups in the suburbs.[1]

The most important innovation in this legislation was the conveyance to UDC of authority to initiate development. The legislation declared it a public purpose "to attract and house new industries" and to "plan, finance, and coordinate industrial and commercial development with residential development for persons and families of low income and with public services and mass transit facilities." Thus UDC could, on its own initiative, undertake anything from a fifty-unit residential development to a complete new town with the attendant public, residential, commercial, and industrial facilities.

[1] For further discussion of the politics involved in the creation of the Urban Development Corporation see above, pp. 11-12.

Subject only to the consent of its board of directors, UDC could exercise the following powers in carrying out its functions: condemn real property; override local building codes, zoning ordinances, building permits, and occupancy certificate requirements; substitute the state's building code and issue its own building permits and certificates of occupancy; acquire sites and finance the planning and construction or rehabilitation of residential, industrial, commercial, or civic projects; create subsidiary corporations, lend or give them funds, and enter into contracts for the purchase, lease, sale, or mortgage of property; and borrow up to $1 billion (subsequently increased to $2 billion) in the open market.

The only major lack in UDC's arsenal of powers was the ability to subsidize its projects. The corporation might utilize all existing public subsidy programs such as the Mitchell-Lama program, public housing, public housing leasing, FHA 236, and rent supplements. Aside from these aids, the corporation's activities had to be financially self-supporting. This requirement was not quite equivalent to the whiplash of the "bottom line" of private firms, since it was accompanied by an escape clause that permitted appeals to the state legislature for financial succour if required; however, it was a bar to financial irresponsibility.

After an organization period of one and a half years, UDC placed in construction from 1970 through 1972 some 30,000 housing units in one hundred developments in thirty communities across the state and $50 million of industrial, commercial, and civic construction. The processing time from the project proposal to the start of construction averaged about one and a half years.

Included in the activities of UDC were a 2,700-acre new town in Lysander Township, thirteen miles northwest of Syracuse, with 800 acres allocated to industrial use. Two hundred of these acres were recently contracted by the Schlitz Brewing Company. Further UDC activities include a 2,000-acre tract in Amherst Township designed to provide supporting new-town residential facilities for the adjoining new Buffalo campus of SUNY now under construction and a 5,000-unit new-town-in-town under construction on Franklin Roosevelt Island (formerly Welfare Island) in New York City. Some 2,000 of these apartments are already part of a new skyline emerging from the East River.

In 1973 the corporation's approved construction program exceeded $1 billion, of which $600 million already had been raised in three bond issues floated between January 1971 and July 1973; a fourth issue for $100 million was offered in December 1973. An additional $175 million of short-term bond anticipation notes were outstanding. In addition, UDC had commitments from the Federal Department of Housing and Urban Development, aggregating some $2.1 billion over the life of the mortgage, for Section 236 subsidies to reduce rents from an average of $78 a room to $43 a room for 27,000 of the 30,000 housing units under construction. The pace of residential construction rose from 6,900 units in 1970 to 11,300 in 1971 and 12,000 in 1972. Early estimates indicated that in 1973 the total would drop sharply as a result of the president's suspension of new funding of the subsidized housing programs in January of 1973.

In short, the ability of this new agency to utilize its powers effectively has been impressive. It is one of the rare occasions in which governmental performance has approached theoretical capacity. For the private sector this is not only desirable but a necessary expectation; for the public sector it is, in a word, unprecedented.

What Does the Urban Development Corporation Prove?

The ultimate point of this discussion lies in the answer to the question, Is there something to be learned from the performance of the Urban Development Corporation? Can some principles about public agency development be drawn from its record? Or is UDC a unique personal triumph of its president and chief executive, Edward J. Logue, who in four and a half years built the corporation from a base of three persons—himself, his secretary, and the present general counsel—to a structure of 550 persons and seventeen offices across the state?

Without question, the corporation bears the strong imprint of Edward J. Logue's personality, especially two of his characteristics. The first is a willingness, seldom found in the public sector, to make difficult decisions. Coupled with UDC's vast powers, this proclivity has taken the corporation farther and faster than most executives are willing to travel. The second Logue characteristic is a flair for quality of design that makes UDC's publicly assisted housing projects collectively the most outstanding in the nation. Both characteristics make UDC different, but not necessarily more successful than it would have been under a different personality. In short, it can be posited that there are principles that may be drawn from UDC's performance that are replicable under any able leadership.

Important elements of UDC's successful performance are inherent in UDC's powers and in the structuring of its activities, both of which are replicable. First, the assembly of a competent professional staff with a mixture of able, experienced talent and young, enthusiastic, bright individuals provides the vital energy necessary to the success of an agency with heavy responsibilities in untried areas of activity. An important concomitant is that recruitment of able talent not be hobbled by conventional, restrictive civil service requirements that sharply constrain the acquisition of personnel with necessary skills. The corporation's ability to acquire personnel with required skills in an expeditious manner has made a major contribution to its ability to carry out its function effectively. Second, a review of its powers reveals that a number of statutory and administrative requirements made of private developers are waived for UDC. Among these requirements are most approvals by municipal agencies, including the planning commission (zoning approvals), the building department (plans review, building permits, and certificates of completion), and the municipal council. About half of the processing steps discussed earlier are thus removed. Third, the agency assumes as a routine function complete responsibility for carrying out all statutory and administrative requirements, at any level of government, that have to be met as part of the urban development process. This function requires dealings with agencies at the municipal, state, and federal level. Difficult as such responsibilities may be, certain significant benefits accrue in the process. When dealing with sister government agencies, irrespective of level, representatives of a state development agency have an advantage no private developer can expect: they are presumed to be acting in the public interest. The danger of adversary relationships that can, fairly or unfairly, be experienced by private developers is thus almost completely removed. Assumption of these responsibilities by the state development agency thereby facilitates resolution of difficult technical and legal problems with other public agencies.

Since UDC is the supervisory agency for its own projects, many of the essential approvals required for project processing are internal. Once a project proposal has been accepted and has passed preliminary market and financial feasibility tests, four main lines of activity take place simultaneously. First are the architectural activities, which include selection of the architect, schematic design, design development, and preparation of working drawings. Economic considerations are agreement on the construction budget, setting up of a financial structure, and arranging for required subsidies. For construction of the project, arrangement for a contractor has to be made, a contract must be negotiated, and the architectural and construction work has to be supervised. Legal activities include arranging for site acquisition, the construction contract, mortgage closing, and subsidy contracts.

The fundamental assumption behind simultaneous track processing is that once the internal decision is made relative to the acceptability and feasibility of the project, all other interagency approvals are obtained as a procedural matter rather than through the exercise of independent external judgments. Differences between HUD and UDC about either the advisability or feasibility of proposed UDC projects usually have been satisfactorily resolved. It is through this process that enormous time savings have been realized. It should be noted, however, that most of the ability to undertake simultaneous track processing is inherent first in UDC's powers and second in the judicious use of this authority.

The private developer who is responsible for constructing, owning, and operating UDC projects is brought into the picture at the earliest possible date to review preliminary designs and suggest construction economies consistent with good design. No processing requirements are made of the developer. His only function is to arrive at a satisfactory agreement on an upset construction price and to undertake construction at the earliest possible date.

From the inception of UDC's program, one cardinal rule was established: once a project was approved, all staff energies were aimed at meeting the established construction start date. In most instances, target dates turned out to be much too tight, but the effort never ceased. In many instances UDC did not own the land, lacked a construction contract, and had no working drawings but simply foundation drawings; nevertheless, the construction start date was met. Of the initial 1970 wave of construction starts, some projects were nearly ready for occupancy before title to the land was acquired and the mortgage closed. This attention to the preciousness of time was well accepted by developers and enabled the corporation to obtain more favorable bids from them in 1971 and 1972 construction contract negotiations.

In summation, after five years of effort, UDC mastered the technique of efficient prosecution of a large-scale, new construction program—a major breakthrough in the public development field that involved negotiations with agencies at the municipal, state, and federal level. To accomplish this breakthrough required a superbureaucracy to overcome normal bureaucratic problems that frequently defeat private entrepreneurs and the assembly and successful coordination of many technical and professional skills.

The UDC and Larger Public Objectives

Although this description of the principles that underlie the operation of the UDC may be accepted as accurate, questions may still be raised about the agency's goals and responsiveness. Has the creation of an efficient public development production machine justified the five years of intensive efforts expended to achieve this result? To those familiar with the low level of normal bureaucratic performance, the answer is a flat yes—UDC has demonstrated something that many persons in the public sector considered impossible.

To the thoughtful observer, efficiency may not be sufficient justification for the resources allocated to UDC. The very mastery of the production process raises serious challenges: production for whom, for what location, and under what circumstances?

The state development agency, with its skills and resources, has both an opportunity and the responsibility to undertake those analyses necessary to answer, with much better perception than so far, questions about the nature, scope, and seriousness of the housing and development problems throughout the state. In such researches, the type and range of programs most likely to be effective should be explored and tested even while normal agency responsibilities are pursued.

UDC has supported efforts in this direction. Long-range program planning is a major function within its structure and some useful contributions have been made to UDC's activities from this division. The corporation's new-town activities are closely related to its long-range planning function. The corporation also takes seriously the function of economic and housing market analysis. Its executives clearly recognize the distinction between housing "need" and "demand" and the constraints of the latter in dealing with the former, even though the distinction is occasionally blurred in practice. Nevertheless, this distinction still constitutes a major intellectual breakthrough for an agency in which nearly half of the professional personnel are architects and planners.

Finally, it may be posited that there are many useful activities for a state agency such as UDC that have not yet been approached. One is the area of rehabilitation and neighborhood preservation. Although UDC has an interest in this area, it has not acted because it lacks the resources to deal effectively with this complex problem. Even if the necessary resources were provided, this subject would require total cooperation and coordination of all levels of government in many more areas of public activity than housing production. It remains a challenge for the future as to whether an efficient production entity such as UDC may make a useful contribution.

The Politics of Public Development

Some observers contend that state agencies are not a useful route in dealing with essentially local problems. The history of state-local relationships suggests that such fears are not totally unwarranted. On the other hand, a large part of UDC's success is attributable to a careful cultivation of local relationships, which are reflected by its administrative structure of regional offices and subsidiaries across the state. Consequently, it may be assumed that the problem consists of a combination of personalities, politics, and the administrative approach rather than something indigenous to state-local relationships. It suffices to note that UDC has totally avoided any partisan political overtones in working with local housing and planning officials of communities with which it has relationships.

No matter how many powers the state legislature may grant to a state development agency in attempts to improve performance, the legislature can withdraw them tomorrow should political realities be ignored. There has been ready acceptance of the exercise of UDC's power in virtually every community where the agency was invited to help solve some development problem. When it was pointed out that a community's proposals could not be developed without a change in its zoning ordinance, the city or village fathers usually suggested that UDC use its zoning override because they were reluctant to change their zoning ordinance. In short, UDC's override powers are most often used with the knowledge and consent of the local community.

UDC proposed in 1972 to develop a small amount of low- and moderate-income housing in the outer suburbs of Westchester County. It was an effort to test a social theory that some modest-cost housing should be provided even in affluent but not well-settled areas to meet the housing needs of lower-income service workers and thus reduce the necessity for extensive cross-commuting. The test of this social theory turned out to be premature. The reaction was so violent that UDC withdrew the proposals, and in 1973 the legislature amended the UDC statute to require that proposed UDC projects in towns and villages be undertaken only after a thirty-day grace period during which the community may exercise a veto of the proposal. This requirement will not essentially affect UDC operations since it has been normal practice in most cases to start with such assent. It is a useful reminder that government cannot pursue goals that its constituents are not ready to accept.

Attica and Prison Reform

GERALD BENJAMIN
STEPHEN P. RAPPAPORT

In the early morning of September 9, 1971, cell block A of New York State's Attica Correctional Facility exploded in an uprising that quickly spread throughout the prison. Within two hours, forty-two correction officers and civilians had been taken hostage by the inmates. After leaving matters in the hands of local administrators for five hours, Russell G. Oswald, commissioner of the Department of Correctional Services, arrived from Albany and assumed the task of handling the uprising. After five frantic days, on September 13, negotiations between Oswald and the inmates broke down. Acting under gubernatorial orders, the state police seized control of the prison by force. Forty-three inmates and hostages died in the process.

As a consequence of the tragedies at Attica and other correctional institutions across the country, prison reform became a major public issue. The rebellions focused attention not only on prison conditions, but also on the American correctional system's lack of success in rehabilitating prisoners. One reason for this failure was that prison life and routine had changed little since the early nineteenth century. At that time, confinement, isolation from other individiuals, and unremitting hard work were seen as the keys to reform. According to the first report of the Select Committee on Correctional Institutions and Programs (the Jones committee), appointed by Governor Rockefeller and the legislative leaders to review the state's prison system and suggest reforms in the wake of Attica, the nineteenth century system:

featured the comprehensive subordination of the prisoner in every aspect of his life, the unyielding silence rule at work, while eating in the solitary cells. All movements were in solid columns with the lock-step. Work was characterized by unremitting prisoner industry. . . . The objectives then were salvation of the prisoner through work, subordination, meditation, and Bible reading, and prevention of crime among the general public through the unending drama of a civilized nineteenth century earthly hell reeking of dread and horror.

This so-called Auburn system, originated in New York in 1826, became a model for the world. Among its legacies were the large, grim, maximum security prisons located in remote areas that constituted much of New York's correctional system. To be sure, there were significant reforms in the past century and a half. Many of them were part of the rehabilitative approach that took hold in the early twentieth century and of the more recent emphasis on probation and parole. Yet prisons were still characterized by a social system that demanded absolute obedience and subordination. Most inmates were still confined to their cells for fourteen to sixteen hours daily. In 1971, Attica inmates spent only five hours a day out of their cells, and during this time they were working or attending school.

The consequence of this system was an atmosphere of despair among inmates, many of whom felt caught in an unending cycle of crime and punishment. They believed that penal institutions provided little help in breaking out of this cycle. Much of their resentment against the entire criminal justice system—particularly its plea bargaining and its unjust, largely arbitrary sentencing procedures—was focused on the institutions that held them. Some argued that the prison system simply trained a man for survival in prison; it did not prepare him for life in the larger society.

As the inmate population in New York became increasingly black and Puerto Rican over the past two decades, the already tense relationship between prisoners and correction officers became complicated by racial differences. Racism, compounded by differences in generations and cultures, at times led to a breakdown of communication between prisoners and staff and some apparent discrimination in prison jobs and treatment. Matters were further complicated by the emergence of more militant black inmates, who believed themselves to be political prisoners and were less likely to abide by strict and seemingly senseless rules. Prisons worked only because of the tacit cooperation of the prisoners; prison officials were ill prepared to handle prisoners who refused this cooperation.

Prisons today do have some pilot programs geared to extensive rehabilitation. Attica's Division of Vocational Rehabilitation (DVR) was such an effort. Originally established for rehabilitation of physically disabled inmates, this special school was operated on three different levels and stressed long-term vocational rehabilitation. Its activities included extensive psychological and group counseling, a monthly newspaper, a token economy system that immediately rewarded inmates for good work, and, perhaps most important, continuing services for prisoners after parole or release. Because the per capita cost of the program was three times that of the cost to keep other inmates, however, the program was restricted to only 4 percent of the inmate population. Thus, for most individuals, prison life was dehumanizing, and a meaningful program of rehabilitation was nonexistent. As Dr. E. Preston Sharp, general secretary of the American Correctional Association, noted, "For years our institutions have been built away from populous areas, swept under a rug of a starvation budget, and, especially in the Northeast, given a heavy emphasis on custody."[1]

It was ironic that the Attica uprising occurred in a state penal system that was already moving toward reform. In an effort to change the state prison system's emphasis from custodial to rehabilitative care, a special commission on criminal offenders appointed by Governor Rockefeller in 1966 recommended reorganization. On January 1, 1971, the Department of Correction and the Division of Parole were consolidated into the Department of Correctional Services. The purpose of this consolidation was to achieve continuity from arrest to release. It was hoped that many persons convicted of crimes would be admitted to a work release program after a short time in an institution. Should they prove unsatisfactory in these work release programs, they would then be returned to a prison. The reorganization also removed the Division of Probation from the Department of Correction and placed it in the Executive Department. It was planned that the state's training program for probation officers would be made more extensive to ensure that all probationary officers had social work training. The plan also envisioned that the state would reimburse cities and counties for 50 percent of the cost of probationary services, which would increase salaries in some rural counties.

Upon taking office as the state's new commissioner of correctional services in January 1971, Oswald vowed to institute additional reform programs that would restructure the state correctional system. His first reforms included granting the news media greater access to state pris-

[1] Fred Cohen and Gerald Wagner, interview, *Criminal Law Bulletin* 7 (December 1971), 836.

ons, revising censorship rules to liberalize mail and visiting privileges for inmates, directing that more nutritional food be purchased even if a deficit resulted, providing an alternative to pork for Muslims, and generally relaxing the rules of tight discipline.

Oswald's actions, however, did not go unnoticed or unopposed. Correction officers and many administrators were concerned about the liberalization of rules and the relaxation of discipline. In raising these objections, Oswald's critics were revealing the basic tension in prison administration, the tension between rehabilitation and correction. An administrator who emphasizes reform is automatically open to charges of "coddling criminals" and endangering the lives of prison personnel by relaxing discipline.

Soon after his appointment, Oswald also found that, like other state services and programs, the institution of massive rehabilitative programs for the prisons was governed by the iron grip of economics. The state was going through the worst fiscal crisis in its history. In Oswald's words, the prison system was simply "fiscally starved." Without money to pay additional officers, Oswald argued, prisoners could not be released from their cells for long periods, and rehabilitative programs like DVR could not be developed. Although state appropriations for correctional services increased by $19 million between 1967 and 1971, most of the increase was spent on administrative overhead. In fact, the percent of the state budget appropriated for correctional services decreased from 4.8 to 3.0 percent. Nonetheless, in 1971, more than $8 million was spent on the Attica correctional facility.

Thus, while the state was making efforts to reform the prison system, Attica exploded. Apart from the state investigation into the criminal aspect of the rebellion at Attica, Governor Rockefeller and state legislative leaders asked Chief Judge Stanley H. Fuld of the Court of Appeals and Presiding Justices Harold A. Stevens, Samuel Rabin, J. Clarence Herlihy, and Harry D. Goldman to appoint a citizen's committee to investigate all aspects of the uprising. On September 30, 1971, nine citizens were selected for the New York State Special Commission on Attica (the McKay commission). In addition to this group, which was to focus specifically upon Attica, state leaders appointed the Select Committee on Correctional Institutions and Programs under the chairmanship of Hugh R. Jones to conduct a "searching examination" into correctional problems, identify "short- and long-term practices," and make "recommendations for improvements in the total correction process."

As a result of these events and the studies of them, a number of questions arise: Why did Attica explode? What have other correctional institutions done in similar situations? What was New York's response? What gubernatorial action was taken? What has New York State done since Attica? The state's response to this massive prison revolt can be understood by integrating the sequence of events at Attica with the various commissions' findings and recommendations.

The Negotiations

For four days after the takeover of Attica, the state, through Commissioner Oswald, pursued intense negotiations with the inmates. Discussions centered on the release of the hostages pending the acceptance of the prisoners' list of thirty demands. As the McKay commission noted, such negotiations were a clear break with the standard procedure of nonnegotiation enunciated by governors and state correction commissioners. According to a poll taken by the *New York Times*, correction commissioners throughout the country generally agreed that negotiations with prisoners during a rebellion should not be undertaken. Governor Warren E. Hearnes of Missouri maintained that "state officials must not negotiate with convicts who seize control or take hostages to enforce demands." Ronald Reagan, governor of California, asserted: "In California, we will not compromise with rioting prisoners." These general views conformed with the expectations of local correctional officials who were on the scene at Attica. Appearing before the House Select Committee on Crime on November 28, 1971, Vincent R. Mancusi, superintendent of the Attica correctional facility, testified that he would not have tried to negotiate the release of the hostages but would have attempted to retake the prison by force. Later Rockefeller testified before the McKay commission that he too expected Oswald to follow the usual pattern of reestablishing order without negotiation, but, when Oswald chose "the unorthodox course," the governor decided not to overrule his commissioner, despite his personal conviction. This decision, Rockefeller said, was in accord with his own long-standing administrative policy of delegating authority to key aides and then backing them fully.

During the first two days of negotiations, little progress was made. Then, at the request of the prisoners, a citizens' observers committee was formed to serve as an ad hoc mediating body.[2] The prisoners' list

---

[2] Among the members of the observers' committee were Representative Herman Badillo, Senator John Dunne, Assemblyman Arthur O. Eve, Clarence Jones, William Kunstler, Bobby Seale, and Tom Wicker.

of thirty demands covering a complete updating of the prison system at Attica was drawn up under the committee's direction. Throughout this early period, the possibility existed that the governor might go to Attica to negotiate personally. Rockefeller declined, stating: "I firmly believe that a duly elected official, sworn to defend the constitution and the laws of the state and the nation, would be betraying his trust to the people he serves if he were to sanction or condone such criminal acts by negotiating under such circumstances." Commenting on this rationale, the commission said that it could "readily understand why the governor was unwilling to go to Attica prior to Oswald's request Sunday evening. The governor's presence could have undermined Oswald's authority in dealing with the observers and inmates."

After lengthy discussion, Oswald agreed to implement twenty-eight of the thirty demands pending the release of the hostages and the restoration of order in the prison. The concessions the state was unwilling to make concerned complete amnesty from criminal prosecution for the prisoners with passage to a "nonimperialist" country and the removal of Superintendent Vincent R. Mancusi. The prisoners' insistence on complete amnesty came one day after the death of prison guard William Quinn, who was injured by the prisoners during the takeover and died two days later at a Rochester hospital. Unconditional amnesty, therefore, was seen by the McKay commission as a way in which the prisoners could avoid prosecution for the death of Quinn as well as the deaths of three prisoners placed on house arrest by inmate leaders and found murdered when the prison was retaken.

In the view of the commission, negotiations broke off when the prisoners rejected the state's concessions which did not include unconditional amnesty. Governor Rockefeller asked Oswald to request observers to leave and inform the inmates that amnesty was not negotiable. Rockefeller explained: "It seemed to me that we had now passed the last possible vestige of hope that this uprising was going to be settled on the basis of a desire for prison reform." Nonetheless, after a final request that the governor go to Attica, Rockefeller directed that there be no immediate assault and that the inmates be allowed another day to accept the points. He then issued a statement which reiterated that amnesty was not negotiable, was outside his constitutional authority, and would undermine "the essence of our free society." The McKay commission later concluded: "Even if the Governor had the power, the Commission agrees that total amnesty should not have been granted in the circumstances of Attica. . . . In these circumstances, the Commission believes that state officials would have undermined public confidence in the rule of law had they excused serious crimes under the threat that there would be additional acts of violence if amnesty were not granted."

In later hearings, Rockefeller emphasized another obstacle that prevented him from going to Attica. He argued that the inmates would demand that he go into the yard, and added that they might next demand the president. Oswald also told the commission of his fears that the governor might be taken hostage if he went inside the prison. The McKay commission concurred, stating: "It is probable that the presence of the Governor at Attica would have precipitated a demand by inmates that he enter the yard. The pressure would have been intense, as the Governor's refusal to comply with the request could have been characterized by the inmates as indication of bad faith, precluding a peaceful settlement and jeopardizing the lives of the hostages."

However, the most far-reaching reason for Rockefeller's refusal to negotiate was the widespread tradition of nonnegotiation that is intended to discourage the taking of hostages by prison inmates throughout the country. Indeed, throughout the entire ordeal Rockefeller appeared deeply concerned about the future implications of an unprecedented attempt of a governor to negotiate personally with rebelling prisoners who were holding hostages. Rockefeller said that it was not easy for him to face a hard decision when human lives were involved. He maintained: "I was trying to do the best I could to save the hostages, save the prisoners, restore order, and preserve our system without undertaking actions which could set a precedent which would go across this country like wildfire."

Rockefeller's failure to go to Attica has been the focus of much criticism. Tom Wicker and others claimed that, if the governor had been present, he might have felt differently about the situation and allowed more time for the negotiations. It has also been argued that Rockefeller's presence would at least have demonstrated concern for the lives at stake. Although Oswald believed that going to Attica would have been good for the governor's image, he did not believe that it would be productive. "I was convinced that amnesty was the key issue," Oswald said, but added that neither the governor nor the prisoners were likely to change their positions.

As for Rockefeller's failure to go to Attica, the McKay commission concluded: "No one can be sure whether the Governor's presence would have succeeded in producing a settlement that eluded Oswald and the observers. Present or not, the Governor was unwilling to grant amnesty, the critical inmate demand." Interestingly, the commission added that it would not "have ruled out some concessions on amnesty," but concluded further that "full amnesty was the paramount issue at all times and there was no evidence before the Governor that the inmates were prepared to accept less"; that "none of the remarks in the yard which were recorded on tape gave any indication of inmate willingness to compromise amnesty"; that "Oswald left the meeting believing that the inmates were still demanding full amnesty"; and that Tom Wicker, "who was present in the yard on Sunday, testified that the inmates were insistent on complete amnesty throughout" the ordeal. Nonetheless, in emphasizing the need for prison reform, the commission believed that the governor "should not have committed the state's armed forces against the rebels without first appearing on the scene" in light of the fact that the "prison system was in need of major reform," which was "a major contributing factor to the uprising."

After Rockefeller declined to go to the prison, he instructed Oswald to attempt to renegotiate as a final effort. At the second meeting between Oswald and the prisoners, eight hostages were lined up, blindfolded, and tied. An executioner held a knife at each one's throat. Oswald, with the govenor's concurrence, then ordered the assault. Four days had passed since the prison erupted.

The commission reported Oswald's description of nineteen separate factors that had influenced his decision to order the assault: "Among them were the brutality of the take-over; Dr. Hanson's observations of increased tension on Saturday evening; the threat to take Oswald hostage; the fear expressed by some observers for their own safety following Oswald's Saturday ultimatum; . . . the release from the yard on Sunday night of an inmate with a stab wound"; and the criminal records of the inmates. Perhaps one of the most important factors in Oswald's decision was that the inmates were making a large number of weapons and constructing defenses. After the assault, the police recovered over 1,400 weapons, including Molotov cocktails, spears, teargas guns, razors, knives, and metal bludgeons. In their recommendations for the conduct of future negotiations, therefore, the McKay commission warned against allowing such a weapons buildup.

The commission was also highly critical of the manner in which the negotiations were conducted. In its view, Oswald was remiss in going forward with negotiations in the presence of 1,200 inmates and with the press and observers present. The commission argued:

There was no effective mechanism to conduct the negotiations. . . . The observers' committee was unwieldy in number—over 30 members—and racked with ideological differences between those who identified completely with the inmates and those who were proponents of the position of the state. . . . Prisons have traditionally been off limits to the press. The admission of newsmen and television cameras to D yard not only provided inmates with an unparalleled opportunity to tell the public about prison conditions, but gave them a sense of importance, dignity, and power . . . [which] made it almost impossible to persuade them to give up the limelight and return to anonymity.

The commission recommended that in the future negotiations not be conducted before hundreds of inmates, that they not be carried on in the presence of the press, that they be conducted without the use of outsiders (or only when the function and authority of a mediating group was clearly defined and agreed upon by all parties), and that a regular procedure for dispelling rumors be established. With specific regard to retaking the prison, the commission argued that "before terminating negotiations, and commencing an assault, the inmates must be made to understand that the alternative to a settlement is an armed assault with guns," although the commission recognized "the possible tactical importance of surprise." The report added that "even at the outset, the authorities may be unwilling to send unarmed men to confront and subdue rebelling inmates" and that "in these circumstances . . . the possibility of a negotiated settlement must be fully explored before using lethal force." This strategy mirrors the sequence of events at Attica.

The Assault

Plans for dealing with fires and riots, however modest, were developed by Oswald when he took office in April 1971. In an interview with Walter Cronkite, Oswald said, "The plan . . . was that in any emergency of this kind, the State Police would lead the way because it is always assumed that correction officers, being embroiled in a situation such as this, might be vindictive in going in and the State Police, who are a tremendously well-disciplined group, would go in coolly." He added that "correction officers would follow behind for mop-up operations and the National Guard and local officials would be on the outside." The McKay commission echoed this view and stated specifically that the governor's order "to exclude correction officers from the assault force was sound, not only because of the doubts about their ability to control their personal feelings, but also because they are not trained in military maneuvers or in the use of weapons." The commission noted, however, that this order somehow never reached the state police or correctional supervisors.

Police action to retake the prison was placed under the direction of the state police troop commander. It was ordered that the assault forces not engage in hand-to-hand combat with the inmates and shoot when resistance was encountered so that inmates would be unable to take the troopers' weapons. It seemed evident that such an order would result in numerous casualities; the tactical plan employed to retake the prison added to what seemed to be an inevitable occurrence.

Four passageways in the shape of a *T* led to a middle courtyard called Times Square, where the prisoners held the hostages. On top of these passageways, the prisoners had erected barricades. Tear gas was released over Times Square by helicopters in a fog, while the state police stormed the passageways and converged upon the prisoners. Shooting continued for six minutes. Not only were sharpshooters firing at the executioners, but the police were shooting at prisoners who were impeding their passage or standing in front of the hostages.

From the description of the circumstances surrounding the assault on the prison, it appears that the tactical plan produced much crossfire that ultimately caused death and injury. With regard to the hostages, the commission found that "no official, including the police commanders, believed that the hostages could be saved if the inmates were intent upon killing them." Indeed, Governor Rockefeller, who was in touch by telephone with officials at Attica during the assault, expressed disbelief that so many persons emerged unharmed.

One clear lesson of Attica is that state police were not adequately trained or equipped for dealing with a prison rebellion. Normal techniques for dispersing large crowds are not suitable for such circumstances, and the police did not have the necessary nonlethal weapons to quell the rioters. Some officers fired prematurely and indiscriminately, and shotguns were used. However, the McKay commission did note that "had the majority of the assault force not acted with restraint, the toll of dead and wounded would undoubtedly have been greater." Though the commission recommended further police training, the development of new prison riot procedures, and the development of adequate nonlethal weapons, there is little evidence that their recommendations have been carried out.

The McKay commission also levelled harsh criticism against the state for what it considered to be inadequate preparation for the large number of casualties that were anticipated. The report noted that the state failed to make adequate arrangements for sufficient numbers of doctors, nurses, and ambulances, and it did not have an efficient procedure for the removal of casualties from the prison to nearby hospitals.

The commission did conclude, however, that no individual died because of a delay in receiving medical treatment.

After Attica

Events at Attica in September 1971 made prison reform a major issue in the 1972 session of the New York State Legislature. In proposing his budget for 1973, Rockefeller exempted the Department of Correctional Services from expenditure restrictions placed on all other state agencies and, in anticipation of the report of the Select Committee on Correctional Institutions and Programs (the Jones committee), called for significant reforms in the prison system. Later, in April, Rockefeller proposed an additional $12 million for the Department of Correctional Services, $1.3 million to be spent for a "maximum program, maximum security" facility requested by the department and the rest for additional personnel and the upgrading of prison services.

The Jones committee's first preliminary report was released on January 24, 1973. In it the committee recommended the development of new, smaller community-based facilities that would encompass a wide range of security in or near urban areas. (Almost all of New York's institutions are maximum security.) The report also stressed the need to provide adequate training for prison personnel, to improve professional and medical services for prisoners, to reorganize the Commission of Correction and provide an inspector general service, to recruit minority personnel, and to improve vocational training and educational services in prisons. Finally, it was suggested that certain steps could be taken to improve day-to-day living conditions for inmates, including improving food services, reducing cell time, easing mail censorship and visiting privileges, establishing a prisoner council to facilitate communications between prisoners and prison authorities, and developing work release and furlough programs.

A second report, released two months later on March 15, 1973, reduced the number of firm recommendations to thirty and established a procedure by which the committee would monitor the progress of the Department of Correctional Services toward the changes suggested. In this document, stress was again laid upon the development of institutions with varying degrees of security, the recognition of civil rights of prisoners, recruitment of minority staff members, provision of adequate training for the staff, and the upgrading of the atmosphere and quality of prison life. Suggested changes, however, were generally less extensive than those sought by the American Civil Liberties Union in a statement in February. Early in April, Rockefeller endorsed the Jones committee report and reaffirmed his commitment to reform.

As a result of this recognition of the need for change, over 150 prison-reform bills were introduced in the legislature during the 1972 session, and eight were passed. The most important of these included the governor's $12 million package of new funds (with the $1.3 million for a maximum security, maximum service institution deleted because of intense opposition), a bill authorizing short furloughs for carefully screened inmates within a year of their release date, a measure equalizing parole eligibility for men convicted before and after penal law reform in 1967, an increase in clothing allowances, an authorization for the Dormitory Authority to help finance new prison facilities, and the first passage of a constitutional amendment to remove the commissioner of Correctional Services as head of the Commission of Correction that was charged with overseeing the operations of the department.

Changes were also made by administrative action. A survey by the *New York Times* at Attica a year after the rebellion indicated that most of the grievances had been redressed by the Department of Correctional Services. Visiting restrictions and censorship of mail and reading matter had been eased, new clothing provided, commissary and food services improved, and a law library opened. Racial tensions had eased considerably. The number of inmates had been reduced from 2,200 to 1,158. Nineteen black and two Spanish-speaking correction officers had been hired.

Some grievances, however, remained. Inmates were still not told the reasons for denial of parole by the parole board, pay for work was still quite low, and the vocational program remained inadequate. In addition, some reforms faced resistance inside the system, both from prisoners and from correctional officers. At Attica, the inmate liaison committee had a constantly changing membership, and because it could not entertain complaints about individual officers, it lost the respect of many of the prisoners. At Greenhaven in 1973, refusal of inmates to vote in elections because of reservations about the powers of the proposed liaison committee prevented its formation. In another area, the hiring of minority personnel, lawsuits which challenged racial criteria in job descriptions slowed the recruiting process.

Often administrators, correctional officers, and their political supporters looked askance at proposed changes. Guards expressed mixed feelings to a *New York Times* reporter on the "inmates trying to run the prison," and Oswald received a great deal of criticism from state legislators when he authorized a packet of candy for prisoners attending new evening educational programs. With regard to liaison committees, the superintendent at Greenhaven said: "I honestly don't know what they want. They can't seem to get organized. And you have to remember that we got along for years without a liaison committee."

With the help of federal funds, major changes have been made in officers' training. A thirteen-week course is now offered to all new correction officers, and all other officers completed a fifty-two-hour in-service course stressing human and ethnic relations by March 31, 1973. A new thirty-two-hour in-service course, also federally funded, was begun in April of that year. The problem remains, however, of how to encourage the use of this training on the job. Federal money also helped in the recruitment of minority officers. By September 1973 the number of black officers in the system had increased from 250 to 481, and the number of Hispanic officers from 23 to 133. These men, however, remained concentrated in the less remote, downstate facilities. Despite department efforts, the reluctance of minority officers to serve in rural, largely white upstate communities remained a problem.

The Department of Correctional Services has also attempted to diversify its facilities and humanize the prison environment. In addition to changes already mentioned, it has reduced lockup time, engaged a Muslim minister, recognized religious dietary practices in food preparation, increased academic opportunities, expanded temporary release for furlough and compassionate leave to encompass 7,000 inmates over the last two years, began to diversify and modernize its facilities, and created residential and community correction facilities. Under Peter Preiser, commissioner since April 1973, the department has improved the prison health care delivery system, has attempted to rebuild the vocational training system, and has instituted positive incentives within the prison environment. Preiser has also stressed the citizen volunteer program; there are now about 7,000 volunteers cooperating in departmental efforts.

Despite these changes, criticism continues. The final auditing report of the Jones committee, released in May 1973, noted that "the Department's efforts since January, 1972 . . . have achieved mixed results. . . . Change which has a fundamental impact on the day-to-day existence of the inmate population remains elusive." In April 1973 the Department of Correctional Services offered a $276.8 million master plan designed to diversify facilities. One prime objective of the plan was to reduce the number of prisoners held in maximum security facilities from 80 percent, the current figure, to 20 percent and to establish smaller community-based facilities. Yet, in that year, the legislature reduced authorizations for new minimum security, community-based facilities by $15 million, effectively killing four of six proposed centers. In addition, the legislature in the 1973 session killed a major package of prison reform measures proposed by a bipartisan group of legislators. As Attica passed into history, political commitment to prison reform began to wane. Outside of the immediate context of violence, prison officials remain disadvantaged participants in the scramble for limited state funds; their programs have little direct impact in legislative districts or upon the gubernatorial electorate.

Between 1970 and 1973, state general-fund expenditures for prisons rose from $90 million to $128 million, an increase of about 42 percent. The governor's budget for 1974 reflects a further increase of about $20 million. In addition, available federal funds increased from $125,000 in 1970 to over $6 million in 1973. Much of this money has been spent on personnel. There are 2,329 more people working in the state prison system in 1974 than there were three years ago. Federal funds have also been used for innovative training, recruitment, and prisoner service programs. Though New York has demonstrated some commitment to change, the question of whether the state will carry on programs begun with federal seed money in a more restrictive fiscal environment remains an open one.

The mandatory minimum sentences required by New York's new drug laws, new second felony legislation, increased return of parole violators, and increased average length of sentences point to an expanding inmate population as the decade proceeds. As inflation and increased population drive costs up and as the public again grows indifferent to prison reform, will the Department of Correctional Services be able to maintain more expensive experimental programs in the face of internal pressures for economy and a renewed "hard line" against inmates? The lesson of Attica is that it must.

Public Transportation

JOSEPH F. ZIMMERMAN

The transportation system is undoubtedly the major force among the dynamic forces that influence the rate and pattern of the development of urban areas. A natural harbor facilitated the settlement and rapid development of New York City, and the construction of the Erie Canal—now part of the New York State Barge Canal System—was a major force in promoting the settlement and development of the New York City-Albany-Buffalo corridor. The canal was the principal passenger and freight route between the Northeast and the Midwest from 1825 until competition from railroads in the midnineteenth century began to reduce its commercial importance and change the nature of urban development in the state.

The invention of the motor vehicle and its widespread use increased the mobility of citizens and lessened dependence upon railroads for the transportation of people, raw materials, and manufactured products. The automobile and truck had an even greater impact than the railroad on the pattern of urban development by making possible the rapid and relatively uncontrolled growth of suburban areas since 1945. This development often resulted in an injudicious use of land and the creation of serious public transportation problems, especially in central cities of metropolitan areas.

Although a few perceptive observers had earlier called attention to

The assistance of Albert R. Pacer in assembling information for this paper is gratefully acknowledged. Executive Deputy Commissioner John K. Mladinov of the New York State Department of Transportation and Ronald C. Kane, special services manager of the Metropolitan Transportation Authority, read the manuscript and offered valuable comments for its improvement.

the growing imbalance between highways and public transportation in New York State, important public officials did not become concerned until the early 1960s. In New York, as in other states, the imbalance was partly due to heavy federal and state funding of highway construction. The federal government, in particular, had been loathe to appropriate funds for public transportation but has willingly appropriated billions of dollars for the construction of new highawys. It has spent over $200 billion on highways since 1956 when the federal Highway Trust Fund was established; less than $4 billion has been spent on public transportation during the same period. Even in 1972 nearly 63 percent of the federal transportation budget was devoted to highways compared to 3.4 percent for public transportation and intercity rail. Urban areas have obviously been shortchanged by federal highway policies since these areas provide 51 percent of the total federal motor fuel tax revenue but have only 10 percent of the federal-aid highway mileage.

While highway building had accelerated since World War II, subway, commuter rail, and local bus systems were allowed to deteriorate. Because the New York City subway system suffered from a lack of proper financing for decades, maintenance was neglected, and hundreds of subway cars were forty or more years old. The bankruptcy of the New York, New Haven, and Hartford railroads and the deterioration of the Long Island Rail Road (which carries approximately 25 percent of all rail commuters in the United States) contributed to the public transportation problem. Half of the buses in transit service in the state were more than ten years old, many terminals and garages were dilapidated, and private bus operators experienced serious financial problems. Increases in operating expenses caused a rise in fares, which generally resulted in fewer riders and sometimes forced bus companies out of business.

Initial State Action

Recognizing the complexity of transporation operations when he came into office in 1959, Governor Rockefeller was reluctant to involve the state in day to day transit problems. Rather he hoped that tax relief for private companies would be sufficient. Consequently, at his suggestion, in 1959 the legislature established the New York State Railroad Tax Relief Program, which granted tax benefits to railroads operating in the state, provided they met specified standards of service. A later provision, enacted in 1961, exempted real property of privately owned commuter railroads from taxation under the same conditions. Moreover, they were permitted to lease new commuter cars purchased by the Port Authority. Thus some millions of dollars were provided to aid the railroads and especially commuter lines serving the state's major urban area.

On August 20, 1961, the governors of Connecticut, New Jersey, and New York organized the Tri-State Transportation Committee and charged it with responsibility for conducting a comprehensive study and developing plans to meet the transportation needs of a twenty-two county area—centering on New York City—the population of which was projected to increase by 29 percent by 1985. Dr. William J. Ronan, secretary to Governor Rockefeller, served as chairman of the committee. In 1966, Connecticut, New Jersey, and New York enacted legislation converting the committee into the Tri-State Transportation Commission, the first interstate metropolitan planning commission in the United States. After considerable opposition from New Jersey, the commission was converted into the Tri-State Regional Planning Commission.

Tax relief, however, proved insufficient to keep the commuter lines operating. In 1962 the bankruptcy of the Hudson and Manhattan Railroad led New York and New Jersey to authorize the Port Authority to construct the World Trade Center in Manhattan, provided that the Authority purchased the bankrupt railroad and modernized it. Immediately following acquisition of the railroad on September 1, 1962, the Authority launched a $100 million capital improvement program. To operate the railroad, the Port Authority established a subsidiary corporation, the Port Authority Trans-Hudson (PATH); members of the Authority serve *ex officio* as the PATH's board. By 1973, PATH carried 145,000 passengers daily on the first completely air-conditioned fleet of rail commuter cars (298) in the world.

The next crisis developed in 1964 when the Pennsylvania Railroad, in financial difficulties, proposed to abandon the Long Island Rail Road. The state's response was to create in 1965 the Metropolitan Commuter Transportation Authority (MCTA). This agency was charged with responsibility for improving commuter transportation services in the Metropolitan Commuter Transportation District—the city of New York and the counties of Dutchess, Nassau, Orange, Putnam, Rockland, Suffolk, and Westchester. In June 1965 the legislature authorized the MCTA to purchase all the stock of the ailing Long Island Rail Road from the Pennsylvania Railroad for $65 million. The state assumed ownership on January 20, 1966. Step by step the force of circumstances was pushing Rockefeller into direct operation of public transportation facilities.

Conditions on the commuter lines of the New Haven Railroad were also deteriorating further in the mid-1960s. New York State and Connecticut worked to preserve the commuter service on the New Haven Railroad when the bankrupt railroad in 1965 sought to abandon four stations in Westchester County and reduce nonrush-hour service at ten other stations. In the spring of 1965, Governor Rockefeller and Governor John N. Dempsey of Connecticut proposed a federally assisted public transportation project to find a solution for the financial problems of the New Haven, a facility that was used by 24,000 persons daily.

On June 28, 1965, the Housing and Home Finance Agency (later the U.S. Department of Housing and Urban Development) approved the proposal. Trustees of the railroad entered into a contract, effective July 1, 1965, to continue existing service between several Connecticut cities and New York City. Federal support for the project ended on December 31, 1966, and it was supported by the two states during 1967 and 1968. The New Haven Railroad was merged with the bankrupt Penn Central on December 31, 1968.

The 1967 Transportation Revolution

Hardening of ground and air arteries in New York had proceeded to the point that by 1967 drastic action was needed to prevent the economic decline of the state and to improve the mobility of citizens dependent upon public transportation. The deepening public transportation problem and the growing recognition of its complexity led Governor Rockefeller to propose and the legislature to pass two laws containing several innovative provisions to cope with the problem. The most dramatic law was one authorizing a $2.5-billion Transportation Capital Facilities Bond Issue subject to a referendum.

Voter ratification of the bond issue on November 7, 1967, was a landmark step in launching a state program to develop a balanced statewide transportation system with an efficient, modern, and economical public transportation system as one of its key elements.

The 1967 law created new organizational entities to facilitate solutions to the manifold transportation problems. The State Department of Transportation (DOT) was established and assumed functions that had been scattered among several state agencies.

Prior to 1967, the attack upon transportation problems in the state tended to be piecemeal. Corrective action was not initiated on the basis of a comprehensive plan providing for the coordination of various modes of transportation. The 1967 law directed DOT to prepare a long-range, comprehensive, statewide plan for balanced transportation and submit it to the governor.

Rockefeller officially approved the Statewide Master Plan for Transportation on May 7, 1973, "as a guide to the public and publicly assisted development of transportation facilities and services in the State."

The most serious public transportation problems in the state in 1967 were in the New York City metropolitan area. Compounding the problems in the New York State portion of this area was the lack of a single governmental agency with adequate authority to develop and implement a coordinated public transportation program. In 1967 there were three major public transportation authorities operating somewhat autonomously—the Metropolitan Commuter Transportation Authority (MCTA), the New York City Transit Authority (TA), and the Triborough Bridge and Tunnel Authority (TBTA). The TA controlled a major bus subsidiary corporation, the Manhattan and Bronx Surface Transit Operating Authority (MBSTOA).

Since the United States Constitution forbids the impairment of contracts by states and since the older authorities had bonds outstanding, the legislature was unable to abolish the existing authorities and replace them with a single agency. The governor and legislature, however, were able to achieve their objective of providing unified direction to public transportation in the area by the use of an innovative device—the interlocking directorate—borrowed from private industry.

MCTA was converted into the Metropolitan Transportation Authority (MTA) and made responsible for the development and implementation of a unified public transportation policy in the twelve-county Metropolitan Commuter Transportation District. The MTA was established as the governing board of a holding company composed of four subsidiary corporations—three transportation authorities and the Long Island Rail Road.

MTA was also authorized to establish subsidiary corporations. It organized the Staten Island Rapid Transit Operating Authority (SIRTOA) and the Stewart Airport Land Authority (SALA) in 1971 and the Metropolitan Suburban Bus Authority (MSBA) in 1973 to operate the bus system in Nassau County. MTA members serve as the *ex officio* board of directors of these three subsidiary authorities, bringing to a total of seven the number of subsidiary transportation organizations linked to the MTA by means of interlocking directorates.

Commuter Rail Service

One of the MTA's major responsibilities was the preservation and improvement of commuter rail service. The most serious rail problem facing New York State in the mid-1960s was the 334-mile LIRR, whose antiquated trains frequently broke down or were late. The huge MTA investment in track improvements and new equipment has begun to pay dividends. Improvements in facilities partly financed with 1967 bond issue funds included the extension of electrification, the purchase of 770 cars, construction of the 63rd Street Tunnel, upgrading of tracks, new high-level platforms, and various station improvements.

As of March 30, 1973, capital improvements totaled $416,087,866. Of this amount, the bond issue provided $286,582,000. Clearly, the modernization and expansion program could not have been undertaken without bond issue funds. Additional modernization of the LIRR's property and equipment, however, continued to be a pressing need.

While service on the New Haven line was continued with financial support by Connecticut and New York State in 1967 and 1968, a review of policy alternatives was conducted. The lease of the line by the two states along with a service contract for its management was considered the best alternative, and Governor John N. Dempsey of Connecticut and Governor Rockefeller signed final contracts on October 27, 1970.

The poor service on Penn Central's Harlem and Hudson Divisions—the result of years of neglect—had been a matter of great concern to Governor Rockefeller, the legislature, and the MTA. On February 28, 1968, the governor and the MTA chairman announced a $2.9 billion plan for improving the transportation system. The first major phase included a modernization plan for the Harlem Division in Westchester. Phase two projects included extension of electrified service to Peekskill, modernization of the signal system, purchase of electric and dual powered cars, and track improvements.

The governor sent a message to the legislature in 1970 requesting that a major portion of the modernization program be financed with bond issue funds. The legislature responded by appropriating $44.4 million of bond issue funds for rehabilitation and modernization of the commuter lines. The remaining $22.8 million cost of the program will be financed by the New York State Commuter Car Program administered by the Port Authority.

New York City Subways

In 1968 the Metropolitan Transit Authority (MTA) inherited an antiquated and rundown New York City subway system suffering from decades of neglect. The New York City Transit Authority as part of the MTA operates an $8 billion subway-elevated system with 6,800 cars, maintains 462 stations on 232 miles of line, and employs 27,805 persons on the subway system. A total of 3.9 million passengers ride the subway daily and account for 80 percent of the subway ridership and 20 percent of total public transit ridership in the United States. Ridership has been declining for many years and has declined 14 percent since the MTA became the TA's *ex officio* board. In fiscal 1974, ridership is projected to decline another 2 percent.

Between 1968 and 1973, subway and bus fares had increased by 75 percent, from 20 cents to 35 cents, and the TA's deficit grew from $44 million to a projected $250 million a year by 1974. Under MTA's aegis, the TA's budget increased 90 percent, from $416 million in fiscal 1968 to $793 million in fiscal 1974. A $1.4 billion construction program has been launched, including an immediate action project to construct an additional fifty-two miles of line. Six hundred million dollars in bond issue funds are helping to finance the program. In 1969, for the first time the state made a direct financial grant to the subway system by providing $99 million for construction of the new Second Avenue subway line from 34th Street to 126th Street in Manhattan. The total cost of this project will be approximately $1 billion. Although substantial progress has been made in renovating and modernizing the subway system, additional billions of dollars will have to be invested to enable it to provide first class service.

The Problem of Finance

By the end of the 1960s it was apparent that forthcoming federal financial assistance would not be sufficient to supplement state and local funds and permit the achievement of a balanced transportation system. Experience demonstrated that the fare box, even aided by capital grants from the 1967 bond issue, could not finance a statewide public transportation system providing comfortable, convenient, dependable, and fast service. To provide additional funds for the support of public transportation, the 1971 legislature authorized a second $2.5 billion bond issue subject to voter approval.

The 1967 bond issue received widespread support by organizations throughout the state, and a special committee, Action for Transportation in New York State, spent large sums urging voter approval. In 1971 the situation was different when the state was experiencing financial difficulties, state and local tax rates were rising, and opposition to the bond issue was better organized. As a result, the proposed issue was defeated by almost a million votes.

The defeat of the proposed bond issue set back the state's balanced transportation program. The problem of financing the program was compounded since $1.35 billion in state funds were not available for public transit projects already planned, and fears were expressed that federal funds might be lost because of the lack of state matching funds.

To assist the financing of public transportation projects in the downstate area, the 1972 legislature established the New York City Transit Construction Fund with power to issue up to $250 million in bonds to aid the city in financing its share of the cost of new public transit facilities without exceeding the constitutional debt limit.

On June 6, 1972, the Special Commission on the Financing of Mass Transportation (the Yunich commission) in the Tri-State Metropolitan Region released its final report which stated that the gap between revenues from passenger fares and operating expenses, depreciation, and debt service of mass transit operations increased from $177 million in 1962-63 to $420 million in 1969-70. More than half of this $243 million increase in the deficit was recorded during the period 1968-70. Forecasts for the period 1970-85 indicate substantial further increases in the magnitude of the deficit.

On October 11, 1973, the New York State Office for Local Government released a report, "Urban Area Bus Transit: A 57-County Survey," which revealed that thirty-nine private bus companies went out of business in the period 1960-72, and most public and private bus operators were still losing money. The situation would have been bleaker if 1967 bond issue funds had not been available to help purchase 600 new buses in seventeen upstate communities. In early 1973, subway and bus riders in New York City were informed that fares would increase to 60 cents unless additional nonfare sources of revenue became available. Rail commuters were warned that fares might be increased by as much as 70 percent.

To help solve the growing public transportation crisis, on July 26, 1973, Governor Rockefeller called upon a special session of the legislature to approve a $3.5 billion Transportation Capital Facilities Bond Issue, which would enable the state to "shoulder its fair share of the burden of meeting transit operating deficits on a 50-50 sharing basis for the next two years," and provide $150 million in each of the following years to help stabilize fares.

Approval of the bond issue would free funds normally reserved for capital projects and use them to hold down fares. These funds would be provided only if a 35-cent fare was in effect, necessitating a fare rollback in some upstate areas and matching by local governments of state funds.

The 1973 bond issue differed from the 1967 and the proposed 1971 issues in that a greater proportion of the proceeds would be used for public transportation—$2.1 billion for public transportation and $1.4 billion for highways. One-half of the proceeds from the 1967 bond issue was used for highways, two-fifths for public transportation, and one-tenth for aviation. The governor and legislative leaders hoped that the allocation of a larger share of the proceeds of the proposed bond issue to public transportation and the provision of statewide operating subsidies would make the issue sufficiently attractive to ensure its ratification by the voters.

On September 21, 1973, Governor Rockefeller announced the formation of a nonpartisan and broadly representative Citizens' Coalition for Total Transportation to support the proposed bond issue. Concluding that the expensive 1971 hard-sell campaign relying heavily on radio and television spots had backfired and a soft-sell campaign helped to secure voter approval of a proposed 1972 Environmental Conservation Bond Issue, organizers of the 1973 campaign decided to use the soft-sell approach. Significantly, Governor Rockefeller did not campaign for voter approval of his proposed bond issue. In his judgment, a photograph of Mayor Lindsay, Dr. Ronan, and the governor sharing a subway strap contributed more to the defeat of the 1971 proposed issue than any other event.

Every major newspaper in the state, except *Newsday* and the *Syracuse Herald Journal*, endorsed the bond issue as did Mayor Lindsay and the candidates for mayor of New York City, Abraham Beame (Democrat) and John Marchi (Republican). Organized opposition was not widespread but included the New York Taxpayers Association and the Anti-Bond Coalition composed of the City Club of New York, the West Side Highway Group, the Committee for Better Transit, and the Sierra Club. This coalition charged that the threat of a 60-cent subway and bus fare was being used as blackmail to persuade the New York

City electorate to approve the issue and that the state surplus could be used to hold down the fare.

As anticipated, the bond issue referendum campaign pitted areas outside metropolitan New York City against the downstate area. Support for the issue was strongest in New York City where approximately 60 percent of the employed residents use public transportation. However, apathy in New York City, as reflected in a low voter turnout, worked against the bond issue. The most effective argument used by opponents in the upstate area was that the issue was designed to bail out public transit lines in the New York City area. Interestingly, many environmentalists and New York City area residents opposed the issue because 40 percent of the proceeds were dedicated to highways, and the bond issue was defeated in the referendum in November 1973.

Conclusions

The heart of the public transportation problem is financial. Even a wealthy state such as New York lacks the resources required to expand and upgrade public transportation systems. Additional federal capital assistance is needed as well as federal operating assistance. In 1973 for the first time both houses of Congress approved operating assistance for public transit, yet it is improbable that sufficient assistance will materialize for New York in the near future because of the president's threat to veto an act proposing such assistance.

Defeat of the proposed 1973 bond issue makes more difficult the establishment of first class public transit systems at a time when two other developments necessitate much less reliance on the private automobile. First, federal air quality standards, unless lowered by Congress, will force a reduction in vehicular traffic. In December 1972 the United States Environmental Protection Agency released a briefing document, "Transportation Controls: Urban Strategies for Clean Air," reporting that exhaust controls on motor vehicles will not solve the problem of carbon monoxide pollution. In order to meet air quality standards by the May 1975 deadline mandated by the Clean Air Amendments of 1970, New York State may have to restrict motor vehicle traffic in certain urban areas and greatly expand the public transportation system in metropolitan areas to ensure that individual mobility is not seriously impeded.

The second development—the energy shortage—will curtail the use of the private automobile, which consumes on the average five times more fuel to move an individual one mile than a bus and ten times more than a subway or train. Petroleum provides about 97 percent of the energy utilized by the transportation sector of the economy, and 75 to 80 percent of the petroleum consumed is gasoline. Even a small diversion of motorists to public transportation would result in significant gasoline conservation.

Action must be taken immediately by the New York State Legislature to expand public transportation systems and prevent a fare escalation, which hurts the quarter of the population most dependent upon public transportation and least able to pay higher fares—children, the handicapped, the unemployed, the underemployed, and senior citizens. To reduce private automobile usage, conserve fuel, and raise revenue for public transit, the legislature should consider levying an automotive emission tax, increasing sharply the motor fuel tax, and significantly raising registration fees for large automobiles. Proceeds should be dedicated to the support of public transportation.

Elementary and Secondary Education

MICHAEL D. USDAN

Elementary and secondary education was a priority policy area for New York State during the years of the Rockefeller governorship. Between 1960 and 1972, state expenditures for education increased almost 400 percent, rising from $633 million to $2,534.6 million. The increase reflected a substantial growth in educational expenditures by the state, although state support dropped from 47 percent of total school expenditures in 1968–69 to 41 percent in 1972–73. Such an impressive state effort is at least partially responsible for New York's leading position among the states in almost every category of educational expenditures.

Until recently, decisions allocating the vast resources involved in New York's support of education were made through relatively stable processes and occurred in a political environment that was dominated by a small group of influential participants representing schoolmen and political leaders. The major policy inputs were provided by the State Education Department and major educational interest groups, such as the teachers, school boards, and administrators. The varied educational interests coalesced on the transcendent issue of school finance and articulated their common position on state aid for three decades through the New York State Educational Conference Board, a cooperative body of educational organizations that periodically presented state aid proposals which had vital grassroots support from its component groups.[1]

[1] Among the member organizations of the New York State Educational Conference Board are the New York State School Boards Association, the New York State Congress of Parents and Teachers, the New York State United Teachers, and the New York State Council of School District Administrators.

This consensual and somewhat closed style of educational politics, with professional educators themselves playing paramount roles, has undergone dramatic changes. Indeed, in the words of one long-time participant on the educational scene in Albany, "It's become a brand new ball game!" This judgment is corroborated by legislators, members of the State Education Department, interest group leaders, and others knowledgeable about educational politics in New York. Within a relatively few years major issues such as race, teacher militancy, community control, student activism, inflation and concomitant concerns about escalating school costs, and demands for accountability have cascaded upon public schools. The recent confluence of education and such volatile issues has politicized education in unprecedented ways and irrevocably pulled it deeper into the mainstream of the body politic.

By the late 1960s the public and legislators were growing skeptical while education, despite the thrusts of the Great Society, did not succeed dramatically in mitigating poverty and other social problems. There was growing apprehension about public education's role and effectiveness.

These developments are not unique to New York; they have occurred throughout the nation. Developments in New York, however, have particular saliency because of its size, level of industrialization, wealth, and tradition of relatively enlightened state government. New York has always been recognized as a leader and innovator among the states, especially in public school education. The Board of Regents was the nation's first state board of education, New York appointed the first chief state school officer, and its state teachers association is the oldest continuous organization of its kind. New York's Education Department is regarded widely as one of the nation's leading state educational agencies. In 1972 New York was the first state in which a merger occurred between the teachers union and the state teachers association affiliated with the National Education Association.

New York ranks as a leader among the states in a number of educationally related categories: first in the number of instructional staff in public schools, first in the taxable personal income per pupil in average daily attendance, first in estimated current expenditures per pupil, and second only to California in school age population. New York has the highest tax burden and school expenditures in the nation, but its existing revenue base is not keeping up with the burgeoning financial needs of education and other governmental services. This fiscal crunch has undermined much of the strong political support for education traditionally found in both the legislative and executive branches of state government. In New York, as in other states, education's "halo effect" is diminished, and the demands for accountability intensify as school finance and related concerns become a major, if not *the* major, issue of state government.

New York's financial crisis in education was accompanied by escalating public criticism from numerous and somewhat diverse sources. Many people, for example, vehemently opposed the use of busing to achieve racial desegregation in schools, and the regents and the commissioner of education, as well as local superintendents of schools and boards of education, became embroiled in this volatile issue. Many blacks became increasingly disenchanted with public education, particularly in large cities, because of the schools' failure adequately to educate minority youngsters. Reformers attacked the schools for their inflexibility and unresponsiveness to the needs of youngsters growing up in a technological age in which change was the only constant. Reflecting the rising dissatisfaction, various alternatives to traditional public education, such as voucher plans, performance contracting, and open education, were suggested.

Further to compound education's vulnerability, the once unified front of the educationally related interest groups was shattered by escalating teacher militancy. The Taylor Law, enacted in 1967, which required boards of education to negotiate with teacher organizations, generated conflict between boards and teachers and led to the fragmentation of traditional public school alliances. Local district struggles over negotiations naturally weakened statewide efforts to achieve unity among educational groups. As criticism mounted, the credibility of educators was decreased by their own infighting. Demands for accountability intensified, as did backlashes against militant teachers who, it was alleged, were eschewing their traditional professionalism in the quest for more pay and other perquisites.

The Educational Conference Board, which once unified the state's major educational interests on the state aid issue, was weakened and currently is undergoing an internal reassessment of its structure and modus operandi. Fiscal constraints, reapportionment, internal leadership changes, and unresponsiveness to minority and urban educational problems have all contributed to the decline of the board in the past decade. The board and its constituent organizations were unable to shift their political behavior quickly enough to respond to the dramatic changes of the 1960s, and the governor and the legislature have become more directly involved. The educational coalition's response to acute racial problems and poverty in the cities was inadequate, and the state's Big Six cities (New York, Buffalo, Rochester, Syracuse, Yonkers, and Albany) felt compelled in 1967 to create their own coalition to gain additional resources to meet their special educational needs. Approximately 60 percent of the students in these six cities are black or have Spanish surnames; more than 90 percent of the black and Spanish surnamed students enrolled in New York State public schools are found in these six school systems.

Teacher Organizations

The merger in 1972 between the United Federation of Teachers and the New York State Teachers Association has radically altered the politics of education in New York. In little more than a decade teachers have become a most potent political force. With grassroots strength that permeates the state and the financial resources generated by its 200,000 members, the New York State United Teachers (NYSUT) is now the pivotal force that will shape educational politics in the state.

In the elections of 1972, teachers were deeply involved in political campaigns and used their political muscle in unprecedented ways. Although teacher-backed candidates did not do well outside of New York City, the NYSUT influence in providing finances and campaign assistance is generally acknowledged. In some sections of the state, teacher political committees interviewed candidates and provided large sums of money for state legislative races. While there was a backlash against teacher "overkill" and an acknowledgment that the teachers were often not very politically astute in their first statewide campaign, the potential of a massive, organized, articulate, informed group that would reach into the grassroots of every community was not lost on politicians, many of whom appointed teacher advisory committees. Teachers can be expected to learn from their mistakes and become more sophisticated political participants in the future. They will learn, for example, that politicians are often more interested in campaign workers than in dollars.

This grassroots political power and potential is readily translatable to the state level, as the legislature discovered at the end of the 1972 session. Legislation was suddenly introduced that posed an immediate threat to the collective bargaining rights so vital to teacher interests. Teacher tenure, sabbaticals, and other hard-won rights were at stake. In an almost overnight response the teachers held mass meetings in

Albany and bombarded the legislature with thousands of telegrams. The teachers were successful in saving tenure, but their probationary period was increased from three to five years, and tenure for school administrators was eliminated. These developments became known symbolically to educators as Black Friday.

Black Friday generated even greater political awareness on the part of teachers. Sensitivities caused by a shrinking job market and rising public criticism were further exacerbated by the legislature's actions. Many attributed the extensive involvement of teachers in the 1972 political campaign to the apprehensions caused by Black Friday. Thus there is an apparent paradox concerning teacher power in New York. While teachers have unified into a single, powerful, statewide organization, they are concerned about widespread public criticism of education and the backlash against their new militancy. The NYSUT is also weakened by organizational problems. Some sources contend that many members of the old teachers association are unhappy with the merger and the "unprofessional" modus operandi of their new group.

Though somewhat defensive and uncertain of the future, the NYSUT is still undeniably powerful. One can expect that the teachers will use their influence to strengthen their collective bargaining rights and to support "right to strike" legislation. A few years ago, when New York City was affected by collective bargaining and strikes, there was little impact elsewhere in the state. Currently, collective bargaining occurs everywhere, and teacher strikes can and do develop in suburban areas. Revisions of the Taylor Law will be a focal point of controversy in the immediate future, and subjects like compulsory binding arbitration, criminal fines for striking, and the prohibition against strikes will be debated widely by the legislature and the public.

The membership and resources of the NYSUT will be of paramount significance to the potential renaissance of the Educational Conference Board or the emergence of any other influential statewide educational coalition. Indeed, it is difficult to envision the viability of such a group without the political clout of the teachers. Although other educationally related organizations, such as the School Boards Association, may disagree with the new militant style of teachers, the emergence of the NYSUT reflects a shift of the political center of gravity away from localities to big unions and other major power blocs in Albany. Through its links with organized labor the NYSUT can provide new strength, as well as some political liabilities, to the educational coalition.

In a speech on October 28, 1973, to the New York State School

Boards Association, Albert Shanker, the influential president of New York City's United Federation of Teachers and vice president of the NYSUT, called for the creation of a broader educational coalition that would include representatives from urban and minority groups and labor. While acknowledging that serious differences would continue to exist between teacher and school board groups, Shanker contended that it was necessary for the educational interests to coalesce because of the unprecedented attacks on public schools.

Changes in Educational Decision Making

The phenomenon of rising teacher power and other developments have dramatically affected the various components of New York's educational decision-making structure. The once relatively stable system in which components such as the regents, State Education Department, governor, legislature, and educational interest groups interrelated in more or less predictable ways is in flux.

Prior to discussing the evolving role of these components, however, it is necessary to describe briefly New York's educational structure. At a time when educators are being subjected to growing attacks and questions as to their credibility, education under New York law is still relatively insulated and institutionally sheltered from the mainstream of the body politic.

The regents, the top policy-making body, have a wide and unique range of powers extending beyond formal educational institutions such as schools and colleges and including libraries, museums, and other cultural institutions. Though elected by the legislature, the regents are relatively independent because of their lengthy fifteen-year terms. They appoint the commissioner of education, who serves at their pleasure and who, as head of the State Education Department and president of the University of the State of New York, enjoys authority over a massive and diversified educational system. At a time when schools are asked to be accountable and the expertise of educators is questioned, the unique independence of the regents rankles many elected officials, some of whom feel that educational policy cannot be adequately responsive to the public until the independence of the regents is reduced. The salient question of how independent education should be from the governor and the legislature poses major philosophical, ideological, and political questions for educational and political leaders in New York and other states.

Governor Rockefeller's interest in public school education had increased markedly as the issues became more visible and controversial. As education became more politically volatile, the governor, like his elected colleagues in the legislature, became responsive to public demands and more embroiled in school issues. Historically the governor of New York has been more concerned with higher education than with the public schools. Rockefeller, in particular, was closely identified with the dramatic growth of the State University of New York (SUNY).

Since the days of Thomas E. Dewey, New York governors have been frustrated with the alleged inaccessibility and unresponsiveness of the regents to educational needs in a changing society. The governor's influence on education has been through the Division of the Budget, which sets the initial limits of the executive budget. The governor and his key staff, the legislative leaders and their staffs, and the rank-and-file legislators in their conferences ultimately determine which legislation will pass, the formula for state aid allocation, and the level of support for the Education Department, despite the latter agency's structural autonomy.

Governor Rockefeller took several actions that reflected both his desire to become more active in the school finance issue and his growing concern about the ostensible lack of fiscal accountability in education. The most dramatic and controversial manifestation of his concern was the creation of the Office of Education Performance Review within the executive branch. In his annual State of the State Message to the legislature on January 3, 1973, Governor Rockefeller made "recommendations for changes which will bring the policy, management and fiscal responsiblities for education closer together." The governor proposed an office of inspector general for primary and secondary education and stated that, although the regents have full jurisdiction over educational policy, the governor and the legislature had to "take responsibility for determining and imposing the taxes" and could "no longer avoid having some direct share of the responsibility for determining how those taxes are spent." The proposed office of inspector general was "to review performance in relation to expenditures under present programs and to recommend means of improving their effectiveness and efficiency."

This proposal dramatically projected publicly the controversy that had festered for years between the political leadership of the state and the regents and the Education Department. Considerable numbers of elected officials had been alienated by what they considered to be the regents' pronouncements and grandiose positions. The regents, who traditionally met with the governor only annually at a formal meeting and rarely as a group with legislators, were regarded by some critics as being too detached and remote from the political and fiscal realities confronting elected officials. Some elected officials were particularly alienated by the regents' strong advocacy of busing for school desegregation. Under strong pressure from taxpayers in their districts at a time of fiscal crisis, legislators were less than enchanted with the regents' proposals for substantial increases in state aid.

Rockefeller's proposal for an office of inspector general was widely interpreted as an open challenge to the regents. Regents, educators, and their legislative supporters quickly attacked the proposal as a blatant political assault on the regents. Some Republicans as well as Democrats thought that the recommendation went too far and would give the executive inordinate influence over elementary and secondary education, the one major policy area not controlled by the governor. They believed that the office would duplicate functions already being performed by the legislature, the regents, the Education Department, the state comptroller, and the governor's own Division of the Budget.

These negative responses kept the legislature from passing the bill, and Rockefeller had to compromise. An office of inspector general for education with subpoena powers was not created. Instead the governor created, by executive order, the Office of Education Performance Review. This office, headed by Daniel Klepak, started to function late in 1973. Although it operates on a relatively small budget with a limited staff, Klepak's office will be watched closely by politicians and educators. Its creation is significant because it represents a visible effort by an external state-based group to assess the management of New York's $6.5 billion education enterprise. The Klepak operation, which has engendered considerable controversy, may not be permanent, but it is a portent of the future. Many legislators and others who opposed the inspector general proposal supported its underlying rationale but felt that the approach taken by the governor was inappropriate.

Another example of additional executive branch involvement is the active participation of a member of the governor's staff in the Task Force on State Aid to Public Schools, a high level staff group created to respond to pressures generated by court decisions throughout the nation questioning the equity of basing school financing primarily on local property taxes. This task force was created in 1973 to work on the formulation of state aid proposals. It has had both the legislative and executive branches actively involved from the outset in its attempt to improve the state's basic aid formula. This attempt is still in an embryonic stage and may fail, but it is significant in that it deviates from the traditional process in which representatives of educational organizations usually initiated major state aid proposals and presented them for approval to legislative leaders and the governor. Now both the legislative and executive branches have staffs with expertise in school finance and thus no longer are as dependent as they once were upon the State Education Department, educational interest groups, or the Educational Conference Board for the conceptualization and development of state aid proposals.

The potential for a new and uniquely influential school finance coalition exists in this fledgling group because its membership represents the ultimate decision makers. The organizations represented in the Educational Conference Board will no doubt provide inputs, but apparently they are no longer in the front line of action. The creation and quick convening of the task force in the late summer and fall of 1973 bodes well for substantive improvement in state aid. It also indicates that the executive branch, which in the past was largely concerned with how much money was to be spent, is now going to be a more active participant in determining how the revenues are to be distributed.

To be sure, some observers are skeptical about whether the task force can reach agreement, although they believe that its creation was a good idea. They argue that once generalities are converted into specific proposals, opposition will develop. They contend that the school districts and educational interests are so fragmented that it will be difficult to achieve a consensus as the diverse entities seek to enhance their own positions.

It is interesting to note that in this task force effort the regents and the Education Department are working cooperatively with the governor. Some predicted that the task force would succeed only if Rockefeller himself became involved and saw the group as a vehicle for reaffirming New York's leadership in education. Indeed, the school finance issue is of paramount significance nationally, and many envisioned the development of a model in New York that could set a national standard.

The legislature also has become much more directly involved in formulating educational policy. In recent years the New York legislature has built up its staff capacity not only on the major finance committees, Assembly Ways and Means and Senate Finance, but also on the major substantive committees like the education committees of both houses. The legislature has thus developed its own capacity to collect and interpret data and, as with the executive, no longer relies so heavily on the Education Department and professional interest groups for information.

Legislators, confronting taxpayer resistance to escalating school costs, have become more involved in educational problems. Rising teacher militancy and the resulting backlash have also contributed to the growing visibility and controversial nature of school issues in numerous communities. In response to these pressures, education staffs have been strengthened considerably to buttress the ability of legislators to handle school issues. Legislators, thus, are influenced increasingly by staff members on budgetary and other issues. As a result, in recent years representatives of educational organizations, while still participants in the process of developing state aid and other proposals, are no longer major actors in the crucial last minute drafting of legislation and the clearing of details. These functions are now handled by the legislative staff, which works out the final details congruent with fiscal parameters set forth by the governor's budget office. The proposals are then sanctioned by the legislative leaders and then submitted to the rank-and-file membership for final approval.

The state aid issue is of primacy to legislators because every constituent is affected by rising property taxes. Since reapportionment, suburban interests have dominated the legislature, and no issue has greater saliency in suburbia than property tax rates. In recent years, legislators have become increasingly cognizant of their need for comprehensive data on school systems in their districts. The education and fiscal staffs thus play an increasingly significant role in providing information and expertise on school finance and related issues. These staff members obviously have primary loyalty to the legislators who employ them and not to the educational interests. They are trusted not only to provide objective information but also to protect their employers' best interests. These realities of contemporary political life understandably have vitiated the influence of educational groups, which once provided not only most of the information but also the budgetary and programmatic alternatives for legislative consideration.

In the past, legislators would frequently defer to professional educators on matters such as teacher evaluation or program assessment. This is no longer the case, as educational programs have become increasingly controversial and costly, and thus more political. Compensatory education efforts, such as Title I of the federal Elementary and

Secondary Education Act of 1965 and New York State's urban aid program, for example, have attracted considerable legislative attention. Lawmakers passed detailed legislation requiring joint evaluation of Title I and urban aid projects by local school districts.

Another reason for the growth of the legislature's assertiveness and independence in educational matters is the antagonism felt toward the regents and the Education Department by many solons. Like the governor, numerous legislators have been disturbed by some of the regents' costly and purportedly unrealistic recommendations. The regents' and commissioner's liberal posture on the explosive issue of racial integration has further exacerbated relationships with many lawmakers. The regents, it is alleged, have made only minimal efforts to communicate with rank-and-file legislators who resent this lack of concern.

Although both the executive and legislative branches have become considerably more active in educational matters, the political influence and substantive capacity of the New York State Education Department are not to be underestimated. Because of its comprehensive organizational machinery and its staff's expertise and long years of experience, the Education Department continues to exercise great influence in programmatic and legislative matters. Educational problems are increasingly complex, and the department is still a preeminent source of information and expertise for legislators and others interested in educational programs and financing. The department remains a most potent force through its pervasive network of ties to educators at all levels, and its support remains critically important to those who wish to alter New York's educational system.

The legislature, as well as the governor, has frequently initiated efforts to curb the regents and the Education Department. Bills have been introduced to reduce the fifteen-year terms of the regents and to make them elected officials. The regents themselves, only too cognizant of the extensive length of their tenure, introduced legislation in 1973 to reduce their fifteen-year terms. Traditionally, the selection of regents by the legislature has been somewhat pro forma, with the lawmakers usually accepting without extensive discussion the nominees of county and local political leaders. In the past year or two, however, prospective regents have been scrutinized much more carefully by ad hoc and standing legislative committees that interview the candidates and elicit their views on major issues such as finance and integration. Reportedly, a "liberal" regent was persuaded not to seek reappointment in 1972 because his prointegration sentiments precluded his chances of being approved by a majority of legislators. Bills to curb the Education Department, which must carry out the policies of the regents, have also been introduced in recent legislative sessions. Proposals to reduce the commissioner's judicial powers and to make him an elected official are submitted regularly.

Even some legislators who support the "progressive" posture of the regents on major social and educational issues feel that as currently structured it is a "doomed aristocracy." They contend that an unpaid, part-time governing body composed of prestigious citizens serving fifteen-year terms is anachronistic. Current school issues, they believe, are simply too complex, visible, and volatile to be the responsibility of a voluntary, insulated, lay, policy-making body. The regents themselves apparently sense the "cracks in their pedestal." In recent months they are reported to have initiated special efforts to increase communication with legislators and other officials with whom they reportedly have had little or no interaction as a group. In the past few years the regents have also moderated their recommendations in school finance. Defenders of the regents deny that their recent fiscal recommendations have been politically unrealistic. The regents have not been the free spending liberals on finance that they have been portrayed to be. In fact, they have attempted to present realistic middle ground proposals somewhere between the recommendations of the Educational Conference Board and what the legislature will endorse. Supporters of the regents deny the charges of political naivete and indifference. They argue that members of the regents and the State Education Department predicate their proposals on realistic assessments and spend a lot of time calculating both fiscal and political tolerances in the legislative and executive branches.

Efforts by both the executive and legislative branches to curb the powers of the regents are viewed with great apprehension by their supporters. Many attribute New York's leadership position in elementary-secondary education to the structural autonomy of the regents. It is pointed out that the regents have a proud and notable history in their governance of the "most comprehensive educational organization in the world." The New York educational system has been able to flourish because of the wise constitutional provision that ensures the regents' independence and separation from other state governmental units. Supporters maintain that this unique structural autonomy, insulating the regents from immediate political pressures, has given this prestigious body the independence to project candidly and with vision the state's broad and long-range educational needs without fearing political retribution.

Defenders of the regents believe that this independence is more important now than ever because of the political volatility of contemporary educational issues. As an example, they point to the "courageous" and "morally right" yet widely unpopular position taken in support of racial integration by Commissioners James Allen and Ewald Nyquist. Supporters of the regents believe that in no other state would a chief state school officer possess the political independence to take such a consistently forthright, controversial stand on such a volatile social issue and still survive. Because of provincial pressures, legislators and other elected officials are unable or unwilling to take such principled stands on major public policy issues.

Supporters of the Education Department are deeply disturbed by recent efforts of both the legislative and executive branches to undermine the regents' traditional autonomy. Thus far, efforts have failed to change the system by legislation which, for example, would reduce the regents' terms of office, curb the commissioner's judicial powers, or make him an elected official. Some advocates of the regents are fearful that a more subtle and "dangerous" strategy has been employed recently by the legislature in scrutinizing regents' candidates. Within the next five years or so, it is possible that as many as ten of the fifteen regents may leave office. If the legislature uses its approval powers more forcefully in the future than it has in the past, quite conceivably it could substantially affect the educational approaches and philosophy of the regents. By ratifying the nominations of only those candidates who subscribed to its dominant political values, the legislature could virtually control the formulation of educational policy. Indeed, some allege that policy concessions were extracted from recent candidates by the legislature's ad hoc interviewing committee.

Some observers of the New York educational scene contend that the actual power of the regents is exaggerated. It is noted that the regents cannot afford to be too independent because each year the budget of the Education Department is subjected to legislative and executive scrutiny. In recent years, the Education Department, like other state agencies, has been hampered by personnel freezes, cutbacks, and greater line item control over areas such as travel funds and internal personnel reassignments, which were traditionally left to the agency's discretion. The regents and the Education Department are also limited by state statutes that provide the basic policy framework for education in New York. Thus the regents and the Education Department are much more constrained by the legislative and executive branches than their critics are apt to admit.

If education becomes even more intensely politicized, conflict between the regents and elected officials can be predicted with some
assurance. As long as the regents advocate a greater state role in financing education, some tension with a tax-conscious legislature and governor will persist. The scenario is for the regents to continue to project
education's fiscal needs and for elected officials (who must levy taxes
to provide the resources) to resent these projections. Despite the continuing irritation that it will cause the governor and legislators, the
regents will probably continue to attempt to goad the state into meeting its obligations to give further support to education.

A basic question, then, is whether it is in the best interests of the
state to have a constitutionally independent entity (regents or Education Department) establishing parameters of educational policy and
playing an advocacy role. What is the appropriate role of the governor
and the legislature and which facets, if any, of educational policy making should be somewhat insulated from the day-to-day political process?

The extent of conflict between the political actors and the educational establishment in New York can be overstated. Many would contend that day-to-day working relationships between the governor
and his top aides and the commissioner of education and his staff
were closer, more cordial, and more reciprocal in the Rockefeller administration than in previous administrations. Nevertheless, there are
fundamental underlying tensions between the state's major political
actors and the Board of Regents and the Education Department. Insofar as these tensions provide New York with a form of dynamic equilibrium in educational policy, they may be very healthy.

Rising teacher power, school finance, race, and other issues will continue to deepen the intensity of educational politics at all governmental levels. The decisions affecting education will be made increasingly
in the legislative and executive branches in Albany and will thus be
more open to public scrutiny and debate. If one accepts the notion
that education is indeed a unique governmental function and that
elected officials, who are weary of constituent uprisings on seemingly
intractable school issues such as desegregation and finance, really do
not want greater influence in educational policy making, then the
structural autonomy of the regents and the State Education Department may well be preserved. Indeed, the regents and the department
serve as a valuable buffer for elected officials because they often absorb much of the heat on difficult educational issues.

Narcotics Addiction:
The Politics of Frustration

ALAN CHARTOCK

The problem of narcotics addiction has evoked proposals for solutions ranging from hard line punishments to the legalization of heroin. That all of these proposals have been taken seriously at various times is some proof that the politics of addiction is a politics of frustration. As official estimates of the number of addicts on the street climb, as related crime continues to increase, as purported solutions fail, the electorate increasingly seeks a definite and final answer to the problem. These demands are fed by shocking revelations—one out of every forty children delivered in New York City hospitals is addicted at birth; addicted mothers sell their children to get money for their habits. The issue is especially compelling in New York State, home for at least half the nation's addict population.

The political fight for resources from the government for the several different types of addiction treatment programs is dramatic testimony to the fact that treatment has become big business. Because of the general ignorance about the subject, each proponent of a cure can muster tremendous political support. Boards of directors, staffed by well-meaning citizens from every walk of life, become proselytizers for their agency's solution.

Each group plays with statistics to support contentions and applies pressure to have its way. Each group seems to make sense because each spots flaws in the others' arguments. The "drug free group," such as Synanon, Daytop, and Odyssey House, propose withdrawal combined with medical treatment and counseling. The "maintenance group" propose use of another drug but one which permits an addict to lead a normal life. The drug free supporters argue that the methadone people are only curing symptoms and their method encourages another form of addiction. Some of these methadone detractors point to the huge black market for methadone and to the number of addicted methadone babies born every year. Some methadone advocates see the "drug free" people as unwilling to accept a morality that at least allows the addict to function without resorting to illegal acts. In a seemingly contradictory fashion, however, some supporters of methadone maintenance reject the legalization of heroin, either controlled or uncontrolled, as dangerous. Recently another group has emerged that espouses the use of "antagonists"—chemical injections that kill the heroin high by occupying the nerve cell sites in the brain where the heroin would otherwise sit. Critics of antagonists argue that an addict looking for a high will not take a drug that would rob him of his pleasure and escape.

In short, each advocate of a particular treatment has made some very telling points about each of the others. Nevertheless, some clear facts stand out. A great many people become addicted to the use of drugs for many different reasons. For those who wish to overcome the habit voluntarily there are Daytop, Synanon, Odyssey House, and similar programs. For others who wish to try maintenance, there is methadone. There are many arguments about the relative success of these programs. The main problem is that the major programs are only for those who want help, while most addicts do not. Governor Rockefeller and the other political actors have addressed themselves to this majority of addicts.

The latest political approach has focused on these addicts and on pushers or at least their stereotypes, because they are a threat to the public. It is a desperate approach, and its motto is, "If we catch you, we will put you in prison and keep you there."

Enforcement

The politics of frustration is most apparent in the enforcement sector of the narcotics problem. Along with the question of how to rehabilitate addicts is the problem of how to control the illegal flow of heroin. This strategy has always been based on two assumptions: it is possible to cut off the addict's supply, and if his supply is cut off, he will be forced to quit. The enforcement process has generally involved the police, district attorneys, judges, and a mixture of federal and state agencies. In the United States, unlike Great Britain, these groups have seen enforcement as the key to the control and treatment of the addict.

Despite the massive amount of resources that have been thrown into the fight, there are few comforting signs of success. The media regularly report confiscations of huge quantities of heroin. In April 1973, for example, New York City and federal officials announced the arrest of sixty-five persons who, they said, could distribute more than 220 pounds of the drug a week. These announcements are usually accompanied by official claims of progress against the drug traffic. Yet authoritative reports indicate that optimism concerning efforts to curtail the flow of illegal drugs is unwarranted. One study issued jointly by the CIA, the Department of Defense, and the Department of State in July 1972, for example, stated that there was no prospect of controlling the flow of drugs from Southeast Asia "under any conditions that can be realistically projected." In August, the *World Opium Survey,* an official U. S. Government publication, suggested that only "a small fraction" of the international heroin traffic coming into the United States had been seized. The *Survey* also speculated that the available drug supply could meet the large United States demand. This research has led one Harvard professor to suggest that in an area where addiction is "endemic," such as New York City, enforcement cannot prevent the use of heroin.

The antidrug enforcement effort in New York has been compromised in part by graft and corruption throughout the criminal justice system. Examples are widespread. Millions of dollars' worth of heroin disappeared from New York City Police Department vaults. The Knapp commission, appointed by Mayor Lindsay in New York City in 1970 to examine corruption in the criminal justice process, documented the fortunes that could be made by the police narcotics squad members. A New York City district attorney pleaded guilty to accepting "sexual favors" from the girl friend of a defendant in a drug case for whom, in return, he promised to intercede.

Police, for their part, have been highly critical of court sentencing practices with regard to persons arrested on narcotics charges. The New York City Police Department revealed that only about 2 percent of those arrested on narcotics charges in the city were jailed for a year or more. In 1970, for example, there were 20,762 arrests for narcotics felonies; only 481 of those arrested went to prison. The entire process is further complicated by the practice of plea bargaining. Under this practice, which is used to avoid the time and expense of a criminal trial, a defendant pleads guilty in return for having the charges against him reduced. The result, the police claim, is that even "good" arrests of major figures are negated. In 1972, for example, an officer of the

New York City Police Department told a New York State Senate joint legislative committee that a man arrested for possession of a sizeable amount of heroin and five illegal weapons was allowed to plead guilty to "attempted possession of a dangerous weapon."

These few vignettes highlight the immense difficulties that have faced government at all levels in attempting to enforce narcotics control legislation in New York. It seems clear that the enforcement approach has not prevented flourishing criminal organizations that make enormous profits from the heroin market. Whether the result of a legalized market would end these organizations, as happened after prohibition, is only speculatory. What is clear is that the situation could hardly be worse.

Politics

Most of the major political initiatives in the area of drug abuse control in New York over the past decade were taken by Governor Nelson Rockefeller. A consummate politician, the governor was able to read public opinion polls as well as commission them and therefore could anticipate his electorate and emerge as its leader. Those who opposed his programs were unable to unite behind viable alternatives. Even when gubernatorial programs did not work, Rockefeller was able to stake out new positions that foreclosed Democratic adoption of them and made him politically invulnerable to the electorate. Especially in its dealings with the New York City government under John Lindsay, the Rockefeller administration was able to take the offensive with new programs and leave the mayor and city bureaucrats defending ongoing programs of questionable effectiveness.

In February 1966, approximately eight months before he ran for his third term, Rockefeller announced "an all out war on drugs and addiction." Knowing his electorate well, he was fully aware of their frustration and fear. Polls had told him that crime and addiction were two of his constituents' greatest fears. In proposing his new program, the governor showed his determination by opposing the views of civil libertarians and mental health bureaucrats who administered the Metcalf-Volker Law. This law, which allowed addicts to commit themselves for rehabilitation, often instead of being jailed, had not worked. Only addicts facing jail sentences requested rehabilitation. Something stronger was needed, according to Rockefeller, and this coincided with the views of the electorate that he was polling.

In orchestrating the campaign for his legislative package and his election, Rockefeller consistently pushed the theme that crime and addiction were closely related, something he knew his electorate already thought. When he announced his program, the governor noted that New York City's 25,000 addicts were responsible for 50 percent of its crime. In his estimate of the number of addicts in the street, the governor was moderate. No one could call him an alarmist since many believed the number was much larger.

Rockefeller's proposed legislation had two major emphases. One concerned stiffer penalties for peddlers. This was nothing new. New York politicians had long realized that stiffer penalties for pushers was a safe political position. While some people are uncertain whether addiction is a disease or a crime, few people have any sympathy for the pusher. The distinction between seller and user is not a clear one, however, because many addicts support their habit by selling drugs.

Rockefeller's position favoring stiffer penalties found support in the enforcement community. As the governor was publicizing his new program, the State Investigation Commission issued a report that indicated that the state's addict population of 30,000 to 60,000 spent $43 million a year on heroin. The commission joined the governor in asking for longer jail terms for those convicted of selling drugs to persons under twenty-one, and called for federal relaxation of controls against wire tapping in narcotics related investigations. The New York District Attorneys' Association also passed a resolution in favor of Rockefeller's program. Stiffer penalties would strengthen the district attorney's role in the plea bargaining process.

The second and major aspect of the new law, however, was not made public by the governor until February 1966. Recognizing the unpleasant fact that most confirmed addicts would not seek rehabilitation because of the psychological or physiological needs that had caused their addiction, Rockefeller urged that addicts be rehabilitated whether they wanted to be or not. The new procedure, known as civil commitment, could be accomplished either by judicial hearing or trial. A similar procedure had been operative in California for a few years and had had mixed reviews when the 1966 New York State Narcotics Package was passed. Under the New York program, an addict would be committed to a "hospital" or rehabilitation center with or without his consent.

Important medical organizations, such as the New York State Medical Society, were firmly behind the Rockefeller plan. Its chairman, Donald Louria, had long been an important Rockefeller adviser on this subject, and at that time was an announced foe of drug maintenance programs. The governor also announced support from John V. Lindsay, the Republican mayor, though some prominent people in and around the Lindsay administration expressed a good deal of skepticism, both privately and publicly, about the program.

In the legislature, opposition was led by Democratic State Senator Manfred Ohrenstein, who had been espousing a program based primarily on the British model, including the right of doctors to prescribe drugs to patients. Ohrenstein decried the Rockefeller program as a hoax, bureaucratic nonsense, and more punitive than corrective. Other opponents included Dr. Vincent Dole, one of the pioneers of methadone maintenance, who disliked its mandatory aspects, and the American Civil Liberties Union, which claimed that the U. S. Supreme Court had ruled that an addict was not a criminal and could not be called one.

While there was a good deal of rhetoric and bargaining, there was little recorded opposition in the final vote in the legislature on the 1966 drug bill. Democrats and Republicans alike were frightened by constituent perceptions of them as voting against a narcotics solution. One senate Democratic staff worker said, "Some of them were just scared, others genuinely believed in a punitive approach to this problem." The final senate vote was 57-4 and the vote in the assembly was an equally lopsided 151-8. These affirmative voters included some originally fierce in their denunciations of the governor.

In the ensuing election, Rockefeller's Democratic opponent, Frank O'Connor, took the governor to task on the new program and called it outdated and punitive. He argued that Rockefeller was making an issue of narcotics and that experience demonstrated that an addict could not be cured against his will. O'Connor was supported in his views by several experts, including the president of the National Association for the Prevention of Narcotics Addiction and the medical director of Daytop Village, but the electorate generally supported Rockefeller's position. Senior Democratic leaders later observed that O'Connor's position on the drug program had cost him votes in this close election.

The 1973 Program—Escalation

By the time the 1973 session of the legislature had arrived, it was clear to the governor and many other people that the 1966 narcotics initiative had not worked. The whole program administered by the Narcotics Addiction Control Commission, established under the 1966 law, was under fire. Some claimed that the facilities which were built or rented were not adequately staffed. Others reiterated the essential flaw that rehabilitation cannot be forced on those who do not want it. Members of the Democratic party claimed that the whole package had been an election year strategy. Still others argued that the program was more custodial than rehabilitative and pointed to the large number of escapees and dropouts as proof of its ineffectiveness. One index of the seriousness of the problem was evident in a report of the state health commissioner, Hollis Ingraham, which indicated that in 1972 narcotics-related deaths in New York had increased 32 percent, reaching a rate of 5.3 per 10,000 population.

Yet opinion polls showed that people were still concerned and frustrated over the narcotics problem. With another statewide election year approaching, Rockefeller had three reasons to act: the old program was not working, political battles loomed, and the electorate was frustrated and wanted some sign of progress.

In his 1973 State of the State Message to the legislature, Rockefeller urged that drug problems be treated with "brutal honesty." Implicitly admitting failure, Rockefeller pointed out that the state had spent over $1 billion and had achieved very little permanent rehabilitation and complained that "all the laws we have on the books now won't deter the pusher of drugs." As a consequence he returned to a strict enforcement policy, which included mandatory life sentences with no possibility of parole for persons caught possessing or selling drugs. This was an attempt to minimize plea bargaining. In addition, the governor proposed ending youthful-offender treatment of pushers in their late teens and making them face life imprisonment with parole only after fifteen years, a 100 percent tax on drug dealers that allows confiscation of their earnings and property, and a controversial "bounty" to be paid to informants whose information led to drug convictions.

As might be expected, when the Rockefeller program emerged, opposition was vocal. The American and New York Civil Liberties Union, the Consumers Union, the New York State NAACP, the New York State Conservative party, the mayor of New York, New York City agencies, and the Democratic party, more solidified than in 1966, all opposed him. The New York City Health Services Administrator, Gordon Chase, attacked the new program as "simplistic and impractical." Two New York State Appellate Court judges warned that the courts would be unable to operate the new program and called for maintenance experiments with addicts. In a major speech, Mayor Lindsay attacked the governor's program as "impractical, unworkable and vindictive," and charged that it meant "nothing beyond momentary satisfaction and inevitable disillusionment." Even in the governor's own party, legislative leaders were supportive but felt certain distinctions should be made including one between the addict-pushers and the non-addicted, profit-motivated pusher. Nevertheless, the governor's mail indicated five to one in favor of his new program.

Mayor Lindsay, however, argued that there were encouraging signs that the ongoing New York program was working: addict-related crime declined significantly in the first eight months of 1972, and the number of incarcerated criminals needing detoxification was decreasing. The mayor warned against abandoning those in therapy. In addition, Henry Ruth, the head of Lindsay's Criminal Justice Coordinating Council, openly criticized the governor's plan. The *New York Times* editorialized that "Rockefeller's simplistic lock-'em-up-for-life for everyone proposal is a gross disservice, making adoption of a responsible program less likely than ever." A key police figure in the New York City enforcement effort called Rockefeller's proposal "an Archie Bunker law" and completely unworkable. Others objected on the ground that policemen would be endangered because those facing life sentences would have nothing to lose and would shoot to kill. Opponents also predicted a rise in the price of drugs and a compensatory rise in addict-related crime. Benjamin Malcolm, the New York City corrections commissioner, said on television that the new proposal was unrealistic and that it might cause riots in the city jails. Governor William Cahill of New Jersey said he would be opposed to similar legislation for his state because "we must realize that the addicted pusher would do anything regardless of the penalties to support his habit."

The New York State District Attorneys' Association, which had supported the governor's 1966 narcotics legislation, denounced the insistence on mandatory sentences, but commended Rockefeller's "get tough policy in the area of drug addiction." The State Bar Association's Criminal Justice Executive Committee voted 20-1 to oppose the governor's recommendations. Even the New York State court administrator called the proposal "completely unfeasible." He reasoned that the 100 temporary judgeships proposed by Rockefeller to handle the increased work load would not be enough. Still others objected to the governor's lumping many different drugs into single categories and said a distinction should be made between heroin and other drugs.

Rockefeller, however, continued to receive support both in his own and external polls. In one national poll he drew favorable comment across the country. Formal endorsements for Rockefeller's hard line approach included one from a group of Harlem ministers and antidrug administrators. In strongly endorsing the proposed legislation this group noted that it was aimed at "bloodthirsty, money-hungry, death-dealing criminals." The Association of Towns of the State of New York also supported the plan.

On April 12, 1973, approximately four months after he introduced his narcotics package, the governor submitted a new version that included some modification and employed penalties for drug sellers. However, it still included mandatory minimum sentences, limited plea bargaining, and a system of life sentences that would permit parole for the rest of a criminal's life after his mandatory minimum sentence had been served.

Nevertheless, because of the widespread opposition, there was substantial difficulty in obtaining legislative approval for the program. Rockefeller actively lobbied for it. On April 26 he said his narcotics proposal was "the most important [task] facing the legislature" because it went beyond the traditional concepts of the criminal justice structure and made a fundamental change in approach. The governor said it was essential to give the public what it wanted, "namely, to stop the pushing of hard drugs."

On April 27, Rockefeller's program was passed in the New York State Senate, 41-14. Several Democrats defected to vote for the bill, though many of their colleagues expressed annoyance at the techniques used to "steamroll the bill through the senate." The *New York Times* was aghast, chiding the senate and accusing it of having "succumbed to political hysteria over drug abuse." The *Times* called on the assembly to reject the legislation. But on May 3 the assembly passed the bill 80-65 despite a flurry of last minute lobbying by New York City. Interestingly, one of the first new judges named was Richard Brown, former head of Mayor Lindsay's Albany lobbying effort. The New York Civil Liberties Union greeted the assembly's action with the statement that it was "one of the most ignorant, irresponsible and inhuman actions in the history of the state." This time, in the assembly, the minority Democrats were largely recorded opposed to the bill with Minority Leader Stanley Steingut saying it was a "sham and a hoax."

On May 8, 1973, Rockefeller signed his new legislation into law. At the signing he praised the legislature for standing up to "this strange alliance of vested establishment interests, political opportunists and misguided soft liners who joined forces and tried unsuccessfully to stop this program." Rockefeller warned that failure would only occur because many of the same enforcement agencies who opposed the bill would not be committed to implementing it. He called on police departments to arrest drug pushers and on district attorneys to prosecute. Mayor Lindsay and the city criminal justice officials could hardly have missed the message. Lindsay announced that, despite all the misgivings he had about the Rockefeller program, he would do all he could to enforce it.

Solutions

If narcotics addiction is tied to sociological frustrations, as some have claimed, major social change will have to come about before addiction is cured. In the short run, other solutions will be tried. The enforcement model that has been prevalent in the United States has not worked. Nor has the rehabilitative approach worked, for most addicts do not want rehabilitation. The British, who have far fewer addicts (hardly 3,000 by any estimate), have worked out a clinical treatment model. They supply addicts with drugs, but under strict supervision and controls that include close contact with a social worker. The British experience differs from that of the United States in that addiction appears to surface in different ethnic and socioeconomic patterns. In addition, the English administer their program through a socialized medical delivery system. Perhaps a coordinated system of maintenance treatment is impossible in this country. On the other hand, the conclusion is inescapable that heroin continues to pour into the United States and that local, state, and federal efforts in this area have not come close to achieving their stated aims, but rather have created a black market and thus have provided a sure way for the underworld to raise money. The politics of frustration has led the United States into a Vietnam-like morass. It continues to throw its resources into a program that simply will not work.

The first Rockefeller program, Civil Commitment, and the expenditure of large amounts of money failed to abolish drug addiction. It is too early to judge whether the latest hard line approach will have a major impact. Predictions of clogged courts and costly trials are already being proven inaccurate; the addict and seller are simply going further underground.

The next governor, like the last, will be confronted with this problem. He will survey options and find that there is only one dramatic thing he can try, and that will be the creation of some kind of heroin maintenance program for the addict population he has not reached.

Until permanent answers can be found, the solution may be this type of containment in combination with strict enforcement exercised against those who seek drugs outside the provided apparatus, along with drug-free rehabilitation programs for those who wish to overcome the habit completely. When the addict who wants to take drugs has some legitimate way of doing it, the drug problem may be at least partially solved.

Environmental Protection

RICHARD J. KALISH

On April 22, 1970, New York State enacted the Environmental Conservation Law, reorganizing the state administration dealing with the physical environment and creating the New York State Department of Environmental Conservation (DEC). The date of enactment was symbolic, for it was the first observance of Earth Day. Just as Earth Day was to register national concern for the environment and encourage change, so the Environmental Conservation Law was to indicate the commitment of New York State to the achievement of a wise use of the state's natural resources and the attainment of an environment of high quality.

The degree and scope of the state's commitment can be seen from the declaration of policy in the 1970 act. According to the declaration, the state accepts the responsibility "to conserve, improve and protect its natural resources and environment" to "control water, land and air pollution in order to enhance the health, safety and welfare of the people of the state and their overall economic and social well being." In addition, the state also recognizes as one of its functions the improvement and coordination of environmental plans in the state in cooperation with other levels of government or private individuals and groups. It is "to act as the trustee of the environment for present and future generations" and to foster, create, and maintain "conditions under which man and nature can thrive in harmony with each other."

The assumption of these responsibilities is not a small order. Despite the acceptance of general principles, there are many questions regarding the compatibility of the listed goals. Because many policies or goals may conflict, society may have to forego something it wants in order to gain something else it wants more. Government plays a leading role in making choices or mediating among groups with divergent interests.

Governments are involved in environmental decisions in three categories. First, they are consumers and producers of goods and services that have the same impact on the environment as those produced and consumed by private firms and individuals. They use resources and also produce pollutants. Second, governments must act to establish acceptable standards and take steps to ensure uniformity of compliance. Air pollution standards are means of achieving at least a minimal level of uniformity. Finally, governments provide a mechanism to mediate between those with divergent views. In the area of environment, many views are undergoing change, and new mechanisms and procedures for the settlement of disputes need to be developed to meet current and future requirements.

Administration of environmental programs is not a new activity to New York State; rather, recent reorganization is a reflection of needs felt by the public. Previous state actions, reflecting the concerns of the "early" conservation movement, centered upon questions of natural resource quantity or availability. The recent growth of public concern has caused the emphasis to shift to questions of environmental quality and the problems of pollution and environmental degradation.

Water Pollution Control

One area in which this shift of emphasis can be documented is water pollution control. Prior to 1949, state water-pollution control efforts had been either nonexistent or ineffective. Throughout the nineteenth century, control of water pollution was considered a local responsibility. State action was limited to authorizing municipalities to enact their own sanitary regulations. Even after establishment of the State Board of Health in 1880, primary responsibility was left to the localities. Finally, in 1903, growing concern about the health hazards of pollution and the inability of municipalities to control it led to the passage of the state's first antipollution law. Despite the firm tone of the statutes, which were to be enforced by the Health and Conservation Departments, pollution control continued generally uncoordinated and ineffective until 1950. These early statutes were almost useless in preventing pollution.

In 1946 the legislature referred the water-pollution problem to the

Special Committee on Pollution Abatement (the Ostertag committee) and set in motion the chain of events culminating in the 1949 Pollution Control Act. The act unified administrative control of the state's water-pollution control program in a new agency, the Water Pollution Control Board, which operated within the Department of Health, and remedied the defect in the definition of "pollution" by introducing the idea of water-quality standards. Responsibility for establishing these standards was given to the newly created board as part of a comprehensive program requiring the classification of all waters in the state according to the "best usage" in the public interest, the adoption of standards of water purity for each classification, the development of pollution-abatement plans for each area of the state, and the enforcement of the plan. Voluntary compliance was to be the first step, but, when necessary, the use of abatement orders and judicial action were authorized. This newly created program contained no deadline for clean water for New York State. Thus, in the first four years of its operation, the board developed plans for pollution abatement and requested compliance for 2,115 of the 47,654 square miles in the state (4 percent of the area). Ten years later this figure had risen to 52.2 percent.

A variety of factors made it impossible for the Water Pollution Control Board to work effectively for pollution abatement. The agency was short of personnel and funds, and it was faced with rapidly expanding industrial production, increasing population, and consequent volumes of wastes. Also localities raised questions about the legality of the law and the board's administration of it.

There were two other important factors in water-pollution control for New York State. The first was the board's attitude toward enforcement actions. From the start of its deliberations, the special legislative committee had stressed the need for stimulating voluntary compliance. Indeed, the law required attempts to obtain voluntary compliance before the issuance of abatement orders. Since no time limit was set for this "cooperative phase," almost endless delays were possible.

The second factor that seriously damaged New York's control program was its regulatory character. The program was all stick and no carrot. The only financial aid to municipalities was planning grants of up to 2 percent of construction costs of treatment facilities. The Special Committee on Pollution Abatement was aware of the fiscal problems of municipalities. The recognition, however, of "fiscal inability" did not lead to serious discussion of state aid. Moreover, the fiscal difficulties of municipalities, as described by their representatives at public hearings held by the committee, centered on constitutional and legal limitations on municipal debt. The solution to the problem, as seen by the committee, consisted in removing or somehow bypassing these restrictions so as to allow the municipalities themselves to generate needed funds. Indeed, the special committee and succeeding committees supported a number of provisions designed to solve this problem of debt limitations.

The failure of municipalities to build treatment plants and persistent pleas of the State Conference of Mayors for state aid in this endeavor caused legislative leaders in 1957 to direct the Joint Legislative Committee on Natural Resources (successor to the special committee) to establish the Advisory Commission on Municipal Fiscal Problems in Pollution Abatement. After a year and a half of study, the advisory commission decided that "no definite conclusion could be drawn at this time relating to any legislative action on State aid."

The 1948 Water Pollution Control Act was the first major national legislation in this field. It asserted federal authority and authorized $22.5 million yearly for construction. In 1956 the law was amended to provide grants-in-aid for the first time to help local communities build sewage-disposal plants. The federal share of the cost was fixed at $50 million annually with the total cost for localities estimated at almost $500 million. The bill included a provision requiring at least 50 percent of the funds to go to municipalities with a population of 125,000 or less.

According to a report of the Joint Legislative Committee on Natural Resources in 1959, stimulation of construction occurred "to the greatest extent in states with aggressive Water Pollution control programs and with construction needs reasonably in balance with the amount of federal funds available." It was clear that New York's construction needs were not even close to being "reasonably in balance" with available federal funds. With the ceiling of $250,000 on any one project and the requirement that half of all funds be alloted to communties with a population of 125,000 or less, the federal grants program was too small to make a significant difference in an urban state like New York. According to the committee's report, it impeded New York water-pollution control by generating a long waiting line of municipal applicants who put off further action on the grounds that they had applied for a federal grant. In short, when Rockefeller became governor, there was a federal grant-in-aid program of limited and, for New York, inadequate scope. New York City's needs alone were estimated to be over $1 billion.

The issues of state aid and the federal role were major influences defining the situation for gubernatorial action. Governor Rockefeller had definite views on the proper role of the states in the federal system. He believed that states should vigorously assert their rights, which could be justified only by carrying out their responsibilities. Rockefeller called for major state action buttressed by federal aid, but opposed further federal enforcement efforts. Consequently, in December 1960 the governor commissioned the Office for Local Government to conduct a study of sewage-works costs and financing and to make recommendations for state action. This study came to be considered the real start of the state's program because it finally gave a realistic estimate of the tremendous costs involved. Acting on the recommendations of the study, in 1962 Rockefeller introduced legislation for a comprehensive ten-year program of state aid for water-pollution control in New York. The legislature's failure to appropriate the necessary funds and Rockefeller's acquiescence in this decision, however, indicate the lack of public support for water-pollution control at that time. It was clear that the extent of public support would be a key factor in the development of any new program.

The decision to push major antipollution legislation in the 1965 session of the state legislature was apparently made by Rockefeller in late 1964. The governor attributed the impetus to his 1964 visit to California, where he realized that New York's water supply was a precious gift and that it was the state's obligation to preserve it. The severe drought that began in 1962 also influenced his decision to act in 1965. William Ronan was given the task of developing a feasible program that was subsequently made public by Robert Hennigan speaking at the HEW Conference on the Hudson River. The keys to the program were fiscal incentives, including direct construction and operation grants for municipalities, and tax relief for industries constructing waste treatment facilities. As Rockefeller himself put it, the major purpose of the program was "to lift much of the crushing financial burden of building sewage treatment systems from the backs of our local communities."

The 1965 Pure Waters Program called for state assumption of 30 percent of project costs; the federal share would be prefinanced with state money if Congress was slow to vote sufficient appropriations. This percentage was reached because it was decided that the localities would be more likely to support the program if they were paying less than half. It was also an ingenious political maneuver. At that time the federal government was providing 50 percent of project costs or

$600,000, whichever was less. For New York's construction needs that amount just about covered the planning costs. With this new state program, New York showed itself willing to fulfill its responsibilities and even, if needed, those it felt were the national government's. This seizure of the initiative put strong pressure on the federal government to act. That it had *some* effect is suggested by the fact that in November 1966 Congress endorsed the principle of retroactive payments. Moreover, prefinancing eliminated the excuse that many municipalities gave for not moving rapidly in the construction of treatment plants.

To assure the plan's acceptance, several thousand color brochures were printed and distributed to business and community leaders throughout the state. Rockefeller also met with the state's newspaper editors to explain the program, and he, along with other state officials, accepted speaking engagements to promote support. The result of these efforts was unanimous approval of the program by the state legislature, on condition that the electorate endorse the $1 billion bond issue in the November election, and it did by an overwhelming four-to-one margin.

In 1967 Rockefeller proposed and the legislature approved the establishment of a public corporation, the Pure Waters Authority, to help municipalities that were having difficulty raising their share of construction costs. By the end of 1969, 117 projects were far enough along in construction to be in operation, 83 more were under construction, and 51 projects were in the final design stage. State aid for these projects was almost $600 million.

As a result of the reorganization and consolidation of the state's environment efforts in 1971, the Pure Waters Authority was reconstituted as the Environmental Facilities Corporation, with an expansion of powers and duties. The corporation was given the capability to finance, construct, and manage a complete package of environmental facilities and services for municipal and state agencies. It was envisioned that the corporation would work closely with the Department of Environmental Conservation (DEC), created in 1970. As a consequence, the commissioner of environmental conservation was made the chairman of the board of directors of the corporation.

As organized, the corporation has four basic functions: financing, project managament, provision of legal services, and general management. Of these four activities, financing is perhaps the most important from the standpoint of both the corporation and its clients. The superior borrowing position of the state allows the corporation to get interest rate savings not available to small communities. The other operations of the corporation are basically service functions and involve the planning, engineering, and administration of projects. The nature and level of services provided by the corporation are largely determined by the local community participating in the project. The range of services offered can extend from a limited review of a project to assumption of full operation responsibilities.

Until recently, corporate activities had largely centered upon sewage treatment and water supply projects, but increasing concern about the disposal of solid wastes caused a shift in emphasis. In January 1972 the DEC reported that only 350 out of 814 refuse disposal areas in New York complied with state regulations. Solid waste disposal has developed into a major problem, particularly in the state's urbanized areas, and the corporation has been charged with meeting these issues. The corporation's initial proposal for the creation of regional environmental facilities parks for resource recovery and sanitary landfill has not met with success, but it is continuing in its efforts to increase resource recovery programs throughout the state.

Preserving Open Spaces

Strict land use controls for both public and private property in relatively undeveloped areas of the state are another area of recent environmental innovation in New York. The state has a long tradition of concern for the preservation of park lands, rooted in opposition during the early nineteenth century to the destruction of forests in the Adirondacks and the concomitant threat to the area's watersheds. In 1885 a law was passed establishing the State Forest Preserve. The Adirondack and Catskill parks were established in 1892 and 1904 respectively. Both parks are made up of a combination of privately owned and state owned land, a unique situation that was to cause a great deal of controversy as the concept was developed. Included in the park's boundaries as originally drawn and later expanded were private residences, farms, businesses, and towns, as well as wilderness and scenic, ecologically unique portions of the Adirondack and Catskill mountains. In 1894 the state lands within the Adirondack and Catskill counties were set aside as "forever wild" by article VII, section 7 of the state constitution for the use and enjoyment of the future population of New York State. Currently, the State Forest Preserve, within the boundaries of the Adirondack and Catskill parks, encompasses some 2.5 million acres. The forest preserve lands make up approximately 40 percent of the Adirondack Park's 6 million acres and

40 percent of the 900,000 acres of the Catskill Park. Almost all remaining lands in these parks are privately owned.

Establishment of these parks did not reduce or eliminate pressures for development. As the forms that these pressures have taken over the years have shifted to reflect the changing needs and tastes of society, their intensity has increased. The need for timber has declined, while outdoor recreational demands have grown. Increasing pressures for recreational development and a swelling tide of unregulated land use prompted Governor Rockefeller to establish the Temporary Study Commission on the Future of the Adirondacks in 1968. The task assigned to the commission by the governor was to review the problems of the area and develop alternatives for the future of the Adirondacks to best serve the people of the state. After conducting what many believed was the most extensive series of field surveys and mapping ever undertaken on the Adirondacks, the commission released its two-year study on January 3, 1971. The core recommendation of the study was for the creation of an independent agency with the power to regulate the use and development of all public and private land in the 6-million-acre Adirondack Park and, where necessary, to override the zoning decisions of local communities and the land use of private property holders. In noting that less than 10 percent of the park land had any zoning regulations, the commission predicted that if unregulated development was not checked immediately, within a generation it would lead to the complete despoilment of private lands that comprise 60 percent of the Adirondacks.

On May 8, 1971, Governor Rockefeller presented the state legislature with a series of bills designed to implement some of the proposals made by the Temporary Study Commission. One month later, on June 8, 1971, the bills were adopted with minor modifications. The bills created an Adirondack Park Agency, composed of the director of the Office of Planning Services, the commissioner of environmental conservation, and seven members to be appointed by the governor with the consent of the senate. The agency was required to present a master plan for the management of state or public lands in the park by June 1, 1972, and a program of land use controls for private lands by January 1, 1973. For the intervening time, the agency was empowered to review and approve land developments that exceeded more than five acres or more than five lots within the park. This measure, the governor claimed, would provide interim safeguards against improvident uses of lands within the park that would threaten its future value.

Some political observers were doubtful that the bill would pass, because of strong pressures exerted by upstate land developers combined with the feeling of many lawmakers that the bills violated the constitutional home rule powers of Adirondack localities. Moreover, others believed that the state legislature would be loathe to create a new state agency and approve the governor's request for a $250,000 appropriation to cover the agency's operating expenses when others were being abolished because of budgetary stringencies.

Throughout the spring of 1972, the Adirondack Park Agency scheduled a series of public hearings across the state so that the people could air their views on the commission's first draft of its master plan for regulating the development of state owned lands in the park. Henry L. Diamond, the commissioner of the Department of Environmental Conservation that controls the state owned lands, claimed that the agency's recommendations for the regulated use of state owned lands would not have to be submitted to the legislature for approval, as would the recommendations for the use of private lands. "Reckoning with public land usage," Diamond said, "is the easier side of the job."

On July 26, 1972, Governor Rockefeller approved the master plan for the regulation of state owned lands by the Adirondack Park Agency. Specifically, the plan placed state owned land that was originally designated as "forever wild" into four broad categories: wild forest, 1,150,300 acres; wilderness, 997,960 acres; primitive, 75,670 acres; and canoe areas, 18,000 acres. The plan also designated smaller areas as intensive use and special management areas, wild, scenic, and recreational rivers and major travel corridors.

On December 21, 1972, the Adirondack Park Agency released its preliminary plan to regulate the development of private land in the Adirondacks. Specifically, the agency's plan provided for six categories of private land use areas with intensity guidelines regulating the maximum number of principal buildings per square mile. The categories and guidelines were rural and urban hamlets, moderate intensity use areas, rural use areas, resource management areas, and industrial use areas. Land development projects in any areas would be classified in one of three categories: regional, special use, and permissible. The plan also asked for a "review and permit system." This review mechanism provided a system whereby the park agency and local governments could engage in negotiations to reconcile local governmental interests with recommendations of the park agency and thus either permit or prevent a particular project in a given land use area. The decision would be based on public concern, existing development, and the physical nature of the area. According to the agency's recommendations, "There would be a two-tiered review process, with the general rule being that the local government may disallow a project even if the agency has approved it."

Public opposition over the proposal to regulate private land use in the Adirondacks was aired at various hearings held throughout the state between January 8 and January 20, 1973. Many north country residents claimed that persons living in the Adirondacks had had little voice in formulating the plan and that a one year delay in legislative action on the plan would allow them better to evaluate its implications. Density guidelines proposed by the park agency also came under attack; some residents argued that they were far too restrictive and others claimed that some areas, such as those designated as resource management, would be better suited for higher population densities. Opponents of the plan also argued that it would erode the tax base of the Adirondack communities and cause great losses in property values and could, in addition, force Adirondack youth to leave the area in search of jobs. Interestingly, the "review and permit system" also came under attack. Opponents of the park agency's proposal claimed that the review system would create an expensive new state bureaucracy.

In response to local criticism, the legislature suggested the delay of action on the agency's proposals for one year. Commenting on the proposed one year delay, Governor Rockefeller argued, "When someone does not like something, he always says that we are pushing too fast and that he has not had time to read it. But I am busy and I have read it. This subject has been around for years."

On March 9, 1973, the Adirondack Park Agency issued its final plan for the use of private lands in the park. The new plan allowed for a maximum population of about 2 million within park limits. This increase of 65 percent over the original plan, which asked for a maximum population of 1.2 million. Consequently, the "intensity guidelines," which established the maximum number of principal buildings per square mile for each major land use category, were altered somewhat. Two weeks later, on March 21, Governor Rockefeller sent a bill implementing the Adirondack Park Agency's Plan for the Use of Private Land in the Adirondacks to the legislature for approval. On March 29, 1973, however, the legislature approved a bill that would delay legislative consideration of the plan for private lands proposed by the park agency until June 1, 1974. On April 27, Governor Rockefeller vetoed the one year extension bill and declared, "No matter how well-intentioned such a delay may be, its inevitable impact would be to create a dangerous time-gap during which irreversible damage can be done to the Adirondacks."

On May 22, 1973, the legislature approved, with a few modifications, the proposal for the regulation of private lands in the Adirondacks. In the modified version a fourth Adirondack resident was to be added to the nine-member park agency and the state commerce commissioner also became a member. Furthermore, it was required that a review board be chosen by county legislators to monitor the activities of the park agency. The board, however, would have no veto power.

The plan, which went into effect on August 1, 1973, basically prevents the establishment of large second home developments within the park. For 53 percent of the private land in the resource management category, an average of only one building for each 42 acres will be permitted. On an additional 32 percent of the land, no more than one building for each 8.5 acres will be permitted; for another 10 percent of private land, the plan calls for no more than one building for each three acres. The remaining 5 percent of private park lands includes areas that are already intensively developed and that will be little affected by the plan. Presently, there are estimated to be 125,000 permanent residents within the park's 6 million acres.

In August 1973, in what was the first action of its kind in New York State, Commissioner Henry L. Diamond of the DEC rejected an application for the construction of a large second home development within the Adirondack Park. In taking this action the commissioner cited the expressed interest of the people for protecting the Adirondacks, as demonstrated by the passage of the Adirondack Park land use plan: "It is clear that the majority of people of the State have mandated a high degree of concern for both public and private land in enacting the recent added protection for the Adirondacks. To grant permits which would dilute this protection runs counter to the intent of the Legislature and the policy of the people of the State."

Like the forest preserve in the Adirodacks, the area in the Catskills is also imperiled. Proximity to the New York City metropolitan area and the ready availability of access highways have generated tremendous pressures upon the Catskills. Once again the competition between development and preservation has become fierce. Recognizing those issues, the legislature established the Temporary State Commission to study the Catskills in February 1971. The commission is to prepare a study of the Catskill region for submission, with its recommendations, to the legislature by March 31, 1975. In its charge to the commission, the legislature asked the commission to study the conservation and development of the natural resources of the region and the strengthening of cultural resources, social organizations, economy, and general well-being of its rural communities. Among other things to be studied are measures necessary to strengthen policy regarding the management, acquisition, and use of public land, as well as policies to be taken by local governments to assure that the development of private lands is consistent with long-range plans.

The Catskill commission is just getting its study under way. Evaluation of its recommendations will have to await the completion of its work. However, even at this stage it is evident that there are major differences between the Adirondack and Catskill projects. While the Adirondack study covered only the Adirondack Park, the Catskill study covers an area of six counties as well as six towns in Albany County, an area smaller than the Adirondack Park but more diverse in land use patterns and population settlement. It includes much good agricultural land and areas of industrial development. Its areas of forest preserve and private wild lands are considerably smaller than the Adirondack region. Most of the state lands in this region are in state forests. Multiple use areas are subject to management and heavy use. Given such factors as these and the differences in population density and private land use patterns, it is highly doubtful that the commission will develop land use regulations of the type developed by the Adirondack agency but will have to establish some compromise that will provide a harmony between private and public interests.

Conclusion

The creation of the Department of Environmental Conservation by New York State in 1970 was a reaffirmation of the state's commitment to making major progress in this area of policy. By consolidating in one department environmentally significant functions formerly performed by the Department of Health, the Department of Agriculture and Markets, the Conservation Department, the Water Resource Commission, and the Natural Beauty Commission, and by giving this new agency statewide planning, investigative, oversight, and enforcement powers, Governor Rockefeller and the legislature created an intragovernment environmental advocate and ensured that the entire state administration would become more responsive to ecological concerns.

The two examples offered here mark significant innovations made by New York in water pollution and land use control. The state, through the DEC, has acted in many other areas of policy with varying degrees of success, and there are, of course, numerous other state agencies whose work either directly or indirectly affects the environment. The Department of Health has responsibilities for dealing with health hazards of air, water, and solid waste pollution. The Department of Transportation is responsible for planning for a balanced transportation policy, including highways, railroads, buses, and rapid transit. If adequate housing should be considered an environmental issue, some attention should be given to the work of the Division of Housing and Community Renewal. By broadening or narrowing the definition of *environment*, the number of agencies that are to be included in the discussion can be greatly varied. Changes in public awareness, sudden shifts in resource availability, and variations in individual demand act to bring forth new environmental crises and shift attention to new areas of concern. In order to meet the shifting public interest, governments must either create new agencies or reorganize existing ones when they do not meet current needs.

A listing of current environmental issues will disclose the wide range of problems faced by governments committed to action. The energy shortage, land use regulation, solid waste disposal, and mass transportation are among the pressing concerns. The ecological approach shows that these are not individual problems but one problem. The world is a closed system in which everything is related to everything else. Energy is related to transportation, land use, and pollution, while pollution is related to energy. It is government's role to aid in the task of bringing man into harmony with the environment. It is a gigantic task, but during the Rockefeller years New York State was committed to acting positively to meet needs as they arose.